TWENTIETH CENTURY VIEWS

The aim of this series is to present the best in
contemporary critical opinion on major authors,
providing a twentieth century perspective on
their changing status in an era of profound
revaluation.

Maynard Mack, *Series Editor*
Yale University

EURIPIDES

EURIPIDES

A COLLECTION OF CRITICAL ESSAYS

Edited by
Erich Segal

Prentice-Hall, Inc. *Englewood Cliffs, N. J.*

Current printing (last number):
10   9   8   7   6   5   4   3   2   1

For Eric Havelock

quod spiro et placeo, si placeo, tuum est

Acknowledgments

Special thanks are due Christian Wolff and Eric Havelock for contributing new essays to this volume. Professor Wolff was also extremely helpful in matters of bibliography, as were my colleagues, A. M. Parry and Kenneth Cavander. All of the scholars here represented were most cooperative in adapting their manuscripts to the format of this series. Translations from the Greek, where not specifically credited, are by the author of the particular essay.

The editor is greatly indebted to Walter Moskalew for his aid in preparing the manuscript, and to Zinta Moskalew for assisting her husband.

Contents

Introduction

by Erich Segal

The progress of Greek tragedy has been likened to the famous fire-relay held at the Panathenaic festival. Aeschylus, nobly bearing the torch lit with the spark of Prometheus, handed it to Sophocles who carried its splendor still further, before giving it to Euripides. But this last playwright was not only too weak to carry the torch, he could not even keep the flame alive.[1] A dramatic simile, but like so much that is said of Euripides, wholly inaccurate. We are led to believe that Euripides "killed tragedy." Aeschylus himself argues as much in the *Frogs*, and this gospel according to Aristophanes has been echoed through the ages, especially by vigorous apostles like Schlegel and Nietzsche. And yet there is a problem here, even for those who believe that the ancient classics never lie. Did not the great Aristotle consider Euripides "the *most* tragic of the tragic poets" because most of his plays end—as the best tragedies should—sadly (*Poetics* XIII 9-10)?

No one would dispute that some of Euripidean drama presents the most unmitigated misery ever witnessed on a stage. The ruthless tyrant Alexander of Pherae was so ashamed to be crying at the sorrows of Hecuba that he had to leave the theater before the *Trojan Women* was over.[2] But then what of the "escape plays" like the *Helen* or the *Andromeda,* in which misery turns suddenly to mirth and—that most comic of catastrophes—marriage? Scholars can provide another convenient explanation for this Euripidean "development" by adducing the example of Shakespeare. After the storms of *King Lear* came the smiling calm of *The Winter's Tale* or *The Tempest*. Likewise, after the tearful *Trojan Women* came the happy *Helen*. Unfortunately, Euripides will not lie still on the literary bed of Procrustes, for after the *Helen* came the *Bacchae*. And before all of them came the *Alcestis*.

To discuss Euripides is to speak in paradoxes, even Aristotelian ones. The *Poetics* insists that the dénouement of a tragedy conform with a

---

[1] This image was surely inspired by Aristophanes' *Frogs* 1085ff.

[2] This "he to Hecuba" incident is recounted by Plutarch, *Pelopidas* 29.

1

certain justice. Good men must not suffer ill and, most important, evil
men must not prosper. This last instance, Aristotle argues, would be
the most *un*tragic situation of all: ἀτραγῳδότατον γὰρ τοῦτ' ἐστὶ πάντων
(*Poetics* XIII 3). In light of this, how can we evaluate Euripides'
Heracles, whose tormented protagonist is not only totally innocent, but
has been constantly hailed as the greatest benefactor of mankind? [3] It
is not a question of a hero being more sinned against than sinning.
Heracles has not "sinned" at all; in fact, even before his heroic quest
he has proved himself a paragon of *pietas.* Similarly, in the *Trojan
Women* the playwright goes to great pains to emphasize that Andromache
has been a saintly wife (cf. lines 643ff), and yet Hector's widow is doomed
to endure what she herself describes as a fate worse than death: a life
without hope. In direct contrast, Helen, who is considered by everyone
to be responsible for all the misery (and indeed *everyone* gets to indict
her during the play), goes scot-free. While the Trojan widows sing sorrow
in sackcloth and ashes, Helen is blithely arranging her *toilette,* so that
she can appear well groomed (and, miraculously, well gowned) for
her happy reunion with Menelaus. By Aristotle's own rules, this play is
a paradox: "most tragic" because of its sad ending, and most "untragic"
because the wicked Helen prospers.

It is important to realize that Euripides was an iconoclast from the
beginning. We have nothing from the earliest years of his creative life,
but we can see that his first extant play was a bold departure from
traditional dramaturgy.[4] In the year 442 or 441, Sophocles' Antigone
marched bravely to her death, lamenting that her tomb was also to be
her wedding chamber (lines 891ff). In 438, Euripides also presented a
self-sacrificing young woman who likewise dies voluntarily, out of family
loyalty, but who goes *to* her tomb and then *back* to her wedding chamber.
And already in the *Alcestis* we see articulated the famous Euripidean
life-in-death paradox which Aristophanes would so often mock.[5] Before
our very eyes, a funeral has turned into a wedding, "tragedy" has suddenly become "comedy." Characteristic of Euripides, the paradox is
vividly visual: the bride wears black. (In the *Iphigenia at Aulis* the
victim is dressed in bridal white.) Moreover, it is no accident that this

[3] Prometheus was also the friend of man, but he stole fire, giving Zeus reasonable
cause for anger. And Sophocles' Heracles does have something of a "tragic flaw" in
the *Trachiniae:* he is in love with Iole.

[4] It is not enough to dismiss the "innovations" of the *Alcestis* by noting that it was
presented in place of the usual satyr-play. Besides, on this same occasion Euripides
presented the *Telephus* which, according to Aristophanes, was even more "scandalous."

[5] E.g., *Alcestis* 242-43: Admetus will "live and not live" for the rest of his days. Also
lines 518-21: Admetus tells Heracles that his wife "has died and not died."

change has been effected by Heracles, half-human, half-divine, a drunken Dionysiac in the service of Apollo. In the *Alcestis* we find innumerable motifs which appear again and again, with differing emphases, throughout Euripides' *oeuvre:* a sudden shift of fortune, demonstrating the potential joy-in-sorrow (and vice versa) all emphasized by verbal paradoxes in the dialogue; Salvation in the Nick of Time; *deus* (in this case, demi-god) *ex machina;* the perplexing problem of what is real and what illusory, and perhaps most important, the evasion of limit.

A longing for escape seems to permeate all the plays of Euripides. But the question of which characters do escape and which do not defies rational analysis. Magically, a flying car arrives to rescue the "villainess" Medea and whisk her to safety. Though her actions are the precise opposite of those of Alcestis, she enjoys the same rewards. Small wonder that Aristotle singled out Medea's *ex machina* exit for special censure (it is, of course, "most untragic"). And yet Phaedra—who is no Alcestis, but surely no Medea either—is denied rescue from her dilemma. The famous "escape ode" from the *Hippolytus* has significance even beyond its context, and bears quoting. Gilbert Murray's somewhat quaint translation may not be the most accurate, but it is the best known piece of Euripides *in English:* [6]

> Could I take me to some cavern for mine hiding,
>   In the hill-tops where the Sun scarce hath trod;
> Or a cloud make the home of mine abiding,
>   As a bird among the bird-droves of God!
>   Could I wing me to my rest amid the roar
>   Of the deep Adriatic on the shore,
>   Where the waters of Eridanus are clear,
>   And Phaëthon's sad sisters by his grave
> Weep into the river, and each tear
>   Gleams, a drop of amber, in the wave.
>
> To the strand of the Daughters of the Sunset,
>   The Apple-tree, the singing and the gold;
> Where the mariner must stay him from his onset,
>   And the red wave is tranquil as of old;

---

[6] *Hippolytus* 732ff. Although T. S. Eliot would later complain that Gilbert Murray "interposed between ourselves and Euripides a barrier more impenetrable than the Greek language," the lines printed above caught the fancy of many English writers (e.g., Galsworthy), who quote them time and again. This is not the place to discuss Murray's idiosyncrasies as translator, except perhaps to note his tendency to ignore the plural of θεός, as in line 751 of the Greek, which he should have at least rendered "the gods' quiet garden."

Yea, beyond that Pillar of the End
That Atlas guardeth, would I wend;
Where a voice of living waters never ceaseth
In God's quiet garden by the sea,
And Earth, the ancient life-giver, increaseth
Joy among the meadows, like a tree.

Faced with the various miseries of life, many of Euripides' choruses yearn
for the wings of a bird (e.g., *Helen* 1478ff), to fly from the face of
disaster. But here in the *Hippolytus,* the cry for escape itself contains
an ironic indication that there will be none at all. The chorus of
Troezenian women wishes to travel to the edge of the earth, the Atlantic
pillars. In a few moments Theseus will wish that he could banish
Hippolytus to this same far-off frontier (line 1053). But the very theme
of this play is no exit; hell hath no limits. In the opening lines of the
prologue, Aphrodite has told us that her power (which is, among other
things, the power to destroy whomever she wishes) extends even as far
as the pillars of Atlas. Moreover, the paradise to which the chorus would
flee has already seen one fatal chariot accident. Would Hippolytus
himself find safety where young Phaëthon fell after losing control of
his horses? Even at the limits of the earth, the situation strangely
resembles what is about to occur on stage. The "Daughters of the Sunset"
are but another—typically Euripidean—chorus of grieving women, who
weep with such sorrow that their tears turn to amber. What good, then,
to fly off like a bird? Grief may be transmuted, but it cannot be tran-
scended.

The second stanza of this escape ode reminds us that the desired
place of refuge was also the scene of one of Heracles' greatest triumphs,
where he gathered golden apples, and shouldered Atlas' burden: the
weight of the world. In a later play, Euripides' chorus can boast that
the protagonist has actually journeyed to this fabled territory (*Heracles*
392ff):

Thence among the singing maidens,
western halls' Hesperides.
Plucked among the metal leaves
the golden fruit, and slew
the orchard's dragon-guard
whose tail of amber coiled the trunk
untouchably. He passed below the sea
and set a calmness in the lives of men
whose living is the oar.
Under bellied heaven next,

> he put his hand as prop:
> there in the halls of Atlas,
> his manliness held up
> heaven's starry halls.
>
> (trans. Arrowsmith)

What is more, just as he did in the *Alcestis*, Heracles has arrived precisely in time to rescue a household menaced with death; this time, it is his own family. But, just as the *Alcestis* turned suddenly from tragedy to triumph after the savior's arrival, here matters take the opposite course. Having successfully gone to the limits of the earth (and beneath it) Heracles is trapped. Hera sends Madness personified against him and he will not escape (line 842). This unexpected demon *ex machina* causes Heracles to murder his own wife and children. When he awakens to the full horror of his deed, he too wishes to escape as a bird:

> οἴμοι, τί δράσω; ποῖ κακῶν ἐρημίαν
> εὕρω, πτερωτός, ἢ κατὰ χθονὸς μολών;
> (lines 1157-58)

> Oh no—what can I do? Where can I find refuge
> from these ills? Fly off with wings? Dive beneath the earth?

But no, he cannot fly. Quite the contrary, as he tells Theseus a few moments later, it is his own happiness that has taken wings and flown from him: οἰχόμεθ᾽ οἰχόμεθα πτανοί (line 1186). And why dive beneath the earth? He has, in fact, just returned from a trip to Hades, but now hell is inside his head (lines 1297ff). No divine epilogue relieves this new misery, not even a goddess like Artemis in the *Hippolytus,* to tell him why things must be as cruel as they are.[7] Heracles is abandoned like Sophocles' Philoctetes, although he must live forever with both wound *and* bow (cf. *Heracles* 1376ff), offered no promise of surcease from pain. There is, moreover, an ironic parallel between Heracles' outcry (quoted above), and *Medea* 1296ff, where Jason, hell-bent on punishing the villainess who has just murdered the King and the Princess of Corinth, shouts that Medea would have to "hide herself beneath the earth, or fly winged into the air" to avoid the retribution she deserves. And yet but a moment later, her hands stained with still more innocent blood, Medea will in fact soar into the sky . . . completely free. Aristotle was

---

[7] And yet Artemis does not even allow Theseus to express his own longings for escape. When she appears at the end of the *Hippolytus,* she says (lines 1290ff) that she knows *he* would like to dive beneath the earth or fly away like a bird, as if, sadistically, to remind him that all routes leading away from torment are sealed off.

understandably outraged by Medea's escape; but he does not even comment upon the horrible fate of Heracles. Indeed, it is beyond the pale
of rational criticism. But the question is its own answer: this is Euripides.
In fact, the *Alcestis* and the *Heracles,* with the same demi-god first as
savior and then as victim, present the polarities of Euripidean drama:
the untragic and the hypertragic.

A similar Euripidean paradox is visible in the figure of Helen. While
often vilified as the oversexed bitch who caused the Trojan War,[8] she
appears in the *Helen* as "virginal" (yes) and pure,[9] waiting to be rescued
by her beloved Menelaus and, though dressed in black, to be rewedded
to him during (of course) a funeral ceremony. Moreover, Helen had
never even been to Troy; an image had gone in her place to cause all
that slaughter.[10] In the *Alcestis,* King Admetus is a widower who is
simultaneously burying his wife and marrying her again. Here Helen is
a widow simultaneously burying (an image of) and marrying (the real)
Menelaus. Moreover, the play concludes with the appearance, *ex machina,*
of Castor and Pollux, earlier described as "both dead and not dead"
(line 138), who absolve Helen from any guilt whatever, noting with
supreme irony that "the world has few like her" (line 1687). It is small
wonder that when scholars tire of calling Euripides "the Greek Ibsen,"
they dub him "the Greek Pirandello."

Dare we ask why, according to Euripides, a "deceitful" Iphigenia
escapes from Tauris, while a "noble" one is immolated at Aulis? We
have earlier been indiscreet enough to broach this matter in the case of
Alcestis and Medea. It is the same question we ask concerning the bad
Helen of the *Troades* (or the *Orestes*) and the "virgin" waiting in Egypt
like patience on a monument. It is not merely a case of comparing plays,
for the dramas themselves abound in contradictory characters and
situations. Every play of Euripides seems to be asking a question or else
boldly stating some mythical and/or visual paradox. It is easy to see
why Euripides was, even in antiquity, branded "the philosopher of the
stage," and linked with men like Protagoras, whose new philosophy
called all in doubt, and who composed, among other things, an *Antilogiai*

---

[8] And in matters of sex, Euripides never minces words. Helen's lust is referred to as
(among other things): ἀπληστία λέχους, "insatiable bed-hunger" (*Andromache* 218).

[9] In the very first line of the play, Helen describes herself as waiting faithfully by
the "beautiful-virginal" (καλλιπάρθενοι) waters of the Nile.

[10] Despite its ostensibly comic aspect, the *Helen* is a far more vehement antiwar
statement than *The Trojan Women.* Helen may have gone to Troy in name only,
but the soldiers who went as men and are *returning* only as names on the casualty
list (cf. lines 399ff) would not be comforted by this.

(*Contradictions*), a kind of paean to paradox, celebrating the power of rhetoric to affirm uncertainty.

All the while Euripides was composing his plays of dubious genre and questionable morality, Sophocles was writing—there is no better term—heroic tragedy. And there are no *antilogiai* in the Sophoclean protagonist; he is a monolith, unyielding and uncompromising. If he is at odds with the world, he will leave it, but "Ajax will 'quit himself like Ajax." The cowardly messenger may run backward and forward while en route to bring Creon the news of Antigone's defiance, but she herself never hesitates for a moment. She never doubts that she is doing the "right" thing. (Hegel grants Creon a case of equal "rightness," but that does not detract from Antigone's self-assurance.) Sophocles' admiration for this sort of heroism, the divine in man, is nowhere more evident than in the well-known choral ode from the *Antigone* (lines 332ff) which begins:

πολλὰ τὰ δεινὰ κοὐδὲν ἀνθρώπου δεινότερον πέλει

There are many awesome things in the world, but nothing more awesome than man.

The sentiment is similar to the Hebrew psalmist's "I will praise Thee; for I am fearfully and wonderfully made: awesome are Thy works." The word *deinon* connotes both admiration and fear, but Sophocles is clearly focusing on what is to be admired. The world of Euripides is also full of *deina*, awesome—if rarely admirable—things, but man is definitely not one of them. In fact, what is *deinon* usually acts upon man. Sometimes this force has a name, like Dionysus:

γνώσεται δὲ τὸν Διὸς
Διόνυσον, ὃς πέφυκεν ἐν τέλει θεὸς
δεινότατος, ἀνθρώποισι δ' ἠπιώτατος.
(*Bacchae* 859-61)

He [Pentheus] shall come to recognize
that Dionysus son of Zeus has come into the world, undeniably a god,
at once most awesome
and gentlest to mankind.

It is the ultimate irony that Greek drama, which began, as Herodotus tells us, with the suffering of Dionysus for humanity, should culminate in a play which presents the suffering of humanity for Dionysus. This new "god" is the supreme paradox, an irrational, self-contradicting force that is at once most benign and most horrible.[11]

But Euripides' Dionysus is not merely an external *deinon* to whom men are as flies to wanton boys (this is Seneca's reinterpretation), it is also a force acting from within. In contrast to the single-minded Sophoclean characters, we have Euripides' Medea, the first expression of what Bernard Knox has called "the unheroic temper." Stricken with doubt, torn by conflicting inner forces, Medea changes her mind four times in twenty lines.[12] Finally darker Dionysiac passions conquer her reason. The denouement of the *Bacchae* demonstrates that Pentheus is lord of nothing, least of all his own actions. And Hippolytus, champion charioteer, is unable to control the horses he has been training his entire life (lines 1355ff). It is a striking coincidence, and all the more striking because it is a coincidence, that Freud uses a similar image of a horse out of control to describe the overwhelming power of the Id.[13]

Our most familiar classical tragedies have a single stage setting: the palace of a king. From play to play the palace remains; only the monarch changes. Today it is the House of Atreus, tomorrow the House of Oedipus—or of any royal family whom Aristotle deemed worthy of tragic treatment. The play might depict the fall and/or rise of princes, but the palace remained intact. Agamemnon is carried out; Orestes soon marches in. If we seek an image to describe what Euripides "did" to classical tragedy, we can do no better than say he destroyed the palace. Two particular instances come to mind. In the *Trojan Women,* Troy lies in ruins *on the stage.* The citadel has already been sacked when the play begins, and the heroes—princes one and all—are dead. We may argue the topicality of this drama, reminding ourselves that the Island of Melos had been sacked the previous year and that the *Trojan Women* was Euripides' castigation of war. But the play is more than a reportage of ruin; it contains as much symbolism as journalism. It is saying that in 415 B.C. the royal palace was a shambles and that Homer's epic heroes no longer have a dwelling place in the Greek theater.

Still another palace was to fall. In the final play of Euripides, Dionysus tears down the palace of Pentheus, before, in fact, he tears the king himself into pieces. Ironically, this ultimate destruction of the dignity of

---

[11] This point was first—and best—articulated by E. R. Dodds, in his epoch-making essay, "Euripides the Irrationalist," *Classical Review,* XLIII (July 1929), 97-104.

[12] *Medea* 1044ff. Professor Schlesinger, in the essay printed in this volume, differs somewhat from the traditional interpretation of this passage.

[13] Sigmund Freud, "The Ego and the Id," *Complete Psychological Works XIX,* ed. James Strachey (London: The Hogarth Press, 1961), p. 25.

man (if not man himself), demonstrates that he is king neither over his
house nor over his mind.[14]

But the theater itself was not destroyed. The Euripidean revolution
merely changed the decor and the *dramatis personae*. In place of the
classical *reges et proelia* ("kings and battles"), Euripides brought to the
stage what Aristophanes derides as οἰκεῖα πράγματα (*Frogs* 959), "familiar
affairs," or still more literally, "household things." The living room replaces the throne room. But he did not wait until his later plays to present
these bourgeois people in their bourgeois surroundings. What is preserved
at the end of his first extant play is not so much the "House of Admetus"
as the *home* of Alcestis.[15] We are back to where this essay—and Euripides
—began.

On the authority of the Parian Marble, we can place the birth of
Euripides at 484 B.C. He was born early enough to know Athens in
its glory and to witness the final plays of Aeschylus, notably the *Oresteia*
in 458. He made his own debut in 455, a year after Aeschylus' death,
with a *Peliades,* clearly some version of the Medea story, but did not
win the first of his (very few) victories until 441. He is said to have
written ninety-two plays, seventy-eight of which were known to the librar-
ians in Alexandria who at the same time, possessed 123 plays by
Sophocles. The fact that we still have eighteen (nineteen if we count
the *Rhesus*) by Euripides and only seven by Sophocles gives some indication of the favor enjoyed by Euripides in later times.

That he was a bold theatrical innovator is indisputable. Sophocles, as
Aristotle quotes him, acknowledged that Euripides presented men as
they actually were—people, not paragons. Euripides therefore owns the
distinction of having brought "realism" to the stage. Visually as well as
verbally, he rejected the "epic" (or perhaps we should say "Homeric")
theater. Gone forever were the Aeschylean red carpet and purple passages.
Euripides' dialogue is extremely simple, although both Aristotle and
"Longinus" recognize a sublime quality in this simplicity.[16]

It is also true that Euripides banished choral drama from the stage.

---

[14] See Norman O. Brown, *Life Against Death,* New York, 1959, p. 16: "True humility,
he [Freud] says, requires that we learn from Copernicus that the human world is not
the purpose or the center of the universe; that we learn from Darwin that man is a
member of the animal kingdom; and that we learn from Freud that the human ego
is not even master in its own house."

[15] And what makes a home is, of course, *philia*. This bond of humanity is all that
remains for a grieving Theseus or Heracles, and even at the conclusion of the *Bacchae*
for Agavê and Cadmus.

[16] Aristotle *Rhetoric* III, 2; "Longinus," *On the Sublime* XV.

His "intrigue" plays made the chorus seem very much out of place. Fifteen Ideal Spectators may look well in a palace, but they considerably clutter up a living room. (Eric Havelock has aptly described the Euripidean revolution as "putting on stage *rooms* never seen before.") Time and again his choruses are cautioned to keep secrets that they have overheard; it becomes increasingly clear that they should not be there in the first place. And yet, as if to confound the scholars, Euripides finishes his career with the *Bacchae*, almost as much a choral drama as the *Oresteia*.

The vast influence of Euripides throughout the ages is ample testimony that what he gave the drama was not a *coup de grâce*, but many *coups de théâtre*. He made a deep impression on everyone, including philosophers, poets, and the apostle Paul (who quotes him in I *Corinthians*). Needless to say, the playwrights worshiped him, comedians as well as tragedians. This awe is reflected in the famous remark by Philemon, writer of Greek New Comedy, who claimed he would hang himself to meet Euripides. Euripides' influence on Seneca is well known, while the romantic comedy he inspired in Menander gave models to Plautus and Terence for their Roman entertainments. Whether Euripides "killed" tragedy is open to debate; that he created melodrama has never been doubted. The long thread from such intrigue-plays as the *Ion* wove innumerable handkerchiefs for centuries of heroines to drop.

And in one way or another, "Euripidean drama" is still being written. There are conscious emulations like O'Neill's *Desire Under the Elms* (from the *Hippolytus*) or T. S. Eliot's *The Cocktail Party* (from the *Alcestis*) and *The Confidential Clerk* (from the *Ion*). But other writers have more forcefully, if unconsciously, presented Euripides *redivivus*. I think especially of García Lorca and Edward Albee. The Spanish poet is justly admired for his portraits of women swept up in the tidal wave of passion. The Novia in *Blood Wedding* is caught in the very same dilemma as Phaedra, her sense of what is right (and honorable) in violent conflict with a sexual desire that is driving her insane.[17] The same author's Yerma, like Medea, is a victim of a passion which "poisons" her, turning love into hate ("me estoy llenando de odio," she cries), and drives her to a bloody act of revenge. Albee's *Who's Afraid of Virginia Woolf?* also deals with the vague boundary between love and hate and culminates, like the *Medea*, with a *Kindermord* (albeit an imaginary one) as the supreme act of vengeance. His *Tiny Alice* expresses the same doubts about reason and faith as does the *Bacchae*, and both plays combine motifs of sexual and religious ecstasy with violent death. All of this

---

[17] In his famous eulogy of Euripides (*On the Sublime* XV), "Longinus" states that the Greek playwright "works hardest and best" at portraying *love* and *madness*.

proves not so much that Euripides was ahead of his time as that the issues he broached were timeless.

One final point. There is a common notion that Euripides was unpopular, unappreciated in his own day. If "success" be measured merely by prizes won, then he surely was a failure, for he received the best-in-festival award only four times in his entire life. But this might indicate, as one ancient scholar suggested, that the judges "were either idiots or bribed." It is easier to argue their aesthetic shortcomings, since this same group of arbiters also failed to give first prize to *Oedipus Rex*. But if we look carefully, we can see evidence that more than justifies Werner Jaeger's statement that in the playwright's own day, the public "adored Euripides like a god." [18] We have Plutarch's authority that the average Athenian sailor could recite whole passages of Euripides by heart. To be singing his odes is *ipso facto* to be singing his praises.[19] And contemporary authors were not loathe to alter their style in the wake of the Euripidean revolution. Sophocles himself owes a stylistic debt to his innovating contemporary, one particularly visible in the *Trachiniae* and *Philoctetes*. Many scholars have even found verbal echoes. On a quiet night they can hear the voice of Alcestis in Sophocles' Deianira. And there is an interesting similarity between *Alcestis* 941ff and *Trachiniae* 900ff, two passages which describe a tearful spouse wandering through the living quarters of a palace, bewailing the death of domestic happiness —with the significant distinction that in Euripides' play it is *King* Admetus who displays "unmanly grief."

But without any doubt the greatest contemporary admirer of Euripides was Aristophanes. His imitation was surely a form of flattery, his parody an expression of reverence. And so much of what Aristophanes had the comic license to utter, Euripides was daring to say on the "serious" stage, not the least of which involved such frightening issues as the death of God, the New Morality, and the changing relations between the sexes. We think immediately of "Cloud-theology" (Euripides in several passages replaces Zeus with "Aether"), as well as the escape theme of the *Birds*. And the significance of Euripides' "appearance" in the *Thesmophoriazusae* far transcends both parody and caricature. These two playwrights

---

[18] *Paideia* I, 380.

[19] In *Nicias* 29, where Plutarch tells the pretty story of how Greek sailors, captured in Sicily, gained their freedom by being able to quote Euripides, he goes on to describe how, after these men returned to Athens, whenever they encountered the playwright, they would warmly thank him "with *love* in their hearts." Such incidents are usually ignored by those who would build a case for "unloved Euripides," the social outcast brooding alone in his cave by the sea.

were so much alike that Cratinus, a contemporary comic author, coined the verb "to Euripidaristophanize." Euripides was always popular. He presented his "familiar affairs" not so much to shock the good burghers of Athens as to please them. It is naïve to argue, as do scholars like H. D. F. Kitto, that the Athenian public preferred art "with themes of importance," and hence rejected Euripides in favor of Aeschylus and Sophocles.[20] Heroic drama, like the epic which inspired it, had run its course. The people wanted Euripides.

It is therefore fruitless to speculate on why Euripides left Athens in the last years of his life.[21] Whatever the reason, it was certainly not because the public—or his wife—rejected him. His "exile" to Macedonia is far more enigmatic than Ovid's to the Black Sea. For one thing, we are at least sure that the Roman poet did not go voluntarily. To consider the various tales of Euripides' misanthropy (or misogyny) is to descend to the level of his scandal-mongering biographers, or to misconstrue Aristophanes, who, we *must* remember, was only joking. The comic poet who had mocked his friend Socrates and seen his comic gibes become tragic accusations surely knew that a Euripidean paradox like "who knows if life is death, or death life" was no laughing matter.

[20] H. D. F. Kitto, *The Greeks*, Baltimore, 1951, p. 129.
[21] It is odd that scholars have not sought for "deeper meanings" in the fact that Aeschylus died in far-off Sicily.

Euripides' Theater of Ideas

by William Arrowsmith

Several years ago I made a plea that scholars and critics should re-
cover a feeling for what I called turbulence in Greek tragedy.[1] By turbulence I meant both "the actual disorder of experience as that experience
gets into Greek drama" and "the impact of ideas under dramatic test."
What I want to do here is to take up the turbulence of ideas, as I see
those ideas expressed by Euripidean drama, with the purpose of showing that the Greeks possessed a theater which we should have no difficulty
in recognizing as a genuine theater of ideas. By theater of ideas I do not
mean, of course, a theater of intellectual *sententiae* or Shavian "talk"
or even the theater of the sophist-poet; I mean a theater of dramatists
whose medium of thought was the stage, who used the whole machinery
of the theater as a way of *thinking,* critically and constructively, about
their world.

In such a theater I assume that the emphasis will be upon ideas rather
than character and that a thesis or problem will normally take precedence
over development of character or heroism; that aesthetic or formal
pleasure will be secondary to intellectual rigor and thought; and that
the complexity of ideas presented may require severe formal dislocations
or intricate blurrings of emotional modes and genres once kept artis-
tically distinct. It is also likely that the moral texture of an action will
be "difficult," and that moral satisfaction will not come easily or even
at all; that problems may be left unresolved; that is, that the effect of a
play may very well be discomfort or even pain, and that the purpose of
this discomfort will be to influence the social rather than the individual
behavior of the spectator. Beyond this, I would expect such a theater to
be commonly concerned with the diagnosis and dramatization of cultural

[1] See "The Criticism of Greek Tragedy," *Tulane Drama Review*, III, No. 3 (Spring,
1959), 31ff.

crisis, and hence that the universe in which the dramatic action takes place would tend to be either irrational or incomprehensible. All of these characteristics are, of course, abstracted at random from the historical theater of ideas from Hebbel to the present, but in their ensemble they serve to give at least a general sense of the kind of theater of ideas I have in mind.

That such a theater—so specifically modern and antitraditional a theater—existed among the Greeks is not, I believe, exactly an article of faith among scholars and critics. To be sure, the Greek theater, like any other great theater, made abundant use of ideas, and the Athenians regarded the theater, not as entertainment, but as the supreme instrument of cultural instruction, a democratic *paideia* complete in itself. Aeschylus, for instance, uses ideas with stunning boldness, showing in play after play how the great post-Hesiodic world order could be compellingly and comprehensively adapted to Athenian history and society; and his theater not only provides a great, and new, theodicy, but dramatically creates the evolving idea of Athens as the supreme achievement of the mind of Zeus and the suffering of mankind. As for Sophocles, I am not of those who believe that he, like Henry James, possessed a mind so fine that no idea could violate it. In Oedipus, for instance, we have Sophocles' image of heroic man, shorn of his old Aeschylean confidence in himself and his world, and relentlessly pursuing the terrible new truth of his, and human, destiny. Oedipus looks into the abyss that yawns beneath him—the frightful knowledge of his nature which fifth century man had learned from the war, the plague and the atrocities, the sophistic revolution, and the collapse of the old world-order—and dashes out his eyes at the unbrookable sight. Similarly in Sophocles' Ajax I think we are meant to see a somewhat earlier symbol of the old aristocratic ethos; caught in new and antiheroic circumstances which degrade him and make him ludicrous, Ajax consistently prefers suicide to a life of absurdity in an alien time.[2] But all this is merely to say that Sophocles, like Aeschylus, uses the perceptions of cultural crisis as framing dramatic ideas or symbolically, not that his theater is in any meaningful sense a theater of ideas. Clearly it is to Euripides—the innovator and experimentalist, the antitraditional "immoralist" and "stage-sophist"—that we must look for any valid fifth century theater of ideas.

That the second half of the fifth century B.C. was a period of immense cultural crisis and political convulsion is, fortunately for my purpose

---

[2] Compare Ajax' situation with Thucydides' statement in the Corcyraean excursus: "The ancient simplicity into which honor so largely entered was laughed down and disappeared."

here, beyond any real doubt. The evidence itself needs only the barest rehearsal, but it should at least be *there*, the real though sketchy weather of my argument. Let me therefore brush it in.

There is, first of all, the breakdown of the old community, the overwhelming destruction of that mythical and coherent world-order which Werner Jaeger has described so fully in *Paideia*. Political convulsion—stasis and revolution—broke out everywhere. If civil war was nothing new among the Greek city-states, civil war on the fifth century scale was absolutely unprecedented in its savagery: city against city, man against man, father against son. Under such conditions the whole kinship structure on which the polis was theoretically and constitutionally founded was irretrievably weakened. In culture the sophistic revolution ushered in something like a transvaluation of morals. In society there was the rise of a new bourgeoisie provided with new sanctions and new theories of human nature, as well as a politically conscious proletariat. In the arts restless innovation was the rule, and throughout the Hellenic world—in literature, thought, and politics—there took place a vast debate whose very terms vividly report the schism in the culture, especially in the great argument between *physis* (nature) and *nomos* (custom, tradition, and law). Men begin to wonder now whether the laws of the state and the state itself, once thought divinely established, are any longer related to *physis* at large or to human *physis* in particular. Thus the great experience of the late fifth century is what can be called "the loss of innocence." Sophocles, Euripides, Aristophanes, and Thucydides are all, each in his different way, haunted by the disappearance of the old integrated culture and the heroic image of man that had incarnated that culture. There is a new spirit of divisiveness abroad in the Hellenic world; appearance and reality, nature and tradition, move steadily apart under the destructive pressure of war and its attendant miseries. Subjected to harsh necessity, human nature now shows itself in a new nakedness, but also in a startling new range of behavior, chaotic and uncontrollable.

How wrenching that conclusion was, how extreme and catastrophic, is told us by no less an authority than Thucydides himself:

> Thus every form of evil took root in the Hellenic countries by reason of the troubles. The ancient simplicity into which honor so largely entered was laughed down and disappeared; and society became divided into camps in which no man trusted his fellow. To put an end to this, there was neither promise to be depended upon, nor oath that could command respect; but all parties dwelling rather in their calculation upon the hopelessness of a permanent state of affairs, were more intent upon self-defense than capable of confidence. In this contest the blunter wits were most successful. Appre-

hensive of their own deficiencies and of the cleverness of their antagonists, they feared to be worsted in debate and to be surprised by the combinations of their more versatile opponents, and so at once boldly had recourse to action; while their adversaries, arrogantly thinking that they should know in time, and that it was unnecessary to secure by action what policy afforded, often fell victims to their want of precaution.

Meanwhile Corcyra gave the first example of most of the crimes alluded to; of the reprisals exacted by the governed who had never experienced equitable treatment or indeed anything except outrage from their rulers when their hour came; of the iniquitous resolves of those who desired to get rid of their accustomed poverty, and ardently coveted their neighbors' possessions; and lastly, of the savage and pitiless excesses into which men who had begun the struggle, not in a class but a party spirit, were hurried by their ungovernable passions. In the confusion into which life was now thrown in the cities, human nature, always rebelling against the law and now its master, gladly showed itself uncontrolled in passion, above respect for justice, and the enemy of all superiority; since revenge would not have been set above religion, and gain above justice, had it not been for the fatal power of envy. Indeed men too often take upon themselves in the prosecution of their revenge to set the example of doing away with those general laws to which all alike can look for salvation in their day of adversity, instead of allowing them to exist against the day of danger when their aid may be required.   (III, 82ff; trans. Crawley)

Every sentence of that account deserves to be read, slowly and meditatively, with due weight given to every phrase, every word, lest we underread, as we so often do with the classics, and translate the greatest cultural crisis of the Hellenic world into a parochial and ephemeral time of troubles. If Thucydides is to be trusted, the culture of his time had been shaken to the roots, and he feared for its survival.

How did this convulsion of a whole culture affect the idea of a theater as we find that idea expressed by Euripides?

The immediate, salient fact of Euripides' theater is the assumption of a universe devoid of rational order or of an order incomprehensible to men. And the influence of Aristotle is nowhere more obvious than in the fact that this aspect of Euripides' theater is the one least often recognized or acted upon by critics. Yet it is stated both explicitly and implicitly from play to play throughout Euripides' lifetime. "The care of god for us is a great thing," says the chorus of the *Hippolytus*, "if a man believe it. . . . So I have a secret hope of someone, a god, who is wise and plans; / but my hopes grow dim when I see / the actions of men and their destinies. / For fortune always veers and the currents of life are shifting, / shifting, forever changing course." "O Zeus, what can I say?"

cries Talthybius in the *Hecuba*. "That you look on men and care? Or do we, holding that the gods exist, / deceive ourselves with unsubstantial dreams / and lies, while random careless chance and change / alone control the world?" Usually desperate, feeble, and skeptical in the first place, it is the fate of these hopes to be destroyed in action. In the *Heracles* the fatal chaos of the moral universe is shown formally; a savage reversal which expresses the flaw in the moral universe splits the entire play into two contrasting actions connected only by sequence. Thus the *propter hoc* structure required by Aristotelian drama is in Euripides everywhere annulled by *created* disorder and formal violence. What we get is *dissonance, disparity, rift, peripeteia;* in Euripides a note of firm tonality is almost always the sign of traditional parody; of the false, the unreal, or lost innocence remembered in anguish. What this assumption of disorder means is: first, that form is not organic; second, that character is not destiny, or at best that only a part of it is; and third, that Aristotelian notions of responsibility, tragic flaw, and heroism are not pertinent.

The central dissonance assumes a variety of forms. But the commonest is a carefully construed clash between myth (or received reality) on the one hand, and fact (or experienced reality) on the other. Λόγῳ μέν . . . ἔργῳ δέ, as the Greeks put it, contrasting theory (*logos*) and fact (*ergon*), appearance (or pretence) and reality, legend and truth. In the *Alcestis*, for instance, Euripides juxtaposes the traditional, magnanimous Admetus with the shabby egotist who results when a "heroic" character is translated into realistic fifth century terms. By making Alcestis take Admetus at his own estimate, Euripides delays the impact of his central idea—the exposure of Admetus' *logos* by his *ergon*—until the appearance of Pheres, whose savage "realistic" denunciation of his son totally exposes the "heroic" Admetus. By a similar translation, Euripides' Odysseus becomes a demagogue of *realpolitik*, Agamemnon a pompous and ineffectual field marshal, and Jason a vulgar adventurer. It was, of course, this technique of realism, this systematic exposure and deflation of traditional heroism, which earned Euripides his reputation for debasing the dignity of the tragic stage. And in some sense the charge is irrefutable. Euripides' whole bent is clearly antitraditional and realistic; his sense of rebelliousness is expressed beyond doubt by the consistency with which he rejects religious tradition, by his restless experiments with new forms and new music, and by his obvious and innocent delight in his own virtuosity— his superior psychology and his naturalistic stagecraft. With justifiable pride he might have seen himself as a dramatic pioneer, breaking new ground, and courageously refusing to write the higher parody of his predecessors which his world—and ours—have demanded of him. There must be, I imagine, very few theaters in the world where the man who writes of "people as they are" is automatically judged inferior to the man who writes of "people as they should be."

But it would be wrong to assume that realism was the whole story or that Euripides was drawn to realism because he knew it would offend the worthies of his day. For it was life, not Euripides, which had abandoned the traditional forms and the traditional heroism. What Euripides reported, with great clarity and honesty, was the widening gulf between reality and tradition; between the operative and the professed values of his culture; between fact and myth; between *nomos* and *physis;* between life and art. That gulf was the greatest and most evident reality of the last half of the fifth century, *the* dramatic subject par excellence, and it is my belief that the theater of Euripides, like Thucydides' history, is a radical and revolutionary attempt to record, analyze, and assess that reality in relation to the new view of human nature which crisis revealed. To both Thucydides and Euripides, the crisis in culture meant that the old world order with its sense of a great humanity and its assumption of an integrated human soul was irrecoverably gone. The true dimensions of the human psyche, newly exposed in the chaos of culture, forbade any return to the old innocence or heroism. Any theater founded on the old psyche or the old idea of fate was to that extent a lie. The task imposed upon the new theater was not merely that of being truthful, of reporting the true dimensions and causes of the crisis, but of coping imaginatively and intellectually with a change in man's very condition.

It is for this reason that Euripides' theater almost always begins with a severe critique of tradition, which necessarily means a critique of his predecessors. Such programmatic criticism is what we expect from any new theater, and in the case of Greek theater, where the dramatist is official *didaskalos,* charged with the *paideia* of his people, it was especially appropriate. Aeschylus and Sophocles were not merely great theatrical predecessors; they were the moral tutors of Athens, and their versions of the myths embodied, as nothing else did, the values of tradition and the old *paideia.* Given such authority and power, polemic and criticism were only to be expected, the only possible response; indeed, were it not for the fact that Euripides' criticism has generally been construed as cultural *lèse-majesté,* the point would hardly be worth making. When Shakespeare or Ibsen or Shaw or Brecht criticizes the theater of his immediate predecessors, we applaud; this is what we expect, the aggressive courage a new theater requires. When Euripides does it, it becomes somehow sacrilege, a crime against the classics. We respond, if at all, with outraged traditionalism, automatically invoking that double standard which we seem to reserve for the classics, that apparent homage which turns out to be nothing but respect for our own prejudices.

In Euripides' case, the prejudice is usually justified by the argument that Euripides' criticism of his predecessors is destructive and negative; that his attack on the old order is finally nothing but the niggling rage for exposure, devoid of constructive order. If this argument were sound, it would be impressive; but it is not enough to offer on Euripides' behalf the reply which Morris Cohen is said to have made to a student who accused him of destroying his religious beliefs: "Young man, it is recorded of Heracles that he was required only to *clean* the Augean stables." Not, that is, if we are serious in maintaining that Euripides was a great dramatist. Negative criticism of dead tradition and inert values is often of positive therapeutic effect, but no really great dramatist, it seems to me, can escape the responsibility for imaginative order. Actually the charge that Euripides is negative is based upon misreading of the plays. For one thing, Euripides did not always expose myth and tradition; this is his bias, to be sure, but there are exceptions in which the received myth and its values are used to criticize contemporary reality and public policy. The obvious example is the *Trojan Women*. A more revealing instance is the *Iphigenia in Tauris,* in which the cult of Artemis of Brauron is reestablished by Athena at the close of the play in order to lay bare the immense human "blood sacrifice" of the Peloponnesian War.

The point here, I believe, is both important and neglected. Let me try to restate it. Euripides' favorite technique for demonstrating the new dissonance in Athenian culture, the disparity between putative values and real values, is simply realism of the pattern λόγῳ μέν . . . ἔργῳ δέ. But it is balanced at times by the converse technique—allowing the myth to criticize the everyday reality—ἔργῳ μέν . . . λόγῳ δέ. And these exceptions are important, since they show us that Euripides' realism is not a matter of simple antitraditionalism, but consistent dramatic technique. What is basic is the mutual criticism, the mutual exposure that occurs when the incongruities of a given culture—its actual behavior and its myth—are juxtaposed in their fullness. That this is everywhere the purpose of Euripidean drama is clear in the very complaints critics bring against the plays: their tendency to fall into inconsistent or opposed parts (*Heracles, Andromache*); their apparent multidimensionality (*Alcestis, Heracles*), the frequency of the *deus ex machina*. This last device is commonly explained by a hostile criticism as Euripides' penchant for archaism and etiology, or as his way of salvaging botched plays. Actually it is *always* functional, a part of the very pattern of juxtaposed incongruities which I have been describing. Thus the appearance of any god in a Euripidean play is invariably the sign of *logos* making its epiphany, counterpointing *ergon*. Most Euripidean gods appear only in order to incriminate themselves (or a fellow god), though some—like Athena in the *Iphigenia in Tauris*—criticize the action and the reality which the action mirrors. But it is a variable, not a fixed, pattern, whose purpose is the critical counterpointing of the elements which Euripides saw everywhere sharply and significantly opposed in his own culture: myth confronted by behavior; tradition exposed by, or exposing, reality; custom and law in conflict with nature. What chiefly interested him was less the indictment of tradition, though that was clearly essential, than the *confrontation*, the *dramatic juxtaposition*, of the split in his culture. This was his basic theatrical perception, *his* reality, a perception which makes him utterly different from Aeschylus and Sophocles, just as it completely alters the nature of his theater.

Is that theater merely analytical then, a dramatic description of a divided culture? I think not. Consider this statement: "As our knowledge becomes increasingly divorced from real life, our culture no longer contains ourselves (or only contains an insignificant part of ourselves) and forms a social context in which we are not 'integrated.' The problem thus becomes that of again reconciling our culture with our life, by making our culture a living culture once more. . . ." That happens to be Ionesco on Artaud, but it could just as well be Euripides' description of the nature and purpose of his own theater. The reconciliation of life and culture is, of course, more than any theater, let alone a single dramatist, can accomplish; and it is perhaps enough that the art of a divided culture should be diagnostic, should describe the new situation in its complexity. Only by so doing can it redefine man's altered fate. It is my own conviction that Euripidean theater is critical and diagnostic, and that, beyond this, it accepts the old artistic burden of constructive order, does not restrict itself to analysis alone. But what concerns me at the moment is the way in which his basic theatrical perceptions altered his theater.

First and most significant after the destruction of *propter hoc* structure is the disappearance of the hero. With the sole exception of the *Heracles* —Euripides' one attempt to define a new heroism—there is no play which is dominated by the single hero, as is Sophocles' *Oedipus* or *Ajax*.

Corresponding to the disappearance of the hero is Euripides' "fragmentation" of the major characters. What we get is typically an *agon* or contest divided between two paired characters (sometimes there are three): Admetus and Alcestis; Jason and Medea; Hippolytus and Phaedra; Andromache and Hermione; Pentheus and Dionysus, etc. In such a theater, the Aristotelian search for a tragic hero is, of course, meaningless. But the significance of the fragmentation is not easy to assess; it is not enough to say merely that Euripides was temperamentally drawn to such conflicts because they afforded him opportunities for psychological analysis. What is striking about the consistently paired antagonists one finds in Euripides is, I think, their obsessional nature. They function like obsessional fragments of a whole human soul: Hippolytus as chastity, Phaedra as sexuality. The wholeness of the old hero is now represented divisively, diffused over several characters; the paired antagonists of the Euripidean stage thus represent both the warring modes of a divided culture and the new incompleteness of the human psyche. Alternatively, as in the *Bacchae,* they embody the principles of conflicting ideas: Pentheus as *nomos,* Dionysus as *physis.*

This fragmentation is also the sign of a new psychological interest. That the convulsion of the late fifth century had revealed new dimensions in the human psyche is sharply expressed by Thucydides, and just as sharply by Euripides. Indeed, Euripides' interest in abnormality and mental derangement is so marked that critics have usually seen it as the very motive of his drama. This, I think, is a mistake. The interest in psychology is strong, but it is always secondary; the real interest lies in the analysis of culture and the relationship between culture and the individual. If I am correct in assuming that Euripides' crucial dramatic device is the juxtaposition and contrast of *logos* and *ergon,* then it follows that the characters of his plays must bear the burden of the cultural disparity involved. I mean: if a myth is bodily transplanted from its native culture to a different one, then the characters of the myth must bear the burden of the transplantation, and that burden is psychological strain. Consider, for example, Euripides' Orestes, a man who murders his mother in an Argos where civil justice already exists; or the heroic Jason translated into the context of a fifth century Corinth; or an Odysseus or Hermione or Electra cut off from the culture in which their actions were once meaningful or moral, and set in an alien time which *immoralizes* or *distorts* them. The very strain that Euripides succeeds in imposing upon his characters is the mark of their modernity, their involvement in a culture under similar strain. And it is the previously unsuspected range of the human psyche, the discovery of its powers, its vulnerability to circumstance, its incompleteness, and its violence, that interest Euripides, not the psychological process itself. The soliloquy in which Medea meditates the murder of her children is much admired; but Euripides' dra-

matic interest is in the collapse or derangement of culture—the gap between *eros* and *sophia*—that makes the murder both possible and
necessary.

Side by side with cultural strain is the striking loneliness of the Euripidean theater. Loneliness is, of course, a feature of traditional tragedy,
but the difference between Euripides and his predecessors in this respect
is marked. In Aeschylus the loneliness of human fate is effectively annulled by the reconciliation which closes trilogies and creates a new
community in which god and man become joint partners in civilization.
In Sophocles the sense of loneliness is extremely strong, but it is always
the distinguishing mark of the hero, the sign of the fate which makes
him an outcast, exiled from the world to the world's advantage and his
own anguish. But in Euripides loneliness is the common fate. Insofar as
the characters are fragmented and obsessional, their loneliness is required.
The one thing they normally cannot do is communicate, and typically,
even such communications as occur (for instance, Heracles' moving reunion with his children) are liable to almost certain destruction by the
malevolence of fate. Again and again Euripides gives us those exquisite,
painterly groupings which stress the impassable gulf which separates the
old from the young, man from god, woman from man, and even hero
from hero. The climax of the *Heracles* comes when Heracles, touched
by Theseus' *philia,* makes his great decision to live; but the understanding is then immediately and deliberately clouded as Theseus fails to
understand the enormous range of his friend's new heroism. The touch
is typically and revealingly Euripidean. The gulf seems to close only to
widen out again.

From the point of view of traditional tragedy nothing is more strik-
ingly novel than the Euripidean fusion and contrast of comic and tragic
effects. Thus at any point in a tragedy the comic, or more accurately,
the pathetic or ludicrous, can erupt with poignant effect, intensifying
the tragic or toughening it with parody. Nor is this a device restricted to
Euripides' so-called "romantic" plays or his tragicomedies; it occurs even
in the most powerful and serious tragedies. Tiresias and Cadmus in the
Bacchae, for instance, are seen simultaneously as tragic and comic, that
is, directly pathetic and incongruous: two old mummers of ecstasy; they
try to dance for Dionysus as the god requires, but their bodies, like their
minds, are incapable of expressing devotion except as a ludicrous mim-
icry. Aegeus, in the *Medea,* has puzzled traditional interpretation from
Aristotle on, precisely because he is Euripides' pathetic and ironic embodiment of Athens—that Athens which the chorus hails later as the
place

where Cypris sailed,
and mild sweet breezes breathed along her path,
and on her hair were flung the sweet-smelling garlands
of flowers of roses by the Lovers, the companions
of Wisdom, her escort, the helpers of men
in every kind of *arete*.

The irony is not, of course, the cutting irony of exposure, but the gentler irony that comes when *logos* and *ergon* of things not too far apart are juxtaposed: we feel it as a light dissonance. Which is merely another way of saying that the new element of the comic in Euripidean tragedy is just one more instance of the dramatist's insistence upon preserving the multiplicity of possible realities in the texture of his action. In the traditional drama, such dissonance is rightly avoided as an offence against seriousness and tragic dignity; Euripides significantly sees both tragedy and comedy as equally valid, equally necessary. A drama of truth will contrive to contain them both; the complex truth requires it.

It is for this same reason that Euripides accentuates what might be called the multiple moral dimension of his characters. Every one of them is in some sense an exhibit of the sophistic perception that human character is altered by suffering or exemption from suffering; that every human disposition contains the possibilities of the species for good or evil. Aristotle objects, for instance, that Euripides' Iphigenia changes character without explanation. And so, in fact, she does, and so does Alcmene in the *Heraclidae*. They change in this way because their function is not that of rounded characters or "heroes" but specifications of the shaping ideas of the play. Besides, if Heraclitus was right, and character is destiny, then the complex or even contradictory destiny which Euripidean drama assumes and describes must mean complex and contradictory characters. But the one kind of character which Euripides' theater cannot afford is that splendid integrated self-knowledge represented by the "old fantastical Duke of dark corners" in *Measure for Measure*; Euripides' theater is all Angelos, Lucios, and Claudios—average, maimed, irresolute, incomplete human nature. The case of Heracles himself, the most integrated hero Euripides ever created, is darkened by Euripides' insistence that we observe, without passing judgment, that even the culture-hero has murder in his heart. This fact does not, of course, compose a tragic flaw, but rather what Nietzsche called "the indispensable dark spring" of action. Moral judgment is, as Euripides tried to show, no less precarious and difficult than the comprehensive description of reality. How could it be otherwise?

This does not mean that Euripides avoids judgment or that his plays

are attempts to put the problematic in the place of dramatic resolution.
It means merely that his theater everywhere insists upon scrupulous and
detailed recreation of the complexity of reality and the difficulty of
moral judgment. The truth is concealed, but not impenetrably concealed.
There can be little doubt, for instance, that Euripides meant his *Medea*
to end in a way which must have shocked his contemporaries and which
still shocks today. His purpose was, of course, not merely to shock, but
to force the audience to the recognition that Medea, mortally hurt in
her *eros*, her defining and enabling human passion, must act as she does,
and that her action has behind it, like the sun, the power of sacred
physis. There is no more savage moral oxymoron in Greek drama. But
if Euripides here speaks up for *physis* against a corrupt *nomos*, he is
capable elsewhere of defending *nomos* and insisting that those who prostrate themselves before *physis*, like the Old Nurse in the *Hippolytus*, are
the enemies of humanity. Necessity requires submission, but any necessity
that requires a man to sacrifice the morality that makes him human must
be resisted to the end, even if it cost him—as it will—his life. Better
death than the mutilation of his specifically human skill, that *sophia*
which in Euripides is mankind's claim to be superior to the gods and
necessity. Only man in this theater makes morality; it is this conviction,
the bedrock classical conviction, that provides the one unmistakable and
fixed reference-point in Euripides' dramatic world. Above that point all
truths are purposely played off against one another in endless and detailed exactness of observation.

Within this new context of changed reality, Euripides' whole theater
of ideas is set.[3]

*   *   *

For example, consider the *Medea*. Traditionally classified as psychological
tragedy, it is better interpreted as a genuine drama of ideas. Superficially
it is a critique of relations between men and women, Greeks and barbarians, and of an *ethos* of hard, prudential self-interest as against passionate love. At a profounder level it is a comprehensive critique of the
quality and state of contemporary culture. Like the *Bacchae*, Euripides'
other great critique of culture, the *Medea* is based upon a central key
term, *sophia*. Inadequately translated "wisdom," *sophia* is an extremely
complex term, including Jason's cool self-interest, the magical and erotic
skills of the sorceress Medea, and that ideal Athenian fusion of moral
and artistic skills which, fostered by *eros*, creates the distinctive *arete* of
the civilized polis. This third sense of *sophia*—nearly synonymous with

---

[3] The author's discussion of the *Iphigenia in Tauris* and the *Orestes*, which followed
in the original essay, has been omitted here—[ED.]

"civilization" and specifically including the compassion[4] for the suppliant and the oppressed for which Athens was famous and which Aegeus significantly shows to Medea—is the standard by which the actions of Jason and Medea are to be judged. Thus the vivid harmony of *eros* and *sophia* which Athens represents is precisely what Jason and Medea are not. Jason's calculating, practical *sophia* is, lacking *eros*, selfish and destructive; Medea's consuming *eros* and psychological *sophia* (an emotional cunning which makes her a supreme artist of revenge) is, without compassion, maimed and destructive. They are both destroyers, destroyers of themselves, of others, of *sophia*, and the polis.[5] And it is this *destructiveness* above all else which Euripides wants his audience to observe: the spirit of brutal self-interest and passionate revenge which threatens both life and culture, and which is purposely set in sharp contrast to life-enhancing Athens where the arts flourish, where *eros* collaborates with *sophia*, and where creative *physis* is gentled by just *nomoi*. Behind Jason and Medea we are clearly meant to see that spreading spirit of expedience and revenge which, unchecked by culture or religion, finally brought about the Peloponnesian War and its attendant atrocities. For it cannot be mere coincidence that a play like this was performed in the first year of the war.

What of Medea herself? Upon our understanding of her depends the final interpretation of the play. Thus those who find in Medea a barbarian woman whose lack of self-control, hunger for revenge, and male courage set her in firm contrast to the Corinthian women of the chorus, with their Greek praise of *sophrosunē* and their fear of excess, usually see the play as a psychological tragedy of revenge. Against this interpretation there are decisive arguments. For one thing, Euripides takes pains to show that Medea is not at all pure barbarian femininity, but rather a barbarian woman who has been partially and imperfectly Hellenized. Thus Medea's first appearance is an intentionally striking one, dominated by her attempt to pass for Greek, to say the right thing; she talks, in fact, the stock language of Greek women, *hēsuchia* and *sophrosunē*. Now this may be a pose, but it may just as well be genuine cultural imitation, the sort of thing a barbarian woman in Corinth might be expected to do.

[4] Cf. Euripides' *Electra*, 294-96, where Orestes says: "Compassion is found in men who are *sophoi*, never in brutal and ignorant men. And to have a truly compassionate mind is not without disadvantage to the *sophoi*."

[5] Just as Medea and Jason between them destroy Creon and his daughter Glauke, so Medea, once she is domiciled in Athens, will attempt to murder Theseus, the son whom Aegeus so passionately desires—a fact which Athenians could be expected to know and hold against Medea, especially in view of Aegeus' generosity to her. Wherever Medea goes, the polis, as represented by the ruling family, is threatened.

But the point is important for, if I am right, this play records the loss of the civilized skills through the conflict of passion; and for this reason Euripides first shows us his Medea making use of those civilized virtues which, in the throes of passion, she promptly loses, reverting to barbarism. Euripides' point is not that Medea *qua* barbarian is different in nature from Greek women, but that her inhibitions are weaker and her passions correspondingly nearer the surface. Thus she can very quickly be reduced to her essential *physis,* and it is this nakedness of *physis,* shorn of all cultural overlay, that Euripides wants displayed. Unimpeded *eros* (or unimpeded hatred) can be shown in Medea with a concentration and naturalness impossible in a Greek woman, not because Greek women were less passionate, but because their culture required them to repress their passions. If culture is truly effective, the control of passion eventually becomes true self-mastery (*sophrosunē*); where culture is less effective or out of joint (as in the Corinth of this play), *physis* is checked only by fear, and reveals itself in resentment of the punishing authorities and ready sympathy with those who rebel against them. Hence the profound resentment which the chorus in this play feels against male domination. This—and not mere theatrical convention or necessity—is why Medea can so easily convince the chorus to become her accomplices in her "crusade" against Jason and male society. Their control over their passions, while greater than Medea's perhaps, is still inadequate and precarious (as their bitter resentment of men makes clear); and Medea's revenge arouses their fullest sympathy, just as war evokes the barbarian in an imperfectly civilized man. And this is Euripides' point, that "one touch of nature" makes kin of Hellene and barbarian. In Medea's barbarism we have a concentrated image of human *physis* and a symbol of the terrible closeness of all human nature to barbarism. In her inadequate *sophrosunē* and her imperfect *sophia* is represented the norm of Hellenic, and most human, society. Thus when Jason cries out, "No Greek woman would have dared this crime," we are meant, not to agree, but to wonder and doubt, and finally to disbelieve him.

The validity of that doubt and disbelief is immediately confirmed by the appearance of the golden chariot of the Sun in which Medea makes her escape to Athens. In this chariot Euripides does two related things: he first restates, vividly and unmistakably, the triumph of Medea over Jason, and secondly he provides the whole action with a symbolic and cosmological framework which forces the private *agon* of Jason and Medea to assume a larger public significance. And by showing Medea, murderess and infanticide, as rescued by the Sun himself—traditionally regarded as the epitome of purity, the unstained god who will not look upon pollution—he drives home his meaning with the shock of near sacrilege. As for the chariot of the Sun, it is the visible cosmic force which blazes through Medea's motives and which her whole *pathos* expresses: the blinding force of life itself, stripped of any mediating morality or humanizing screen; naked, unimpeded, elemental *eros;* intense, chaotic, and cruel; the primitive, premoral, precultural condition of man and the world. If that force vindicates Medea as against Jason, her ardor as against his icy self-interest, it is only because her *eros* is elemental and therefore invincible. But she is vindicated only *vis-à-vis* Jason; and she is not *justified* at all. Of justification there can be no question here, not only because *eros* is, like any elemental necessity, amoral and therefore unjustifiable, but also because Euripides clearly believes the loss of *sophia* to be a tragic defeat for man and human culture.

In the agon of Jason and Medea, passion, vengeance, and self-interest expel *sophia.* That *agon,* as we have seen, stands for the Peloponnesian War—the war which Euripides, like Thucydides, feared would expel *sophia* from civilized cities, thereby barbarizing and brutalizing human behavior. At any time, in both individuals and cities, *sophia* is a delicate and precarious virtue; if anywhere in the Hellenic world, *sophia* flourished in Athens, but even there it bloomed precariously (how precariously the plague which overtook the city in the following year proved). And with the coming of Medea to Athens, Euripides seems to imply, comes the spirit of vengeance and passion, endangering *sophia,* that *sophia* whose creation and growth made Athens, in Thucydides' phrase, "the education of Hellas." For Hellas and humanity a new and terrible day dawns at the close of the *Medea.*

In sum, the Greeks possessed a recognizable and developed form of what we should not scruple to call a classical theater of ideas. And there, in substance, my argument rests. Whatever its critical shortcomings may be, its historical basis is, I think, sufficiently secure. If, historically, the theater of ideas tends to occur in times of severe cultural crisis, then we may properly expect it in late fifth century Athens, for of all the cultural crises of Hellenism, the late fifth century crisis was by far the most profound. Among its casualties are classical tragedy and comedy; the old mythical cosmology and the culture which it mirrored and sanctioned; the gods of the polis; the sense of community on which the polis was based, and therefore in a sense the polis itself. In short, the whole cloth of culture, fabric and design together.

In the fourth century Plato's attempt to repiece the old culture—to reconcile *physis* and *nomos,* myth and behavior, to reweave the moral community of the polis—was heroic but finally unsuccessful. Plato was a great conservative and a great revolutionary, but the Hellas he preserved was only preserved by being radically changed, in fact revolutionized. The old Greek culture—the culture to which the Western world most owes its being and to which it returns for life and freshness when Platonic Hellenism threatens to swamp it—died in the fifth century B.C., and it is this culture in its crisis of disintegration that Euripides records. If Euripides could no longer hold out the old heroic image of man, it is because he preferred to base his theater upon what he actually saw as the prime reality of his time: the new emerging human psyche, tested and defined by crisis, and the apparently uncontrollable chaos of human behavior and therefore the turbulence which any viable culture must know how to contain, but without repressing.

Put it this way. The complex knowledge and experience about politics and culture so evident in the *Hecuba* or the *Bacchae* look forward to Plato and also explain Plato's response to the same crisis. Both men share the conviction that war and greed for power have corrupted culture or deranged it; both are convinced that chaotic human nature, as revealed by crisis, cannot be controlled within the framework of existing culture. But Euripides' liberating perception has become Plato's restrictive premise. For Euripides any new cultural order must somehow contain what is uncontrollable in behavior; the failure to allow for turbulence, the failure to democratize its ethics, was what had made the old culture so susceptible to crisis. The Athenian democracy after Pericles could no more make do on aristocratic *sophrosunē* than industrial England could run on knightly chivalry. The solution, however, was not to reorganize society to operate on *sophrosunē* and the old aristocratic ethos but to revise *sophia* and *sophrosunē* in terms of a more democratic view of human nature. It is for this reason that in the *Bacchae* Pentheus' inability to control his inward turmoil is matched by his incompetence to control the public situation. He is an emblem of his age, attempting out of his ignorance of himself and his culture to cope with chaos by means of an inadequate or corrupted aristocratic *sophrosunē.* For whatever the solution to Dionysiac chaos may be, it is not repression, but perhaps a more responsibly Dionysiac (that is to say, liberated and liberating) society. The new polis may not be quite "polymorphously perverse," but it will at least be free, disciplined by experience of inward and outward chaos to a larger self-mastery.

For Plato the ideal polis can only be based upon a coercion that looks like consent. And it is therefore subject to the fate of Euripides' Pentheus, the terrible revenge which *physis* takes upon a *nomos* that cannot enlarge itself to a true human order. In short, the culture envisaged by Plato rests ultimately upon suppression of the natural, and is to that degree profoundly pessimistic and anti-Hellenic. Euripides' specifications for culture rest upon an extremely realistic judgment of human nature and its potentialities for disorder; but because what is chaotic is seen as the thrust of life itself, as something *below* (or *beyond*) good or evil, morally neutral, culture is always a project for hope, for free order, for the creation of new institutions in which man's society will not be in conflict with his nature. The Athens which Euripides had so triumphantly hailed in the great choral ode of the *Medea* may have betrayed what it stood for, but the creative fusion between the passions (*erotes*) and the civilized and artistic skills (the large sense of *sophia,* nearly synonymous with "culture") which produced *arete—here,* however transient, was a paradigm of ideal social order, the polis which made man's fulfillment possible.

That Euripides is an innovator is, of course, not an altogether new idea; Werner Jaeger's word for him is, flatly, revolutionary. But those who regard Euripides as an innovator or a revolutionary rarely see in him much more than a theatrical sophist or the inventor of a realistic and psychological tragedy. So far as I know, nobody has seriously proposed what I am proposing here: that Euripides' theater is no less revolutionary than his ideas, and that these ideas are implicitly expressed in the assumptions of his theater and his dramatic hypotheses. In short, that his theater *is* his ideas; that his radical critique of crisis in culture is not just Sophoclean tragedy turned topical and sophistic, but a wholly new theater, uneasily based upon the forms and conventions of the old. That is, not tragedy at all, but a critical drama related to Aeschylus and Sophocles in much the same way that Hebbel's theater was, at least in theory, related to Schiller's.[6] And for this very reason, I suppose, the argument will be discounted: Why, it will be objected, has a point like this been somehow missed for twenty-five hundred years?

[6] A comparison I owe to Eric Bentley's *The Playwright as Thinker* (New York, 1955), p. 27. Hebbel described his new theater in this way: "At its every step there throngs around it a world of views and relations, which point both backwards and forwards, and all of which must be carried along; the life-forces cross and destroy one another, the thread of thought snaps in two before it is spun out, the emotion shifts, the very words gain their independence and reveal hidden meaning, annulling the ordinary one, for each is a die marked on more than one face. Here the chaff of little sentences, adding bit to bit and fiber to fiber, would serve the purpose ill. It is a question of presenting conditions in their organic totality. . . . Unevenness of rhythm, complication and confusion of periods, contradiction in the figures are elevated to effective and indispensable rhetorical means."

To this question it is possible to make a great many answers. For one thing, the identification of the theater of ideas is of very recent date, even among critics of the theater. For another, classicists have traditionally been—as they remain—hostile or indifferent to literary criticism. For this reason they have very rarely asked the kind of question which might have led them to a literary answer. Instead of giving the dramatist the customary benefit of the doubt, they have assumed that a hostile tradition was generally sound and that Euripides was an interesting aberration but finally too realistic, irreverent, and vulgar to fill the bill as a bona fide classic. With deplorable regularity scholars have insisted that it was Euripides' fate to be an imitator or higher parodist of his predecessors, and then, just as regularly, have condemned him for bungling the job. I doubt, in fact, that the history of literature can show a more pathological chapter. Surely no great dramatist of the world has ever received less benefit of the critical doubt or been more consistently patronized; a fourth-rate Broadway hack will normally demand, and get, more courtesy from critics than Euripides has received from six centuries of scholarship. Even when he is praised by comparison with other dramatists, the comparison is inevitably patronizing. We do not honor our greatest classics by asserting their modernity; if classicists and critics compare Euripides to Ibsen, this is more to Ibsen's credit than to Euripides'—though this is *not* the assumption. We pay no honor to Shakespeare when we compliment him on his modernity: we merely reveal the true proportions of our contempt for the classics. Having said that, I can now say without being misunderstood: the theater of Brecht and of Sartre, and even the Theater of the Absurd, are in many ways remarkably like the theater of Euripides.

In any traditional perspective, Euripidean theater is complex and uncomfortably strange, almost exasperating to a taste founded on Aeschylus and Sophocles. Its premises, as we have seen, are unlike, and almost the inversion of, those of the traditional Greek theater. Typically it likes to conceal the truth beneath strata of irony because this is the look of truth: layered and elusive. For the same reason it presents its typical actions as problems and thereby involves the audience in a new relation, not as worshipers but as jurors who must resolve the problem by decision. But because the problem is usually incapable of outright resolution, is in fact tragic, the audience is compelled to forfeit the only luxury of making a decision—the luxury of *knowing* that one has decided wisely. Something—innocence, comfort, complacency—is always forfeited, or meant to be forfeited, by the audience of jurors. This suggests that the essential *anagnorisis* of Euripidean theater is not between one actor and another but between the audience and its own experience, as that experience is figured in the plays. *Anagnorisis* here is knowing moral choice, exercised on a problem which aims at mimicking the quandary of a culture. As such, it is a pattern of the way in which the psyche is made whole again, and the hope of a culture.

It is thus a difficult theater, and difficulty in literature, as opposed to textual difficulty or a doubtful manuscript reading, has never quickened the pulses of classical scholars. Indeed, the commonest scholarly response to the suggestion of a complex critical reading is that no classical writer could ever have been so unclear as not to be immediately transparent. If he was unclear or unusually complex or at all contorted, he was clearly unclassical; to such a degree has Winckelmann's criterion of "noble simplicity" seized the imagination of classical scholars. To those who believe that Euripides could not possibly have meant more than the little they are willing to understand, there is no adequate reply. But if it is true that critics who interpret great dramatists often seek to involve themselves in the dramatist's greatness, those who deny the dramatist any ideas but their own clearly involve the dramatist in their own dullness. John Finley's words to those who charge that more is read into Thucydides' speeches than the average Athenian citizen could have understood, are appropriate:

> It might be replied that the mass of the people could not have followed speeches of so general a character, but to make such an objection is to misunderstand the mind of the fifth century, indeed of any great period. The plays of Shakespeare and the sermons of early Protestantism give proof enough of the capacity assumed in an ordinary audience or congregation. It could be argued that any era which offers the ordinary man vast horizons of opportunity demands and receives from him a fresh comprehension proportionate to his fresh self-respect. Attic tragedy, even the philosophical and political subjects treated by Aristophanes, cannot be explained on any other assumption.[7]

As for Euripides, if I am right in assuming that his subject was nothing less than the life of Greek and Athenian culture, respect for the intelligence and good faith of the ordinary audience *must* be forthcoming, since it is the premise of culture itself. If Euripides for the most part failed to win the understanding of his audience, as I think he did, the fact does not disprove the intent. It is, I think, not sufficiently recognized that the very scholars who object that literary criticism means importing modern prejudices into an ancient text are themselves usually the worst

[7] John H. Finley, Jr., *Thucydides* (Cambridge, Mass., 1947), pp. 64-65.

offenders. Utterly unconsciously they take for granted all the cramping prejudices which a culture like ours can confer upon an uncritical man, and confer them in turn upon antiquity. "The classicist's attitude toward the ancient world," wrote Nietzsche, "is either apologetic or derives from the notion that what our age values highly can also be found in antiquity. The right starting-point is the opposite, i.e., to start from the perception of modern absurdity and to look backward from that viewpoint—and many things regarded as offensive in the ancient world will appear as profound necessities. We must make it clear to ourselves that we are acting absurdly when we justify or beautify antiquity: who are *we?*"

Among literary men and critics of literature, as opposed to scholars, it might be assumed that a Greek theater of ideas would find favor, if only as a sanction and precedent for the new intellectual theater. But I suspect that this is not the case, precisely because contemporary critics are so stubbornly and unreasonably convinced that the entire Greek theater from Aeschylus to Euripides is firmly ritualistic. In saying this, I am thinking of the fact that the modern poetic theater, in searching for antinaturalistic models, turned significantly to Greek drama. What interested contemporaries in Greek drama was, of course, the belief that they would find in it those features—ritual, stylization, gesture, a sacramental sense of life and community—which promised release from the restrictions of the naturalistic theater. They were confirmed in this by the literary vogue of anthropology, and the apparent success of the so-called Cambridge school, especially Francis Cornford and Jane Harrison. But the strongest argument for the ritual view of Greek drama came, I think, from the inability of the classicists themselves to give any substantial meaning to Greek drama. Thus literary men, always a little nervous when confronted with a Greek text and seldom inclined to quarrel with scholarship, eagerly accepted a scholarly view of the Greek plays that at least had the merit of making them mean *something* and which also suited their own theatrical programs. Ritual for them was a "find." For Greek drama it was, as I have tried to show elsewhere, an unqualified disaster.

But because its basis is "need," ritual interpretation is particularly insidious. My own objections to it are threefold; first, the belief that developed tragedy still bears the visible structural and aesthetic effects of its origin is a clear case of the genetic fallacy; second, there is so little evidence for it in extant tragedy that its own originator, Gilbert Murray, recanted it; and third, it is really Cornford's argument for comedy—a far sounder argument in view of comedy's late nationalization—that gives it cogency. My critical objection to the ritual approach is that it tends to diminish rather than enhance the literary value of the plays; in short, it tends to make priests of tragedians and worshipers of audiences. This is not, of course, to deny the religious importance of the Greek tragedian or his religious concern. But it is to deny that his subject was prescribed, his treatment wholly conventional or stylized, and his thought unimportant or unadventurous. Whatever value the ritual approach may have for Aeschylus or Sophocles (and I think the value is small), its application has obscured even further the nature and originality of the Euripidean theater of ideas, since it is precisely discursive, *critical* thought, the complex dialectic of Euripidean drama, that ritualist interpretation regularly suppresses. Thus the only result of the ritual criticism of Greek drama has been, in my opinion, a further falsification.

But the essential, the crucial reason for our misunderstanding of Greek drama in general, and Euripidean theater in particular, is one which classicists and literary men alike share with the whole modern world. And this is our special cultural need of the classics, our own crucial myth of classical culture. A tradition is, after all, like love; we "crystalize" it, endow it with the perfections it must have in order to justify our need and our love. And classical Greek culture has for some time stood in relation to modern culture as a measure of our own chaos—a cultural Eden by which we measure our fall from grace and innocence. Thus we view the Greeks with the same envious and needful wonder that Nietzsche and Thomas Mann reserved for Goethe—that integrated soul—and which Euripides' age felt for the age of Aeschylus. To our modern dissonance, the Greeks play the role of old tonality, the abiding image of a great humanity. They are our lost power; lost wholeness; the pure *presence* and certainty of reality our culture has lost.

Against a need like this and a myth like this, argument may be futile. But we should not, I think, be allowed to mythologize unawares. If we first deprive classical culture of its true turbulence in order to make ourselves a myth of what we have lost, and then hedge that myth with false ritual, we are depriving ourselves of that community of interest and danger that makes the twentieth century true kin to the Greeks. We deprive ourselves, in short, of access to what the past can teach us in order to take only what we want. And that is a cultural loss of the first magnitude.

Euripides and the Gods

by G. M. A. Grube

The nature and character of Euripides' gods should not be deduced merely, or even primarily, from the passages in which they appear in person. The main question raised by these epiphanies is their dramatic relevance, a problem that more properly belongs to a discussion of the function and purpose of the "prologues" and "epilogues" in the dramas. Here we are concerned with a wider and more fundamental subject. Throughout the plays there is a divine background to the human conflicts, the presence and power of the gods is felt nearly everywhere, their influence frequently motivates the actions and feelings of the *dramatis personae;* they are discussed, prayed to, and cursed. The divine framework is, in fact, as integral a part of Euripidean drama as it is of the *Iliad* itself. What, then, do these gods represent? What is their moral, as well as their dramatic value? Are they so obviously immoral and the presentation of them so inconsistent that we are driven to conclude that the poet is all the time, implicitly or explicitly, bent on destroying belief in them? Is this purpose so strong with him that he deliberately sacrifices dramatic consistency in order to achieve this end?

We cannot hope to answer these questions adequately unless we are fully awake to the differences between the pagan and the Christian attitudes to divinity. Nowhere is an effort of historical imagination on our part more essential, nothing is more likely to lead to misunderstanding, than a failure to adjust ourselves here. Such failure has, in fact, been responsible for serious errors of interpretation in Euripides, as in other Greek writers.[1]

Let us first clearly realize that the word θεός does not carry either the same meaning or the same associations as the word "God" in English, or its equivalent in any modern language. "Theos" primarily means

[1] See the chapter on The Gods in my *Plato's Thought*. The following discussion of θεός, largely repeats what I have already said there, pp. 150ff.

something that is eternal; it can be freely applied to all that is greater than man because it lasts for ever. A "god" is the personification of any more than human power in nature, or any force within the heart of man which is also greater than the individual because it is shared by all individuals. Euripides frequently uses "Theos" in an extremely vague and, to us, startling manner; the word does not necessarily imply any full degree of personification. The most notorious, and the vaguest, example is where Helen says that "to recognize friends is a god";[2] but many other things are also called by that name: Ambition, Equality, Struggle, Reverence, Sorrow, Hope, and the like.[3] And—what is even more surprising—such things can be called bad in the same breath as they are called "gods" or divine. "Why do you long for Ambition, that worst of all divinities (δαιμόνων), my child? Refrain, for she is an evil goddess (ἄδικος ἡ θεός)"exclaims Jocasta; "Reverence will lead you no-where," says Creusa, "she is a sluggish goddess" (ἀργὸς ἡ θεός). Aphrodite complains that Hippolytus calls her "the most wicked of divinities" (κακίστην δαιμόνων). These passages are of the greatest interest, for they show quite clearly that goodness is not an inevitable quality of a "god," it does not, as it were, belong to the divinities by definition. Even the most anthropomorphized gods of Homer are not good: they lie and they cheat, not to mention their more boisterous sins such as quarrel-someness, cruelty, and adultery.

It is quite true that the religious teachers of Greece were constantly engaged in a process of purification, constantly trying to free the more respectable inhabitants of Olympus, and the word Theos, from the amorality of natural forces, which becomes immorality once the gods are endowed with human minds and personality. The need to justify the ways of gods to men is a necessary consequence of creating gods after man's own image, until finally man's natural desire for order in the universe led Greek poets and philosophers to enforce order on Olympus under the sovereignty of Zeus. But the gods of Euripides' contemporaries were still definitely many, and retained a great deal of their earlier amorality; a god could thus be called bad, and bad things could be called gods. This is true of the great Olympians as well as of the mass of lesser gods, divinities, and spirits of all kinds below them, though the Olympians were greater than the lesser spirits in power and more definitely anthropomorphized. We must realize that a god may be shown to have behaved in an improper manner without ceasing

---

[2] *Helen*, 560: ὦ θεοί· θεὸς γὰρ τὸ γιγνώσκειν φίλους.

[3] *Phoenician Women*, 532 (φιλοτιμία), 536 (ἰσότης), 798 (ἔρις); *Ion*, 337, and *Heracles*, 557 (αἰδώς); *Orestes*, 399 (λύπη); *Iphigenia at Aulis*, 392 (ἐλπίς).

to be a "theos." For, if Aphrodite in the *Hippolytus* is a mightier being than Madness in the *Heracles* or Death in the *Alcestis*, they are essentially of the same nature.

Nor should it ever be forgotten that Olympian religion had no fixed creed, no accepted version of consecrated books. The result was that men could, as long as they conformed to ritual, think what they liked about the nature of their divinities and disbelieve as many as they pleased of the stories told concerning them, without necessarily denying the existence of those divinities, or being considered atheists. If, for example, a play leads one to doubt the story of Apollo's fatherhood of Ion, it is not necessarily an attack upon the god whom men called Apollo, but at most on that story. The same is true of any other single myth.

Besides, several of the Olympians have so obvious a significance that even if you deny their divinity, you cannot deny their existence. As Death stands for something real, so—indeed more so—do Aphrodite, Ares, Apollo, and Dionysus. Nor would a Greek think it necessary to deny their divinity, since divinity to him was not inevitably tied up with the notion of moral behavior. To us, God is good or He is not God, for an evil god we call a devil. But to a Greek, Aphrodite and Dionysus exist; they may be good or evil, but gods they are. Such at least was the general attitude of the people, though some of their teachers were struggling toward the conception, found also in a fragment of Euripides (29) that "if the gods do evil, they are not gods." This fragment tells us only that one character in Euripides gave expression to this more Platonic conception, that the poet knew of it, not that it was his own.

Further, the Olympians never inspired their worshipers with the same kind of awe and adoration as Jehovah did and does. The Greek gods were not remote beyond human comprehension: the gods of Homer —and we should never forget that Euripides and his contemporaries were brought up on Homer—are far too human for that. There was no impassable gulf fixed between gods and men: as the gods came down to fight men on the plain of Troy, so human heroes became objects of religious worship, and the great Olympians themselves are but glorified humans. Not one of them could claim to have created the world, even Zeus is but rarely thought of as omnipotent; his power is, as a rule, restricted by that of other gods. The very idea of worship, in the stricter sense that implies a mixture of awe, anxiety, and adoration, is foreign to the Olympian religion; the usual words applied to the cult of these gods have a far less awful meaning and indicate a less sublime and more homely relationship. Nor does the sense of sin appear as a religious concept; indeed there is no Greek word for "sin" as a religious attitude to God; they spoke of mistake or error (ἁμαρτία), of injustice (ἀδικία), or harm (βλάβη). They could and did feel guilt and remorse—Phaedra does—but the religious associations of the modern conception, based at it is on the doctrine of original sin, was absent. The gods were powerful, they could be angry and jealous; but, if man was often powerless before them, he, too, could be angry and reproach his gods.[4] It is against this background of common belief that we must understand the philosophers' struggle toward a higher, or at any rate a simpler, conception of divinity, toward monotheism with Zeus as the supreme ruler, and toward a God who can do no wrong. They had to work with the ideas of their time, and we should avoid thinking of them as merely struggling toward a Christianity never quite realized. Some things in Christianity they might very definitely have rejected and by no means considered as a higher view of things. They were following a different path, even if they sometimes arrive at the same conclusion.

Euripides was, as we have seen, well versed in the new thought and new teaching. We find in his plays the most startlingly "modern" utterances, about the gods as about everything else. We can be certain that he understood contemporary religious criticism, reflected as it is in the words of his characters. He knew his Xenophanes and his Anaxagoras as well as his Aeschylus, and cannot have shared the cruder beliefs of many of his contemporaries. No educated Athenian did believe in an Athena who looked exactly like her statue, nor can Euripides have had any faith in the literal truth of some of the stories he dramatized. But a dramatist must use the mythological apparatus of his time: when Euripides dramatizes Aphrodite, it must be in human shape. It does not, admittedly, follow that he believes in the human shape of the goddess, but neither does it follow (and this we are much more apt to forget) that he does not believe her to be a goddess at all. The symbol of human form may not mean to him what it meant to some of his contemporaries, but it certainly meant to him a great deal more than it means to us. Exactly how much, we cannot tell. You cannot, on reading *Macbeth,* decide whether Shakespeare believed in ghosts and witches. As for the nature of Euripides' belief in the myths, it would be interesting if some commentators who scorn the idea that Heracles' divine birth could have any meaning for Euripides would back their opinion by explaining how far the Christian myth of divine birth has any meaning for

---

[4] And he did, without hesitation, from Homer down. See *Iliad,* III, 365; II, 110, etc. and Wolfgang Schadewaldt, *Monolog und Selbstgespräch* (Berlin: Weidmann, 1926), p. 21, note.

themselves. An average audience, even a modern audience, would, as a rule, be a far better judge of at least the dramatic efficacy of the mythical apparatus in Euripides than some of his most learned critics.

We may grant, then, that Euripides had to represent his gods, whether they appear in person or remain in the background, in a manner intelligible in his day, and therefore in the customary manner, with human shape and personality, and that this method of presentation was probably not to him the mere literary symbol that it is for us, even though he did not believe in the literal existence of such gods as represented. How far was he willing to accept these divinities as simply part of the story? How far were these Olympian persons and their immoral ways so repulsive to him and contrary to his highest aspirations that he deliberately depicted them in a bad light in order to destroy belief in them, constantly using words and phrases that undermine such belief? Does he go further and, within the body of the play, throw out constant hints that all miracles are capable of rational explanation?

Those who believe that Euripides is a militant atheist who uses miracles only to discredit them seem to magnify the religious aspect of his drama out of all proportion. By seeking rational explanations for everything supernatural, they turn his plays into antireligious tracts, and the resulting double meanings and hidden solutions seem to add up to something more akin to crossword puzzles than to great drama. For if, while we are actually hearing the messenger's report of the death of Hippolytus or Pentheus, we are expected to be also constantly on the lookout for catch-phrases by which to recognize that there is round the corner, as it were, a perfectly rational explanation of their death, that these miracles exist only in the imagination of the teller—if we are thus to keep our wits awake and our emotions in check, we may find some delight in our cleverness, but we cannot be moved by the tragedy at all. Deep emotion is not compatible with a perpetual laughing up one's sleeve. If Euripidean drama is of this kind, then the sooner we salvage the purple passages into an anthology and throw away the rest, the better.[5]

A dramatist may be an atheist, and yet use the religious symbols of

[5] It is true that in Sophocles' *Electra* there is an account of the supposed death of Orestes, i.e., a moving account which is not true. But there we know with absolute certainty that Orestes is alive; we have seen him, and are therefore not supposed to be moved by the report of his death, but by its effect on Clytemnestra, and it is upon her that our attention is fixed. The tragic value of the scene lies there. There is no confusion in our minds. Nor does the fact that a credulous messenger appears in the *Iphigenia in Tauris* offer any parallel. All the facts he gives are true, the humor is due to his language. This is similar to the paean of joy raised by an old attendant, when the princess dons the fatal robes in *Medea*.

his day with great effect, and without irony. At the very worst, the irony must not be such as to destroy dramatic consistency. Wherever it does so, he is dramatically at fault, though we should be careful to hold Euripides responsible for the effect on *his* audience only, not for the effect on ourselves, which may well differ. If he ever does so on purpose, it is an unforgivable blunder. I do not think this ever happens.

The influence of drama, in matters of religion as elsewhere, is achieved in two ways. First, by the general impression left upon the spectator at the end of the performance; this is its direct influence, and it may be enhanced by further reflection. In the second place, striking lines are widely quoted, often quite out of their context and without regard for the particular character that spoke them. This may well lead to an influence which the author neither intended nor desired. The Greeks were especially prone to learning poetry by heart, and had no scruples in twisting the original meaning to suit fashion or fancy. It is quite likely that Euripides' reputation for atheism rests, both in ancient and in modern times, as much on such isolated quotations as upon the total effect of his plays. Aristophanes set the fashion, and it has been enthusiastically followed ever since.

Aristophanes does make it very clear that Euripides had a reputation as an atheist, even in his lifetime. That, however, does not prove that his dramas were written, the gods in them conceived and dramatized, with the deliberate purpose of propagating disbelief. The effect of the whole play is here a more reliable criterion than isolated passages. Admittedly, we cannot take into account the plays that are lost, and Aristophanes had more to go on than we have. Nevertheless, it is worthwhile to examine the total effect upon the spectator of such plays as we do possess. In two of them the gods are more intimately linked with the action than elsewhere: in the *Bacchae,* where Dionysus is in the unique position of being a character throughout, and in the *Hippolytus.* A complete realization of the part played by the gods in both these tragedies can be attained only by a full analysis of them, but we may ask here with what feelings toward those divinities we put down the book, and hope that these feelings may have something in common with those of Athenian spectators as they left the theater.

After Agave in her madness has torn Pentheus limb from limb, will the spectator not have impressed upon his heart the conviction that there is this thing here called Dionysus, a power that can be terrible, vindictive, and cruel, a power which we ignore at our own risk? He may well, like Cadmus and Agave, feel that gods should not behave like this, and he will find little comfort in the thought of this more than human power, this "theos." He will, however, be profoundly stirred. He will certainly not walk away and mutter, with a superior smile and a shrug of the shouders, that there is no such thing. The exact nature of this divine force is of course the business of the theologian, not that of the poet. Just because the *Bacchae* so obviously does not result in disbelief, the play has sometimes been looked upon as a recantation, the work of an atheist repenting in old age, as death closed in upon him. And yet, if Sophocles had only to read a few passages from his *Oedipus at Colonus* to convince an Athenian court of law that he was still in possession of his faculties, any court of critics should be as easily convinced by a reading of the *Bacchae* that its author was not suffering from senile decay.

Besides, the impression left upon one by other plays is not so very different. The *Hippolytus* ends on a note of reconciliation between father and son, but, at that very moment, Artemis is vowing vengeance— at the expense of another mortal, be it noted—upon Aphrodite. "But," exclaims the modern reader, with the equation "God equals Good" fixed in his mind, "these are not gods, but devils." Unfortunately, the Greek word "god" can also mean "devil." [6] And it is no use saying men cannot believe in devils, because they do. What we feel as the play ends is an intense pity for those poor mortals in the power of terrifying forces, of these gods who have them at their mercy; but we feel pride too that men can at least find reconciliation which the gods cannot or will not know. There is no trace in the play of any doubt cast upon the existence of these beings, so merciless and yet so beautiful, for we are as conscious of the beauty of both Artemis and Aphrodite as we are of their power.

Nor has the most consistent upholder of Euripidean atheism any fault to find with Poseidon and Athena in the *Trojan Women*. They appear at the beginning of the play. Troy has fallen. Poseidon was on the Trojan, Athena on the Greek side. But, angered by the conduct of her favorites, Athena now proposes a deal, and they join forces to destroy the Greek fleet on its return home. The rest of the action takes place before the fleet sails, but the dramatic effect of the whole depends upon our knowledge that the Greeks will suffer later. That knowledge, in turn, depends upon our belief that Poseidon and Athena stand for something real. This is the only place in Euripides where we have a reconciliation between gods. Its sole purpose is to inflict further sorrows upon men!

Then consider the *Heracles*. Here we have the son of Zeus, the mighty

---

[6] There are, of course, Greek words that mean evil spirits, e.g., ἀλάστωρ. My point is that "theos" can be applied to an evil, as well as a good power.

hero whose greatness and origin have aroused the jealousy of Hera. Iris and Madness appear in the middle of the play to carry out her vengeance, and in a fit of madness Heracles kills his own children. At last he finds comfort in the friendship of Theseus. Once more we find that feeling of peace and reconciliation between men under the blows administered by irresponsible gods. But everything depends for its effect upon the reality of those gods.

In all the above plays, the drama consists to some extent in this relation of the human to the divine; though even in these, if we except the *Bacchae*, it is upon the human characters that our attention is focused; it is the human drama which is reinforced, universalized by the appearance of the conflicting forces personified as gods, not the quarrel among the gods that is illustrated by the human tragedy. Where the gods do not directly appear, we have essentially the same type of drama and the same impression of the gods' reality.

The *Medea* is a good example of this. Heaven does not directly enter the picture. Yet obviously Love is the driving force in Medea, as Jason says (527-31), and is celebrated in both the central odes of the chorus (627-41, 835-45). The play ends in an atmosphere of unrelieved vengeance and hatred—there is no peace here, even on earth. And if Medea reaches more than human stature at the end, is it not just because she alone is possessed by a *theos,* an eternal force, until she herself almost becomes a goddess or, if you prefer, a devil? The drama is essentially of the same kind as the *Hippolytus,* and a vindictive Aphrodite could easily have been introduced. Her presence in one play and her absence in the other are more a difference in dramatic presentation and technique than in essential outlook. To regard the *Hippolytus* as a piece of atheistic propaganda is to attach far too much importance to the actual appearance of the gods. Incidentally it may be so, but such is not the purpose of the drama.

The same is true of those plays where some god, whether he appears in person or not, behaves disgracefully or is the inspiration of evil deeds, and gets roundly abused by despairing mortals. The chief example of this is Apollo in the story of Clytemnestra's murder. Aeschylus, recognizing the difficulty, had made a brave attempt to reconcile the matricide with the idea of divine justice—the magnificence of the *Oresteia* is the result. Sophocles ignored the difficulty blandly in his *Electra,* where the murder of Clytemnestra by her son is regarded as a fine action, its justice never questioned. Euripides treats the subject in a manner essentially more akin to the earnest spirit of Aeschylus, however different the result. His purpose is to dramatize the story realistically, to show what such a matricide would mean to real men and women as he knows them. Hence we have an Electra whose whole being is warped by hatred for her mother, an Orestes who looks with horror upon what he believes to be his duty; also, inevitably, an Apollo who, as the inspirer of the deed, appears in a poor light and is severely blamed in the *Electra,* the *Orestes,* and the *Iphigenia in Tauris.*

These plays are not primarily an attack upon the god. They are realistic presentations of men and women in the circumstances dictated by the legend. Apollo was as much part of the story as the murder itself. Euripides did not hesitate to be realistic to the end, whatever consequences followed for Apollo. The position of the god is the result, not the cause, of this presentation, of the dramatist seeing Orestes and Electra as real people. Nor, even there, do we rise from the play with the feeling that Apollo does not exist, though we may, on reflection, come to the conclusion that, if these are the only gods, they do not deserve human worship. Or we may reflect that men are too prone to blame their own instincts and wrongdoings on the gods (a quite orthodox conclusion), or again we may decide that the story is not true. But such ultimate effects of the play are a very different thing—they do not mean that the poet is intent on making us feel, while the play is going on, that the story is all nonsense. Rather was he concerned at all costs to show us real people on the stage. The powerful emotions stirred up in the reader or spectator, on the contrary, depend upon a belief, or at least a suspension of disbelief, in the existence and the reality of those gods, here symbolized in human form.[7]

*   *   *

Misunderstanding . . . may arise also from attaching undue importance to lines isolated from their context and quoted as the opinions of the poet himself. When we now come to deal with some of these, it must again be emphasized that our first concern should be whether the sentiments are dramatically relevant and in character. Euripides clearly aimed to represent life as he saw it. Actual human behavior was his starting-point and he was little concerned, in the first instance at least, with theological considerations. He paints men and women "as they are, not as they ought to be." Now one of the most deeply ingrained human characteristics is that in moments of overwhelming sorrow, when stunned by misfortune, especially if they feel the misfortune to be un-

---

[7] The more extensive discussion of the relationship between men and gods as seen in the *Iphigenia in Tauris,* the *Ion,* and the *Children of Heracles,* which followed in the original essay has been omitted here. [Ed.]

deserved, men do doubt and (if they are pagans) curse their gods. But they do not doubt unless they believe, nor do they curse a god whom they know not to exist. It is not the atheist, but the believer, who can be guilty of blasphemy.

Perhaps the most poignant picture of unrelieved suffering is Hecuba in the *Trojan Women,* and the gods are at times violently rebuked by the old queen. In this case, at least, it is easy to see how dramatically relevant, how well in character, her blasphemies are, just because the whole play depends upon the reality of the gods. If Apollo is not real, Cassandra's threats lose all their power (329, 356). And before turning to other plays, it is well to remember Hecuba's curses (469, 612):

> O Gods!—they are bad allies that I call on
> Yet we are prone to call upon the gods.

> I know the gods' way, how they raise aloft
> Those that are nought, and cast down those
> That seem important.

Yet when she sees the prospect of vengeance, she does not hesitate to invoke "Zeus, whatever he be" (884), and to express a belief in justice, which later events do not justify. Nor does she hesitate to say that Helen is wrong to lay the blame on Aphrodite for the sins she herself committed, and discredits explicitly the whole story of the Judgment of Paris (988):

> Your own mind, when you saw him, became Love
> For men call every madness Aphrodite.
> Truly the goddess' name is Senselessness.

with a pun on the name of the goddess ('Αφροδίτη—ἀφροσύνη). This is not a denial of Aphrodite, but another version of the familiar thought that men are far too ready to blame their sins upon the gods—to *call* their every passion Aphrodite, and then feel no further responsibility. "It is *you* who fell in love and *you* who are responsible," is what Hecuba means. Not that she is careful to avoid blasphemy, but it is incidental. The same thought occurs in the *Iphigenia at Aulis* (1264). So Helen in the *Orestes* blandly blames the gods for Orestes' sins as she does for her own (76). The *Trojan Women* is so terrible a play largely because, while the existence of the gods is beyond doubt, they are utterly deaf to any human appeal.

Essentially of the same kind, though more rebellious, is Amphitryo's famous outburst (*Heracles,* 339-47); when he, Megara, and the children seem to be facing certain death, and no help appears, he exclaims:

'Twas all in vain, O Zeus, you shared my bed,
In vain we two have fathered the same child.
You showed yourself a worse friend than we thought you,
I, a mere mortal, am in virtue greater
Than the great god. It was not I betrayed
Heracles' children. You know how to creep
Into another's bed and steal his wife,
But how to save your own friends, that you know not.
You are a stupid or a sinful god.

The Amphitryo who utters these words is no atheist, he is rather a
believer crazed by suffering and despair—and Heracles does come back
to save them in the end. Amphitryo hurls at Zeus the worst insults he
can think of, for the fifth century was beginning to require from its
gods both knowledge and justice. 'Aμαθία means both stupidity and
loutishness (the word is applied to Lycus shortly before); ἀδικία is both
injustice and wrongdoing. The adjective ἄδικος, unjust, is repeatedly applied to Apollo.[8] All these insults, however, are based either on ignorance
of the god's real conduct as proved by the rest of the story, or due to
impatience at the slowness of divine justice and help, a sentiment so
often expressed as to be a commonplace.[9]

*   *   *

We should not expect from the characters of Euripides a more perfect
confidence in any promise, oracle, or sign given by the gods, than men
had, and have, in real life. Take, for example, Creon in the *Phoenician
Women*. Tiresias has declared that the city is doomed unless Menoeceus,
the son of Creon, is sacrificed to the gods. Contrary to his father's express
command, the boy does kill himself on behalf of the city. When Creon
returns, he does not, we are told, speak like a man who is sure of the
city's salvation. That is quite true, but surely it is also quite natural.
We need not quibble about Tiresias' words, though it might be maintained that he only said the city would definitely be defeated unless the
sacrifice took place, not that victory was certain if Menoeceus was sacrificed. But even if Tiresias did give a definite promise of victory, Creon
is human. There was always the possibility that the seer might be
mistaken. Besides, the purpose of the sacrifice was to placate the gods of
Thebes, Ares in particular (934). The enemy also had gods on their side,
and—since ancient gods were not as ubiquitous as those of modern
combatants—they were different gods. As Iolaus naturally rejoices in the

---

[8] *Orestes*, 27, 161, 418. Cf. 596; *Ion*, 252, 384.
[9] E.g., *Ion*, 1615; *Orestes*, 420, 426, etc.

Children of Heracles that the gods on their side are at least as strong as those of the enemy (247-52), so Creon knew that the invader could count on the support on Hera. Moreover, even if Tiresias had interpreted the god's will correctly and his own gods were overwhelmingly stronger than those of the enemy (which would rarely be the case), even so the gods themselves were not always to be trusted. Men could never be sure that their prayers and their sacrifices would be effective—we have a great example of that in the fall of Troy, as seen in the choral odes of the *Trojan Women*.[10] Finally, whenever he finds himself faced by sorrow and possible defeat, man is never quite sure either of himself or of his gods, whether it be Creon after the sacrifice of Menoeceus or Orestes on his wanderings. In the same way the victory remains doubtful even after the sacrifice of Macaria in the *Children of Heracles*.

All the passages referred to hitherto are, within the drama, effective, appropriate, and in character. We may readily admit that their very number and vitality makes it unlikely that they are the work of an orthodox believer in strictly anthropomorphic gods or the literal truth of the myths, but there is nothing that requires us to read into them more than the dramatic situation demands. It would, however, be surprising if the frequent introduction of fifth century religious thought did not at times clash with the given facts of the legendary situation. Such occasions are very rare; a contemporary spectator would, as a rule, not feel the contradiction as acutely as we; it was so much easier for him to take the familiar legendary framework for granted. *These contradictions, where they do occur, are not deliberate but accidental; they should nowhere be taken to indicate a subtle intention to make nonsense of the story; nor is whatever indirect religious propaganda they may contain a primary concern of the dramatist.*

There is one passage in the *Heracles* which, however, is difficult to account for. When Theseus has at last managed to rouse the hero from his apathy (1255), Heracles launches into a pitiful catalogue of all his miseries. He begins by saying that he inherited the taint of Amphitryo (who killed his grandfather), and immediately afterward adds that, because Zeus was his father, he was hated by Hera. He then turns to Amphitryo and begs him not to be angry, for he really thinks of him, not Zeus, as a father. It is, of course, the inherited curse that is strange, for biologically at least he could hardly inherit anything from Amphitryo if he was the son of Zeus. The explanation is that Heracles is so eager to pile up his misfortune that he exceeds all probability, a

---

[10] Lines 511–50, 820–58, 1060–80; and Hecuba's words, 1240–50.

deliberate sign of his unbalanced state of mind, for he is still the same bombastic and unstable Heracles, as the rest of this speech makes clear. Or we may condemn it as a strained conceit, but we should not suppose that the dramatist is being purposely awkward in order to make us realize, if we are clever enough to see it, that this divine birth business is nonsense, thus destroying in us all emotional response to the real pathos of this beautiful scene.[11] But a worse shock awaits us. Theseus tries to console his stricken friend, and he says (1313):

> I would much rather exhort another than suffer myself, but no man is free from misfortune, nor any god, unless the tales of our poets are lies. Are the gods not guilty of adultery with one another (ἐν ἀλλήλοισι), which no law allows; have they not bound their fathers in chains and dishonor? Yet they live on Olympus, though they have acted wrong. What will you say to justify yourself, a mortal, in bearing your lot so hardly, when the gods endure?

This is the old familiar method of blaming it on the gods, but instead of the argument being used by the wrongdoer to excuse himself, it is addressed to him, in order that he should give up the idea of suicide on realizing that even the happy gods have sinned and suffered as he. It is a direct appeal to Heracles' pride: if not in happiness, at least in endurance, man can equal the gods.

Heracles' reply begins:

> Alas! This has little to do with my evils, but I do not believe that the gods love where they should not, or enchain one another. I never did nor ever will believe it, nor that one god is another's master. The god, if he be truly god, stands not in need of anything. Such tales are but wretched lies of the poets. . . .

How can the son of Zeus by a mortal woman, we wonder, deny that the gods are guilty of adultery? It certainly sounds strange. But Heracles, like Theseus, is thinking of life *on Olympus*. His first words mean simply that these consolations of Theseus' are not to the point, whatever may be the case on Olympus is no help to him. Nonetheless, as a disputatious Greek would, he answers Theseus point by point: he does not believe the poets, there are no adulterous relationships *between gods,* nor do they emprison one another, they cannot be to each other as master to slave. He then goes on to admit that suicide would be cowardly, and to discuss his future.

Neither passage is the main point of the speech in which it occurs,

[11] The descent into Hades must be taken at its face value, both here (1276) and throughout the play.

they are quite incidental. Nor has it been sufficiently noted that the second is a direct answer to the first. The adulterous life of the gods on Olympus, with which is rejected the vile treatment of parents, is a very different, cruder, and earlier kind of mythology than stories of birth by a divine father from a human mother. The latter kind of myth survives long after the other sins of the gods have been rejected with horror, as they are here by Heracles. The middle position he takes up is, therefore, not unreasonable, it does not explicitly deny the story of his own birth; the audience, even the poet, may not have been alive to the implications, because in their own day there must have been many who would accept myths about the divine birth of Heracles without a murmur, but who would never accept the cruder stories of immorality on Olympus or the dethronement of Cronos by Zeus.

Nevertheless, to a modern reader at least, the awkwardness persists, mainly because Heracles is not the *kind of person* who would indulge in these religious speculations, whatever age he lived in, whereas his violent denunciation of Hera at the end of his previous speech (1303-10) is completely in character. Thus the lines seem out of character; an even more serious dramatic blunder, one which, to the extent of those six verses, should probably be admitted. Yet, if we do admit carelessness in this instance, it should be quite clear that no other passage can be condemned with as much justification. The opinion generally held that Euripides is full of this sort of thing, that he perpetually cracks the legendary framework of his plays and steps outside the limits of his own characterization, is quite unjustified, even though critics more sensitive to anachronism, more anxious about the character of the gods, and more hostile to argumentation on the stage, may reasonably condemn more than I.

. . . Yet it should now be clear that Euripides the atheist, who wrote plays with the specific intention to make men cease to believe in such gods, is a myth. He was neither a philosopher nor a religious reformer, but a dramatist first and foremost. On the other hand, he was very much alive to the doubts and speculations of his day, on religion as on all other subjects; these are reflected in his plays wherever the situation or the characters made them appropriate. He may have an occasional moment of carelessness, and we may parallel the above reflections of Heracles to the debate on democracy between Theseus and the Argive herald. But, at the worst, such a criticism can only be made in very few cases; nowhere is the anachronism or the implied contradiction serious enough to vitiate the structure of the play. And the reader should be warned that, if he thinks the poet is deliberately casting doubts on Heracles' birth in the moving scene from which the above extracts were quoted, he will be compelled to follow the Verrallian interpretations of the plays, *and to follow them all the way*. This leads to far more improbabilities than it solves.

About the gods as about everything else, we must allow for a manner of speech and thought that is largely contemporary but we can complain only when this leads to inconsistency within the play itself. If we allow for the realism of the presentation, if we welcome the fact that his characters are live men and women who doubt while they believe, and blaspheme against the gods just because they know them to exist, if we grant them the right to behave in the illogical manner of real life, if we at the same time remember that they are fifth century pagans and that their gods are pagan gods, then and then only can we hope to grasp what Euripides tried to make his contemporaries see, reach a certain intimacy with him, and thereby understand more fully both his contemporaries and our own.

No one would maintain that Euripides believed in the literal existence of the gods such as he represented them on the stage, as definite personalities with human shape. Nor can he have been concerned to encourage such belief in others; if he had been, he could hardly have made his characters speak as they do. As dramatist, he naturally used the current symbols to represent the divine, for these alone could hold any dramatic significance for his audience. *The fundamental point at issue is whether, when he thus represents the gods, he is concerned with the truth of the symbols, or only with their capacity to enhance the emotional appeal and significance of his drama.* When, for example, he represents Aphrodite as a goddess in human shape, was he aiming at destroying the validity of his own presentation—to make people see that *such* a goddess at least could not exist—or does he wish us to accept her for the purpose of the drama and to fix our attention upon the drama itself, i.e., upon the conflict between the very real forces at work in the hearts of Phaedra and Hippolytus? If the first alternative is true, if the *Hippolytus* is deliberately intended to disprove the existence of Aphrodite as she there appears, then it will be difficult for us to be very deeply affected by the drama just because a good deal of our attention is sidetracked into wondering whether this Aphrodite exists at all, perhaps even into discovering rational explanations for all the miracles in the story. Such inevitable splitting of attention must surely detract considerably from the emotional response awakened by the real drama.

If, on the other hand, we take the anthropomorphic presentation of the gods for granted, not as something literally true or untrue, but as an essential part of the myth which is being dramatized before us; as true, that is, for the purposes of the drama, then we are free to receive the full emotional effect of the drama itself. We feel to the fullest extent the appalling power of Aphrodite, the might, whether for good or evil, of Dionysus and Apollo, we can identify ourselves without afterthought with the human characters whose tragedy is being enacted. The whole more than human apparatus of gods and miracles then serves but to intensify, to universalize the particular action, as divine apparatus, when capably used and freely accepted, does on the modern as on the ancient stage.

It can hardly be denied that a good deal of the divine apparatus in Euripides must be so accepted: Athena and Poseidon in the *Trojan Women* are an obvious example, Madness and Iris in the *Heracles,* and *all* the gods who remain in the background. This acceptance should extend everywhere. The question whether Euripides does or does not believe, or wish us to believe, in the gods, does not arise, at least while the play is going on. He wants us to accept the divine framework as part of the story. We should not, while in the theater, reflect upon the particular details of the symbolism employed any more than we should wonder whether the poet intends to encourage perjury when he puts in the mouth of Hippolytus the famous line: "My tongue has sworn, my mind is free from oath." [12]

What our reflections will lead to when the play is over is a very different matter. Many a passage in his plays, remembered in or out of context, will stimulate thought. It was clearly never Euripides' intention to send an audience away mentally happy and contented; he made his hearers think and wonder, about the gods as about everything. A man who could so poignantly express doubt and despair in matters of religion cannot have been a satisfied worshiper of the Olympians; but neither can he have been a satisfied atheist.

Denial of the existence of the gods is not, as we have seen, the impression left upon one by his plays.[13] To ask what, more specifically, that impression is, comes to asking what were Euripides' own beliefs. To this there is no certain, no objective answer. The impression carried away by different students must be different, and any answer is largely conjectural and almost wholly subjective. It cannot be proved, for any attempt to prove it will involve attributing to him the words of certain of his characters, and the principle of subjective selection comes in at once.

My own feeling is that most of his extant plays, especially the greatest

[12] *Hippolytus,* 612.
[13] Cf. Van Lennep, *Euripides* (Amsterdam: Swetzand Zeitlunger, 1935), pp. 123ff.

—the *Hippolytus, Bacchae, Medea, Trojan Women, Electra, Heracles, Hecuba*—show mankind in a very real sense in the power of gods before whom they are all but helpless.[14] These gods, who are neither one nor kindly, cannot be denied without grave risk. Euripides presents the gods also "as they are, not as they ought to be." There is no peace in Heaven, no certain order in the universe. It is customary to represent pagan thinkers rising steadily to a conception of a single omnipotent deity; but Euripides at least must be left outside that development. Scattered passages can no doubt be quoted to support monotheism, as others can be quoted to support every kind of contemporary religious and philosophic speculation, but the general tone of his work is against it, and in this respect he is perhaps the most thoroughly pagan, because the most completely pluralistic, of all classical poets and thinkers. For him the eternal forces remain at war with one another as man, poor creature, is ever at war with his fellows and with himself. And yet, if little or no help is to be expected from these ruthless and inexplicable gods, men and women can find some consolation, some lightening of the burden of sorrow and despair by turning their eyes upon themselves and their fellows, by trying to replace hatred by friendship, by having confidence not so much in the gods as in humanity. Whatever peace may be so found must be a human peace, whatever help is obtained will be human help. The human mind and emotions reflect only too fully the conflicts of the gods—are those conflicts perhaps, at least in part—and a synthesis can be found only by accepting the reality of those conflicting forces and by attempting to reconcile on earth the warring forces of heaven.

Such, or somewhat on these lines, I imagine the Euripidean outlook to have been. One thing is certain, it was upon humanity that his eyes were fixed, it was humanity that he tried to understand. His sight was clear and his glance unafraid; he tried to show his contemporaries what he saw in them and in himself, and this accounts both for their fear of him and their unwilling admiration.

---

[14] Cf. A. S. Way, *The Tragedies of Euripides in English Verse* (New York: The Macmillan Company, 1898), II, xxxv: "Men have always worshipped their gods, not for their goodness but for their power; and the more realistic such stories were, the more they brought home to believers the nearness, the formidable irresponsibility, the readiness to harm if offended, to help if propitiated, of these beings."

The Virtues of Admetus

by Anne Pippin Burnett

The *Alcestis* nowadays is commonly described as a psychological drama which has as its true subject an absurd disparity between outmoded ideals and actual human conduct. It is usually said that Euripides has portrayed the noble action of a fairy-tale heroine, then capped it with ignoble consequences. Some scholars, however, turn a skeptic's eye even upon Alcestis and her sacrifice. Those who admire the queen often assert that she dies disillusioned, while the true debunkers explain that she is dying for base reasons that show her to be as false and calculating as her mate. Critics who believe in Alcestis but find her husband unworthy of her read the play as a bourgeois-realist comedy with a plot that breaks all the rules of realism. Those who find both the king and the queen to be cheap imitations of tragic nobility discover a Shavian marital fable ending with the reunion of a pair who will live unhappily ever after, each a thorn in the other's flesh. Both groups believe that the secret of the play is hypocrisy, conscious or unconscious; they argue that principals and chorus often do not mean what they say, and that Euripides meant only the simpletons in his audience to take his play at face value. These critics seem to forget, in dealing with the *Alcestis,* the enormous spatial candor of the ancient theater, and the difficulty of conveying innuendo from behind a mask.

I should like to play the simpleton, and attempt a naïve reading of Euripides' *Alcestis.* The way has been prepared for many years, ever since Lesky's study of the fable's fairy-tale forms showed that the story itself makes no evaluation of the husband's acceptance of his wife's sacrifice, though it plainly condemns the parents. Euripides, then, in choosing as his *mythos* the mixed tale of the bargain with death and the love sacrifice, was not choosing a story which necessarily dealt with a cad or a coward. It was doubtless within his power to give the king these qualities if he wished, but if the conventional story of a favorite of the

"The Virtues of Admetus" by Anne Pippin Burnett. From *Classical Philology*, LX, No. 4 (October 1965), 240–55. Copyright © 1965 by the University of Chicago. Reprinted by permission of the University of Chicago Press. Notes omitted by permission.

gods was to be given a new tone of moral corruption, the change would
have to be strongly made. A straightforward dramatist would establish
the altered ethical coloring of his king as soon as possible; a writer of
more subtlety might lull his audience for a while, then suddenly force
them to see the baseness of the man they had admired. In this case,
however, the longer the revelation was postponed, the more shocking and
incontrovertible it would have to be when made. Euripides, however,
follows neither of these courses. His opening description of Admetus is of
a king, hero, and favorite of Apollo. At the play's end the entire kingdom, the entire generation, has had its admiration of the man, his wife,
and his friend strengthened and confirmed. The audience has nowhere
been instructed to separate its judgment from that of the chorus. Nor has
its attention ever been directed to what must be, in a reevaluation of the
Admetus story, the crucial moment for revision: the moment when
Admetus accepted his wife's offer to trade her life for his. Euripides, in
fact, has gone to considerable trouble to discourage his audience from
thinking of this moment at all.

In fairy tale the bargain and its fulfilment both belonged to the king's
wedding day; the family refuses, the bride insists, and at once she sinks
away as her dying husband is revived. Euripides has split this single
action in two, making a new chronology that stretches over an indefinite
length of time. No word of his text describes the circumstances of the
past bargain: how Apollo announced it, how Admetus made his canvass,
how Alcestis offered herself, and how Admetus received that offer. All
these matters are ignored, though three passages mysteriously suggest
that Admetus was virtually dead at the time (13, 462-63, 633). The bargain is stated as fact; Apollo's first (and presumably inalterable) arrangement with the Moirai in two lines (14-15), the subsequent actions of
Admetus and his family in three (15-18). The only motivation discussed
is that of Apollo; he sponsored the bargain as a boon for Admetus, to
show his gratitude for that man's pious hospitality. Euripides' new
chronology supplies one new detail, however; in his version of the
bargain, the death that was offered and accepted was not an immediate
death but one set vaguely in the future, allowing a certain amount of
continued common life to both the receiver and the giver. This ameliora-
tion would hardly have been added by a poet bent on condemning the
king.

The play allows us to watch what happened on the day the bargain
was fulfilled, but places behind a veil of time the day when Alcestis made
her promise to the Fates. It was Euripides, as far as we know, who made
this unmeasured chasm of years appear in the middle of the old story,

and the effect of the innovation is plain. The bargain assumes the unquestioned inevitability of historical event. In the course of his play the dramatist explores and evaluates Alcestis' decision by making her, on this later day, repeat her old reasons, but there is no similar exploration in the case of Admetus. He has no decision today, since her death cannot now be prevented, and the audience is not encouraged to think that he was allowed a decision on the long-ago bargain day. That bargain was engineered by Apollo and presented to Admetus in token of gratitude, and one thing Euripides has made his chorus say, at a crucial moment in the denouement, is that one must accept the gift offered by a god (1071, a positive version of Solon's δῶρα δ'ἄφυκτα θεῶν ["inescapable are the gifts of the gods"]).

The visible action of the *Alcestis* represents the bargain's fulfilment, and then its remarkable dissolution. The cost is met, the article secured, then suddenly the price is returned and the purchase becomes a free gift. The audience sees Alcestis die and sees her carried out; it sees her husband take a visitor into his house and drive another away; it sees him refuse to go back into his house alone and refuse to take a strange woman in with him; then suddenly the strange woman proves to be the dead wife, and the man who bought his own life at the price of hers reenters his house, his purchase still secure but with the price paid once more in his hands. This is the skeleton of the *Alcestis*; it acquires its flesh and form, its ugliness or beauty, from the speeches which Euripides has written for his characters. As they speak, the king and queen at least must be heard with the ordinary good faith granted to all the figures who walk the classic stage, for there is nothing in the tradition, nothing in their past, and nothing in the play's overt system of rewards and punishments to suggest that this man and woman are false. If the dramatist is playing a subtle game with the material he has chosen, if in spite of the positive evaluations of the action he himself has created he means his creatures to be doubted, he will label their lies, or show a strong contradiction between their words and their accomplished deeds.

In the *Alcestis* prologue a god and a demon meet at Admetus' threshold; Apollo is just leaving the house Death is about to enter. Apollo toys for a while with the demon, pretending to dissuade him with a courteous plea, then standing aside sardonically to let him pass. He knows that Death is to lose his prey, and ignominiously, submitting to force and getting no thanks for what he will have to grant (64-71). The prologue thus shows the apparent defeat of what is bright and young and good, while promising that in the end these qualities will be victorious over the power that is black and old and evil.

As the two supernatural beings dispute, their speeches investigate the ideas of graciousness, justice, and repayment. Viewed from heaven, this whole affair is merely an incident in a series of repayments, transgression for transgression, made between Zeus and Apollo (3-7). On earth there has been a series of benefactions; Apollo is here because of a positive repayment, the benefaction he returned to Admetus after his kind reception (9). Such chains of repayment must begin somewhere; the heavenly one began, according to Apollo, with Asclepius' raising of the dead—a boon to men but an evil in the eyes of Zeus. The earthly chain began with Admetus' hospitality to Apollo. In the course of the prologue Apollo asks, perhaps not quite seriously, if Death will not perform another such gratuitous initial act (60). If Thanatos had agreed, a continuing courtly exchange of favors between him and Apollo would presumably have been founded (70). Death, however, is interested in justice, in getting and giving exactly what is due on the basis of old debts and established law (30-31). An independent act of graciousness is incomprehensible to him (63).

Apollo suggests, like Athena in the *Eumenides,* that there is more to justice than Death supposes, that the quality of an act is to be considered as well as its quantity, and that repayment is to be made not only in kind but with love or hatred in addition. Admetus' hospitality was technically repaid by the tricking of the Moirai, but in addition Admetus, the man who was *hosios* ("pious"), has become dear to the god. Apollo is interested now in the death of Alcestis, not because he still has any debt to discharge, but because he shares the griefs of his mortal friend (42). In Death's way of thinking, this is contrary to justice (41). And Thanatos' refusal to become Apollo's benefactor provides an opposite case; he is to be repaid exactly, according to his own notion of justice, by receiving no thanks (70), but in addition he will become the enemy of Apollo (71). Thus the motifs of friendship and enmity are added to those of *dikê* ("justice") and repayment while the demon and the god confront each other. The ambiguous word *charis* ("graciousness") is also introduced as they converse; it is used to describe an original, gratuitous benefaction (60), or the necessary return of good for good (70).

The prologue introduces, beyond these abstractions, one concrete concept. Apollo opens the play by stepping forth from the house of Admetus and turning to address it. The house is dear to him (23), and he has acted for its aid and salvation (9, 41). He has in some sense occupied the house ever since he first entered it as a servant, and he now leaves it only because he cannot stay under the same roof with Death. Heracles will enter the house in his stead, and then Death's work will be undone.

There are ten direct references to the house in seventy-six lines; a lighter but still unusual density characterizes the rest of the play, where there are at least sixty mentions of *domos* or *oikos,* and as many more to roofs, walls, gates, etc., in the total of 1163 lines.

The prologue's motifs of house and repayment, *dikê* and *charis,* are— like its symbolic action—prophetic of the play to come. As the prologue begins with an apostrophe to the house, so does the denouement (861ff), and at the center of the whole, marking the beginning of the reversal, is the great House of Admetus Ode (569-605). This house is the formal object of the action, and the action is moved by the mechanism of repayment. Apollo entered the house in repayment of his crime against the Cyclopes. He repaid his host by arranging for his escape from death at the price of another death, which causes Apollo to leave the house and Death to enter. Death's entrance is followed by Alcestis' exit from the house as a corpse, a departure that leaves the house temporarily emptied and diminished. Apollo, moved by his love for Admetus and his respect for the house, and also perhaps by his need to do Zeus a new disservice, brings Heracles upon the scene, and Admetus, repaying old obligations to his friend, opens his house to the agent of the god. Admetus has, in repayment to Alcestis, promised to close the house to a future wife; as part of the same repayment, he closes it also to his father and mother. Finally Heracles, repaying Admetus, keeps Alcestis from entering the House of Hades and restores the House of Admetus by sending her once more within its doors. I hope to demonstrate that this formal structure of action and motivation represents the true action of Euripides' play as a device or an emblem might.

As long as the prologue lasts, Alcestis' approaching death appears to the audience, as it does to Apollo, simply as an event in the history of the House of Admetus. The death is fixed and has been for many years; there is, as Admetus later says, a sense in which it has happened long ago (421; cf. 527). Very soon, however, it becomes immediate.

This death, although it is to be reversed, is the central fact of the drama, and it is at once created and dissected in a fashion typical of Euripides. First the causes of the death are expressed, in the barest possible form, by Apollo. Then the death is represented symbolically, as the god withdraws before its miasma and the demon enters to cut his lock of hair. Next the death is mourned by the citizens of Pherae, as they sing the *parodos,* and only at this point does the dying woman instead of the death itself become important. She is given public praise as the best of women, whose death will be the fullest expression of her *aristeia.* A third shift of focus comes with the speech of the servant woman who in effect forces the eye of the chorus to the keyhole of the women's apartments. She allows them, and the audience with them, to watch what no man could have witnessed, knowing that the purity of Alcestis' private actions will be the more blinding for having been spied upon. After this incomparable glimpse of stately preparations and heart-broken farewells, a brief ode is sung to say that there is no escape from death. The surface of the song is funereal, but the audience simultane-ously anticipates both the terror of death and the joy of revival, since they know that Heracles is somehow to save the queen.

At last Admetus and his dying wife appear, and in the scene that follows the presence, the words, and then the silence of Alcestis drive out all consciousness of artistry or illusion. In a passage of only 150 lines Alcestis first experiences her death, in a brief and pitiful *agon* with an invisible enemy, and then explains it. She gives a crystalline state-ment of the reasons which led her to choose this death and of the results she wishes it to have. Then, as soon as she is assured that her death will be effective, she simply ceases to live. The child's song follows, releasing the emotion of the audience and providing testimony that the woman who spoke so clearly a moment ago is really gone. All memory of Apollo's promise is momentarily lost and the death seems beyond redemption.

Euripides' prismatic technique for dramatizing this death also allows evaluations of it to come from different sources. Apollo made no judg-ment, he simply said the queen was young and not yet ready to die; but the chorus of citizens and the serving woman have saluted the queen as the finest of women. To them her action is a just expression of her superlative virtue. Alcestis says the same of herself, and with her state-ment of reasons and demands the audience is allowed to test all these opinions and to judge the woman and her action for themselves.

Alcestis begins with the fact that her promise to die was freely made, not forced upon her. It was, in the prologue's terms, a gratuitous bene-faction of the sort that inaugurates a repayment chain. Thanatos had objected that such actions are not required by *dikê* and are made at the expense of the benefactor. He refused to perform a minor act of gracious-ness, but Alcestis has decided upon a major one. What can move a human being to a freely chosen act that is in the interest of another but against his own? This is the question that Euripides explores in Alcestis' dis-cussion of her case, a case in which the cost of her action to herself was the highest any human could pay.

The lucid economy of Alcestis' explanation has shocked some moderns, but her secret is that she sees the problem as simple. She knows of course that her action will bring *kleos* and that fame is an honorable thing, but this prize she gives away to her husband and her children as a consolation. For herself she wants only one thing—success. Self-sacrifice has no inherent value since life is good; it is conceivable only when careful calculation has shown that death will bring results that life could not, results that are more valuable even than life.

Alcestis chose to die rather than to live as Admetus' widow (the two existing possibilities, once Pheres and his wife had declined) because she saw that in these circumstances her death would best serve that to which her life was dedicated, her marriage. She states this with cool precision, but Euripides makes her reveal as well her passionate idealism. She would not betray her marriage bed and her husband (180-81); she honored her husband's life more than her own soul, though she loved life well (282ff); her children can be despots in their father's house, though she is dead, as they could not be in the house of a stepfather (280ff). In Alcestis' cosmos Marriage is a pure element to be named with Sun, Air, and Earth (244-49). Husband and bed are one, as are husband and hearth; she confides her children to Hestia (163ff) and to Admetus (375), for the two are inseparable in her thought. Husband, children, house, and marriage make up a single ideal concept which her death will save. It is more valuable to her than her sharp delight in life, and having seen what was best she felt that to choose any course but death would have been shameful (180; cf. Plato *Apology* 28B).

Alcestis' farewells are made to her marriage bed, the symbol of temporal union; her recommendations for the future are made to the goddess of the eternal *foyer,* from whose altar nothing can be taken away. Nothing that she does has any reference to romantic love, for this concept is unknown to her. She is ruled by *philia* (279), the feeling proper among friends and members of the same family. She expects to be forgotten (381, 387) and assumes that another will sleep in her bed (181-82), but these things do not interest her. The success she demands is that her marriage should continue after she is gone; it must not be imitated or replaced, for her death is to make it immortal.

Alcestis dies only when the results she wants have been promised her. What she asks is specific; she says in effect: "I refused to give our children a stepfather; I ask in return that you shall not give them a stepmother." This finely calculated return of like for like which takes no account of the quality of the initial benefaction and which has nothing to do with gratitude or love, this repayment which cannot pretend to be worthy of Alcestis' deed, she labels "just" (302). It is the kind of *dikê* that Death understands. Admetus agrees as a matter of course (note how his reference to Thessalian brides, line 331, echoes hers to Thessalian grooms, line 285; they make exactly paired renunciations), but he is no more satisfied than an Apollo would have been by this mean return of like for like. Hastily he adds extensions and embellishments to his covenant in the attempt to respond to her *philia:* he will not only not marry a new wife, he will grieve for this one forever, sacrificing not only the joy of future sons, but all joys. He will not only close his house to the potential enemy stepmother, he will drive away the actual enemy, the father who has behaved like a stepfather (636ff). A comparison of his parents' action with that of Alcestis has proved to him that they deserve not love but hatred from him (338-41; cf. her accusation of them at 290ff). From this day on he will be a stranger to the pleasures of music and masculine company, nor will he have any female companion to solace him.

Had he simply proposed never to install the concubine Alcestis took for granted, the effect could only have been crude. Admetus instead makes a promise that is positive, delicately stated, and filled with a powerful meaning (348-56):

> Your body's counterfeit as like as art can make
> I shall command, and place upon my bed.
> This will I embrace and this adore,
> Holding it I will call your name
> And thus in semblance will I hold the wife I have no more.
> A pleasure cold as ice I'll know
> But it may lift the weight upon my soul
> And then, perhaps, in dreams
> Your shade will come to bring my heart some cheer.
> For sweet it is in sleep to welcome friends,
> Though all too short their stay.

Since he is not Orpheus (357) this will be his way of bringing his wife back from Hades. He will live in the dream he hopes to induce with the *eidolon* (image), himself a sleeping image of death, host to her phantom imitation of life. She has asked that her marriage be kept alive; Admetus determines as far as possible to keep his wife alive too, as statue and as ghost (cf. 328). At the same time he arranges to die with her; his life will be like death (288, 242-43, 278, 666, 802, 1082, 1084), its goal that moment when his corpse will lie beside death's image of her while his soul seeks her shade in the house she is to prepare below (363-68).

Admetus' promised repayment exceeds Alcestis' bid for justice and attempts to reflect something of the quality of her action. His words are approved by the chorus, which calls his promises, thus extended,

axia, worthy of her sacrifice (370; cf. 300). Whether his actions are likewise worthy of her, whether the play as it continues is worthy of her, are
the questions which next must be considered. Both dramatist and characters must meet the test of Alcestis' death: its motives, its demands, and
its beauty. Alcestis has explained the results she hopes for; the audience
will witness the results the playwright has arranged.

Alcestis' body is carried into the house, and Admetus accompanies it,
to close the first episode. The next phase of the action is expressed in a
pair of scenes in which one visitor is almost violently brought into the
house and another is more violently driven away. These scenes of reception and ejection stand on either side of the axial House of Admetus
Ode, the physical center of the play, a song in celebration of the welcome
once given to Apollo and of the blessedness of wealth that was its reward.
The two scenes occupy the space between the death and the decision to
revive Alcestis and so, unless this is a very foolish play indeed, they
must in some way cause or explain the happy reversal which occurs.

Pheres, as one of the refusing parents, belongs to the love-sacrifice tale,
but Heracles is an intruder. An alternate and probably older version
made Persephone return Alcestis to her lord, and this detail is echoed
in the folk-tale solution of direct divine intervention. Phrynichus had
made use of Heracles in his more primitive drama, but such a precedent
was far from binding, and Euripides emphasizes the technical superfluity
of this visiting hero in his prologue. Apollo has already cheated death
once by making the Fates drunk, and on Admetus' doorstep he teases
Death in the manner of a satyr-play Sisyphus about to trick Hades himself. Clearly the god could save Alcestis at once; instead he announces a
story change: the bargain will be reversed, not by divine interference,
but by the heroic act of a mortal. Even in this form, however, the story
does not need Heracles. If someone is to wrestle with death, Admetus is
on hand, and there is no dramaturgical need to bring in an outsider.
Euripides emphasizes this point too, by making Admetus himself touch
on the possibility of a journey to the underworld.

Heracles is plainly necessary to Euripides' particular intentions toward
his story, and the dramatist as plainly wants us to realize this. The brute
effect of Heracles' introduction is that something of the satyr drama in-
vades the tragedy of Alcestis' death and salvation, echoing the drunken
Moirai in the story of Admetus' escape. A more subtle result is the
restored prominence given to the king. Admetus had figured in a god-
come-to-visit story in which he was rewarded for his piety with wealth, a
beast chariot with which to win a wife, and escape when he was
threatened with death. He had also figured in a love-sacrifice tale. The

two stories had no essential connection, but had been given a point of contact through Apollo when the final reward for hospitality that ended the first became the bargain with death that began the second tale. Euripides succeeds in conflating the two, by refusing Persephone and choosing Heracles, an envoy of Apollo's, to act as Alcestis' savior. By means of this semidivine friend he is able to stage a version of the god-come-to-visit story concurrently with his drama of the love-sacrifice. He can thus consider, in a single play, the characteristic virtues of both Alcestis and Admetus.

As soon as Admetus has sent his friend indoors the audience is reminded of that other, gratuitous act which stands with Alcestis' decision as one of the two mortal causes of everything seen on the stage. The reception of Heracles is the double of Admetus' original reception of Apollo and will have the same sort of consequence; this much is made explicit in the ode which follows (605; cf. Apollo at 68-69). Thus Admetus, making the first move of his new life, is shown to reenact the past. He faces a second test of hospitality, more difficult than the first, since Heracles' arrival is apparently so untimely. However, his new duty to Alcestis (his promise to mourn and yet to live as if his wife were still alive) coincides with his continuing duty as a nobleman. His simple impulse to deny Alcestis' death shows him the way, and he has soon fulfilled Apollo's requirement by offering the hospitality of his house to Heracles. When the traveler's fateful entrance into the guest quarters has been accomplished, Admetus explains his reasons (553-60). He could not have turned his friend away, for to do so would have threatened the reputation of his house and the future reception of its members elsewhere. Whereas Alcestis saw the house from within, an enclosed space with the marriage bed at its center, Admetus honors its outward aspect. For him the house includes the city (553), a city which has obligations toward other cities. The house where Alcestis' children are to rule is also the *polis,* and he values its good name more than his own sharp need to grieve alone for his wife. Even the servant, whose views are much more limited than his master's, recognizes that Admetus was governed by *aidos,* the sense of proper reverence felt toward one's family and the gods (823).

Once, before the play began, Admetus had taken in a guest without realizing the full meaning of his action, and he will do so again, before the play has ended. The three actions are given such heavy echoes that they stand each as a type of the other two. Apollo was presumably unrecognized; Heracles is recognized only as a friend, not as a savior; Alcestis will be veiled. In every case Admetus acts out of respect for his house: the desire to give it its due and to preserve in this way its ideal existence in men's opinion. The first reception resulted in *philia* (42), the second has friendship as its partial cause (1037); in the final case, the desire that a friend shall not become an enemy causes the reception (1106) which has the return of Alcestis' *philia* as its effect.

In the scene that follows, this act of friendship and welcome is matched by an act of enmity, as Pheres is abused and driven away. The primary fairy-tale identification of Pheres is not as father but as one who refused to do what Alcestis did, and Euripides has done his best to preserve this single character for the old man. When he arrives on the scene one fact and only one is known about him, but it has been stated four times over: Pheres, though ripe for death, refused to exchange his life for his son's (Apollo, 16; Alcestis, 290-92; Admetus, 338-39; Chorus, 468-70). His presence now makes possible the completion of the central inquiry of the play; through him the dramatist can consider again what it is that could induce a human being to give up his life for another. The woman who chose to die has given her reasons; now, in the presence of her corpse, the audience hears the explanation of the man who refused.

Pheres begins with a fair speech in praise of Alcestis. If there was a convention for portraying the hypocrite, the actor probably followed it here, for Euripides has made Pheres' own words prove him disingenuous. He begins by saying that he would sympathize and share in his son's misfortunes (614), but soon he admits that whether Admetus be wretched or joyful is no concern of his (685-86). Alcestis he calls wise (615) when he thinks he has benefited from her action (625), an idiot (728) when it is suggested that he might have done as she did. The noble deed (623) becomes a stupid error when he imagines himself performing it (710). He congratulates Alcestis on her most glorious life in his first speech (623), but reveals in his next that he does not believe in glory (726). He wishes her well in Hades (627), then states his own conviction that the time below is long but never sweet (692-93). With each self-contradiction he proves what Admetus had earlier said (339)—he is a friend only in words.

When his trumpery offering of praise has been rejected, Pheres states his reasons for refusing to save his son, beginning at the same point that Alcestis had chosen. No debt bound him to die for Admetus, and he loved life. *Dikê* was enough for him, and *dikê* meant holding on to the same tangible things that Alcestis had decided to relinquish. The house, for him, was a complex of lands and flocks (687) to be counted and consumed, not a complex of ideals to be preserved. He values only the sweets of this earth (693) and thus the best life is the longest one.

Pheres does not care for reputation and he admits that he knows nothing of sympathy; it is his own fate a man cares about, not that of anyone else (712). And in so denying *philia* he isolates himself from every other being in the play save Death alone; all the rest, from god to slave, experience what it is to live with two souls instead of one (Admetus, 883-84; cf. Apollo, 42; the household, 192-93 and 825; the chorus, 210-12; Alcestis, 313-19; Heracles, 1010). Thus the problem posed by Apollo was even simpler for Pheres than it had been for Alcestis, since self-sacrifice is inconceivable to a man who stands outside society, recognizing nothing but material goods. Such a man could easily allow his own kin to be protected by one who was not of their blood, though he thus betrayed his house as well as his son.

Pheres freely admits that his present good fortune is owed to Alcestis (620-21; 625), and he comes with a token repayment. She, however, had not intended to be his benefactor, and so his gift is refused. Admetus then proceeds to withdraw the advantages which had come to the old people through Alcestis' sacrifice, and as he explains himself he repeats words that she had spoken (651-52; cf. 295-96). He charges Pheres with responsibility for Alcestis' death, and honoring the symmachy of marriage makes her enemy his and that of his house. Pheres is forbidden access to the hearth where her spirit resides, and is driven away from the halls that belong now to her children. The old parents will have, however, exactly what they bargained for (662-66, 735-36). Pheres had chosen, not honorable death for himself and survival for his son, but continued life for himself and death for his son. Burial at the hands of his son had not then seemed important to him. Now Admetus says in effect: "You have the continuing life that you wanted; you will have also the rest of your choice, the dead son and a burial by strangers." He renders his father the sort of justice the old man had proclaimed, the calculated *dikê* of Thanatos, and could say now in his father's words, "How do I wrong you? What do I deprive you of?" (689) Admetus casts off his father, not by doing any violence to the man, but by announcing his own symbolic death (666). At the same time he declares that he will substitute Alcestis, although she is dead and an outsider, for his living father and mother; she will receive the honor and care due by tradition to Pheres and his wife (646-47). And so Admetus states again the two fictions of the paradoxical dream in which he will live if live he must: Alcestis remains alive and he is dead. When Pheres is gone, Admetus moves away at his wife's side to the grave where he would join her (897-99).

In receiving Heracles, Admetus repeated his original reception of Apollo; in refusing Pheres he seems to repeat Apollo's confrontation with

Death. As in the earlier scene, a young and powerful figure comes out of the house, meets an old man who has entered from the *parodos,* and a dispute about Alcestis ensues. Admetus, like Apollo, argues that the old are meetest for death, while Pheres, like Thanatos, denies it. Pheres accuses Admetus of having too little respect for established custom, as Death had reproached Apollo. Apollo asked a favor; Thanatos refused; Apollo answered, "It will happen anyway, by another agency, and you will get no thanks but become my enemy." Admetus had long ago asked a favor and Pheres had refused; now Admetus says, "It has happened anyway, by another agency, and you will get no thanks but be my enemy." The visual and verbal parallelism suggests that the Pheres scene has been constructed with a special intention. This scene is the play's *agon* in the technical sense, and it is made to seem almost a life and death struggle. One of the curiosities of the *Alcestis* is that it has four separate *agons,* all reflections of the heroine's central match with death. She gives in after the briefest resistance (259-63), but Apollo teases Thanatos, Heracles wrestles with the greedy demon, and Admetus drives off her human enemy, the immediate cause of her demise. In so doing he duplicates one of Heracles' other exploits, the defeat of the demon Old Age (a figure scarcely distinguishable from a Ker or from Death himself). The spectator is left with the subrational sense that the ugly figure whom Apollo allowed to enter the house has now been driven off by Admetus.

In the paired scenes upon which the plot of the *Alcestis* turns the spectator watches Admetus begin to act. He repays a friend of the house with a benefaction and its enemy with enmity; the one who has threatened his house is driven away and the one who will save it is taken in. Since Heracles is young and jolly, a banqueter and a bringer of life, while Pheres is old and mean and associated with death, the king has shown himself truly king by driving out old Hunger and bringing in Wealth and Health. Like a celebrant at the Anthesteria he has said to Pheres, θύραζε κῆρ ("Get out, Death"); to Heracles, like the citizens of Thasos, ἐνθάδε κατοικεῖ ("Come dwell with us," 1151). These actions strengthen his house, and likewise strengthen his alliance with Alcestis, as he makes her friends his friends, her enemies his.

As Admetus has an *agon* in Alcestis' name, so he also has a *pathos.* *Philia* means sharing both the good fortune and the suffering of another being (1054, 1103, etc.), living with two souls (see 900, where Admetus would have given Hades two souls instead of one, and its contradiction to 54), and the full experience of what this can mean reaches Admetus on his return from the tomb. In spite of his fictions, he is to suffer life, not death, and he realizes that here, at last, he has outstripped his wife in unhappiness (935-36). The scene (861-961) in which he greets the humiliating actuality of an unwanted life is the mirror image of her farewell to a richly desirable world. She, before, with face unstained by any tear, had moved serenely through a much-loved house where linen lay folded in orderly chests. Admetus now loathes the very walls of the building and cannot enter where she is not; he cries out and longs for death, as he imagines the sordid minutiae of the life that awaits him in this ill-kept house filled only with emptiness. Her tears fell only once, in farewell to the bed she would not betray; in the service of that same bed, now deserted (925), he must waste his spirit in a struggle with each day's petty lusts (950-53). She willed the joy of her good fame to those she left behind, but Admetus looks forward to the agony of knowing himself slandered by enemy tongues (954-60).

At this point the natural results of Alcestis' death have had their full description. The sacrifice is a success, as far as mortal endeavor can make it so, for Admetus has maintained the external life of the house she died to preserve. Her action has found its *dikê*, its narrow due, but the real has not become the ideal. The immortal marriage will be a grievous phantom thing at best and the continuing house will be shadowed by slurs on its master's reputation. But the world is not fully defined by the natural, and Euripides will not allow the story to end this way. Apollo has sent Heracles and he by a miracle brings to husband and wife a true *charis* (1101; cf. 1074), something far beyond the limits of mere justice.

Heracles reenters, the first words in his mouth a description of the reciprocal duties of friendship (1008-11); as Pheres is the false kinsman so Heracles is the true friend. His protestations, unlike those of the old man, are borne out by his actions. He claims that Admetus' deceit has caused him to fail in his own friendly duty of sympathy; it has also laid him under a new obligation to his host, since Admetus had meant with his deception to serve their friendship (855-60). By returning Alcestis he can erase the evil fortune he had failed to share, and he can repay the host who so honored his arrival. And by keeping what he is doing a secret, he can even return in kind Admetus' well-meaning deceit. Here the direction of Apollo is more than ever evident, for Heracles' heavy sprightliness serves many more purposes than he can suppose. The disguise of Alcestis allows Admetus a symbolic repetition of the act that first earned him Apollo's patronage as, for the third time, he receives a god-sent guest. The veil causes Alcestis, whose death had deprived the house of its spirit, to return in the guise of Hestia herself; it also allows her to witness a test of her husband's promised faithfulness. Only her corpse was present when Admetus, for her sake, quarreled with his father; now she hears him make public his plan to love and honor her, though she is dead, until he dies himself (1085-96).

The trick being played on Admetus creates the peculiar, happy tension of this scene. It makes this third test of friendship, hospitality, and faith by far the most difficult of all. Admetus must close his door to betrayal of his wife and yet open it to the gift of his friend and the gods (1071). He must reject what he takes to be a False Alcestis without depriving himself and his house of the true presence of his wife. The audience watches Admetus' nobility guide him once again in a situation he does not wholly understand. The entertainment of this woman will, he believes, bring him a grief more bitter than any he has felt (1069), but rather than damage his friendship with Heracles (1106) he will accept this further suffering. Heracles' ironical offer of a joyful reward does not tempt him (1101); his resistance breaks only when his friend urgently begs the favor (1107). His plain statements that he can have nothing to do with the girl (1056, 1090) have served to separate the threat to Alcestis from the threat to himself, and thus he agrees to receive the property of Heracles (at the cost of pain to himself), while he refuses to accept a substitute for his wife. In so acting he completes the salvation of Alcestis (1020, 1119) and bears out the chorus' prediction that his aristocratic piety, incomprehensible to themselves, will find a reward at last (600-605, the close of the House of Admetus Ode). And in fact Admetus crosses his threshold not with his friend's property but with his own wife restored, for Heracles sees to it that he shall receive the recognition token, the touch of Alcestis, before the eyes of the audience. Husband and wife step back into their restored house each in his own character and each aware of his new felicity. Their alliance has been strengthened, the false friendship of Pheres is at an end, the true friendship of Heracles is firmer than before (he will return, 1152), and the reputations of king, queen, and house have been fixed forever by the miracle. Admetus and Alcestis are harbored now in a better life than any they had known before (1157), and at last the ideal is become real. The Homeric description of the best of marriages has found its perfect illustration (*Odyssey* VI 182-85):

. . . for a better and higher gift than this there cannot be, when with accordant aims man and wife have a home. Great grief it is to foes and joy to friends; but they themselves best know its meaning.

(trans. Palmer)

When Admetus and Alcestis close the play by walking back into their castle, they do not merely exit through a conventional palace-front set. They enter a place altogether different from those dim and planless tragic palaces which seem to contain no more than a noose or a blood-filled bath. They have idealized the House of Admetus, but Euripides has made it real, no longer a façade but an interior. The House of Admetus has storerooms and chests, household altars, throne room, guests' quarters, men's hall, and a *thalamos* with its marriage bed. In it one may bathe or feast or play the lyre, scold a servant or listen for a woman's call of greeting. It is a house where dust can gather and children cry. It was not the poet's vulgarity that dictated these details, though Aristophanes would have it so. The subject of the play is the salvation of this house, and by a miracle it, like Alcestis, has been saved whole, an ideal clothed again in full reality.

The play has shown a pair of human beings faced with a number of choices. Each was able to discriminate between real and apparent qualities and each valued certain timeless things above the joy or pain of the moment. Both follow the path of virtue and it brings them grief and separation, but a god is interested in their case and he, by reversing nature, reunites the pair, restores their happiness, and gives their ideal transcendent reality. This is not the sort of tale we have been taught to expect from Euripides, but he has told it. The pleasure he took in dramatizing it is evident, for the pathetic emotion of the death scene, the hard accuracy of the quarrel, the bitterness of Admetus' return from the burial, and the complicated sport of the final moments all display the characteristic Euripidean talents at their height. In addition, the pervasive recurrence of a bit of wordplay suggests that Euripides saw in the Admetus-Alcestis *mythos* other opportunities not strictly drama-turgical.

"Who can say if what we call life is not death, and death life?" (Frag. 638 Nauck) sounds fully as foolish out of context as Aristophanes intended it should. In the *Alcestis,* however, Euripides shows the kind of profit he could make from such a paradox. He uses it as if for decorative effect, but in fact it lies at the heart of his subject, with Alcestis herself its embodiment. When Admetus begins his ambiguities about the state of his wife with διπλοῦς ἐπ' αὐτῇ μῦθος ἔστι μοι λέγειν ("of her I have a double tale to tell," 519; cf. 521 and 525), he is only repeating the play's initial description of Alcestis: "You could say that she was living and you could say that she was dead" (141). The two conditions are always mixed in her. She has in a sense been dead for many years (527); when she first enters the chorus has already described her funeral, and when she returns to the house in the end she still has the touch of Death upon her. While she is in her tomb, the living declare that they too are dead (825, 1082); she on the other hand is to be treated as if she were yet on earth (329, 992-99, 1096). They lead a life that is not life (242-43), she lies in a tomb that is no tomb (995). The only ease Admetus hopes to find in life is death (1086), though by his own definition he and all mortals with him are dead already (527). Everywhere this "double tale" is told. When Heracles, like the impatient comic poet, objects that there is generally thought to be considerable difference between the two states, Admetus answers, "You indeed may think so, but I see the matter otherwise" (528-29).

Euripides constructed his drama so that there would be at its core a time when life and death, Heracles and Thanatos, were housed under a single roof. This is the situation within, while the House of Admetus Ode is sung, and this is the situation which provides the technical causation of the plot's reversal. The simultaneous celebration of banquet and funeral serves to provoke the outraged slave, producing the revelation that moves Heracles to save Alcestis. The sounds of mourning and rejoicing have been kept from sacrilegious mingling by the ritual foresight of Admetus, bent on carrying out to the letter his promise to Alcestis (548). Nevertheless they have risen from the house in the same moment (760) in a double strain that finds a fanciful echo later just before the miracle of Alcestis' return, when Admetus mixes the remembered music of his wedding with the present music of his grief (915ff).

A house in which a corpse is laid out while a feast goes forward is a plain but profoundly suggestive image in a drama of death and its reversal. Heracles, the satyrlike glutton, creates this symbolic situation, and Euripides makes him also its exegete. Fallen upon an elegiac mood, he decides to share the secret of life with the man who serves him; his speech is remarkably close to another, put into Apollo's mouth by Bacchylides as the moral of Admetus' escape from death (782-91; cf. Bacchylides III 76ff):

> Every man must die;
> There's not a living soul who knows
> If he'll be here tomorrow.
> Fate creeps on unseen
> And neither book nor spell can teach you
> When the end will come.
> Since what I say is true,
> Be of good cheer and drink!
> Make today your own

> And leave the rest to fate.
> Honor Kypris, that sweet god,
> For she is fond of men.

Anyone who will not live this way, he concludes, ends with a life that is no life at all. He thus repeats the old lesson in Dionysiac terms, his own example (added to that of the drunken Moirai) enforcing the notion that this is the way, not just to happiness but to salvation. He has hardly finished when he learns of Alcestis' death. Off he goes to surprise Thanatos, hardly sober, still wreathed, his tuneless song echoing yet. He makes the day his own by sharing his victory with a friend, honoring the Aphrodite of Admetus' marriage.

Even Heracles at his most buffoonish slips into the paradoxical way of talking which assumes that life may not be life; even for him there is an ideal life to be sought. He states the commonplace, positive side of the proposition, in contrast to Alcestis' heroic negative statement. The ordinary man is to take what best pleasure the day may offer and not count the number or the rewards of the days to come, since he may die tomorrow. This is the exact opposite of Pheres' rule of life; the old man, who ends with a life that is no life at all, thinks always of tomorrows—how sweet, how few, they are. Heracles on the contrary says, "Today is sweet: live as if there were no tomorrow." The noble man is to follow the same lesson, according to Heracles' example, in a bolder and more elevated form. Heracles' victory and Alcestis' sacrifice teach him that the day's best pleasure may be an exercise of virtue, even though choosing it should mean counting the days to come at precisely naught, risking death today or fixing it for tomorrow. The difference between life and death is nominal, that between a virtuous act and a shameful one absolute.

Euripides has made of his *Alcestis* an elegant mystery play for the uninitiate, the revelation of a world in which friendship may resurrect and virtue is the key to miraculous blessedness. This saving virtue is bred in a mind that makes life and death its simultaneous guests; the virtuous man hears always the mixed strains of dirge and revelry, for the knowledge that he may die tomorrow is also the knowledge that he may be snatched from death. A man who understands what Heracles taught will not argue always from *dikê*, but will be free to perform the uncalculated act of graciousness, and such a man may attract the favor of the gods, who know how to be gracious in return. Gods do sometimes befriend mortals, for there is an aspect of divinity that interests itself in man, cutting simples for Asclepius or urging the Moirai to tipple, opposing the will of Death and the justice of a jealous Zeus. His own play becomes a final figure for what Euripides says about life under the dominion of such a company of gods, for in it tragedy, comedy, and satyr drama touch and intermingle. Death and Old Age are real, and are only temporarily defeated, but this time, at least, Heracles the satyr-savior did appear, as if in answer to the hymn addressed to him by Orphic votaries (*Orphic Hymn* 12):

> Come, blessed one, purveyor of all healing means,
> Evil demons exorcise with waving wand;
> Loose your feathered arrows and harsh death remove from us.

On Euripides' *Medea*

by *Eilhard Schlesinger*

I

In the past twenty years critics have fastened their attention upon the great monologue of Medea (1021-80) and found therein the essence of the tragedy. This speech is undoubtedly the drama's poetic culmination, but at the same time we should realize that this is not the whole play but only one of several speeches of the protagonist. We are dealing with the words in the fifth *episode* which Medea directs first to her children and the chorus, but then more and more to herself. The structure and style of this speech has been brilliantly studied by Schadewaldt.[1] The children return from Creusa to whom they have given the deadly gifts in accordance with their mother's plan. Medea sees that her revenge has begun to materialize, that now it will inevitably take the course which she herself had determined, and that the fate of her children has thereby been irrevocably decided. Yet at the same time the sight of her children makes her also feel the whole monstrosity of her design.

Because actors wore masks and performed at a great distance from the audience, an ancient dramatist could not convey his meaning through the sort of facial expression, which would be effective in the cinema today. Euripides, however, in a masterly fashion is able to achieve the same effect through the words of the heroine: "Why, children, do you look upon me with your eyes?" cries Medea (1040f), "why do you smile so sweetly that last smile of all?" They have carried out their task and now must inevitably die. At this point her maternal instincts rebel once more, and in the ensuing verses of the monologue we find two Medeas

"On Euripides' *Medea*" (German title: "Zu Euripides *Medea*") by Eilhard Schlesinger. From *Hermes: Zeitschrift für Klassische Philologie*, XCIV (January 1966), 26-53. Copyright © 1966 by *Hermes*. Reprinted in slightly abridged form by permission of *Hermes*. Translated by Walter Moskalew.

[1] Wolfgang Schadewaldt, *Monolog und Selbstgespräch* (Berlin: Weidmann, 1926), pp. 193ff.

70

opposing one another, or rather the two forces that are fighting for control over her: the *bouleumata* "reason" and the *thymos* "passion." The opposition is so strong that at the climax of the soliloquy Medea plainly identifies herself with the *bouleumata,* while the *thymos* becomes a second person whom she resists and addresses in the vocative: "You must not do these things! Poor heart, let them go, have pity upon the children" (1056f).

The word *thymos* here certainly means passion or a passionate temperament—a usage also found among Pre-Socratic philosophers like Heraclitus and Democritus.[2] Yet we should not overlook the fact that this passage, despite its strongly rhetorical coloration, is nevertheless a transformation of an old poetic device.[3] Even in the *Iliad* a hero addresses his μεγαλήτωρ θυμός "proud spirit." [4] But here *thymos* is not unbridled emotion, what Plato calls *thymoeidês,* nor do the *bouleumata* stand in direct opposition to it as a rational principle, in the manner of the charioteer in the *Phaedrus* who keeps a tight rein on the two horses, *thymos* and *epithymia.*[5] For Medea at one point refers to her revenge plan as *bouleumata* (1044) and then later uses the same term for her thoughts opposing the revenge and especially the murder of her children (1079). This word therefore can not refer to a specific part of the soul or a specific psychic force.[6] *Bouleumata* are rather thoughts, considerations, or plans that serve various and even opposing aspects of the soul. Nor should one regard *thymos* as a narrowly psychological term, for the old meaning it has in epic poetry—vitality, vital energy—is still strongly felt.

One often compares this utterance of Medea to the soliloquy of Wallenstein: "Wär's möglich? Könnt ich nicht mehr, wie ich wollte, nicht mehr zurück, wie mirs beliebt? Ich müsste die Tat vollbringen, weil ich sie gedacht, nicht die Versuchung von mir wies?" "Could it be possible? Could I no longer, as I wished, could I not turn back? Must I commit the deed, because I have thought it—did not dismiss temptation?" The

---

[2] Heraclitus *Diels-Kranz* 22B85, Democritus *Diels-Kranz* 68B236. See also the other occurrences listed in Kranz' index.

[3] See Page's commentary on this passage.

[4] E.g. *Iliad* X 98.

[5] According to Lesky in "Zur Problematik des Psychologischen in der Tragödie des Euripides," *Gymnasium,* LXVII (1960), 10ff., the tragedy of Medea lies in the conflict of *thymos = hedonai* and *bouleumata = gnome.*

[6] This question is examined in detail by Hans-Dieter Voigtländer, "Spätere Überarbeitungen im grossen Medeamonolog," *Philologus,* CI (1957), 217ff. See also Lesky's reply to A. Rivier, *Entretiens sur l'antiquité classique,* tome VI (Vandoeuvres-Genève, 1960), p. 83.

situation is similar, for both characters at a certain point notice that what they themselves have set in motion is now independently developing in accordance with its own inevitable laws and can no longer be stopped. But there is a fundamental difference. In contrast to Wallenstein's constant indecision, Medea is determined to act; she has not merely thought of it, nor has she struggled to the decision. In a sense the revenge is imposed upon her by her own nature. She must will it of necessity, and this she knows very well. Even before the great monologue begins, the revenge is already a closed matter, and so is the murder of her children, for *this* is the essence of her revenge. But it is very important that she herself come to grips with this fact. The force within Medea that reacts to this necessity is not an opposing will, but rather a simple longing for happiness struggling against a destiny that has forced her to perform deeds of superhuman proportion, "heroic" deeds in the Greek sense of the word. What is said here in the language of the latter half of the fifth century differs very little from the sentiments expressed in Hector's monologue in *Iliad* XXII and in the great speech of Achilles in *Iliad* IX. It has therefore been incorrectly maintained that in this monologue Medea struggles with the decision to murder her children, that the tragic conflict of the whole drama lies essentially in the assault of passion on her maternal feelings, which here in the monologue finally impels her to decide to kill her children. Such is generally the view of those who adhere to the theory that this is "psychological drama." Yet the interpretation of their opponents is equally unsatisfactory, even though we cannot deny that they have helped interpret the tragedy by vigorously pointing out certain inconsistencies.

Zürcher sees in Medea's monologue a proof of his theory that the Euripidean characters are not psychologically consistent creations.* He feels that Medea's motivation to kill her children is complex; that it is not *exclusively* her innate passions which drive her to this, for she herself speaks of her children's death as a *necessity*. Euripides presumably had joined two motifs: infanticide as both *revenge and inevitability*. In the second part of the monologue, as the heroine gradually comes to her senses, she says (1062f): "Force in every way must have it they must die, and since this must be so, then I, their mother, shall kill them." That these verses create a problem of interpretation is of course no new discovery. In addition to this they are also repeated in 1240f. Most editors, among them Page in the latest edition of his commentary, simply bracket them. The question belongs first of all to the realm of verse repetitions

* [W. Zürcher, *Die Darstellung des Menschen im Drama des Euripides*, Basel, 1947.]

in our text of Euripides, and it has in fact been already examined in that context.[7] We also pass over the textual problem, which we can do more readily, because bracketing only lessens the difficulty pointed out by Zürcher, but does not remove it altogether. These verses certainly remain in the speech which Medea delivers at the end of this *episode,* when she prepares to go inside and actually carry out her plan (1240f). Admittedly this is somewhat less awkward than having the motifs of *revenge* and *inevitability* placed side by side, but the problem can in no way be eliminated through brackets. *At least once* in this scene Medea maintains that in every way it is inevitable that the children die, in which case it is better that *she* rather than her enemies kill them. She herself expresses this thought for the first time here, but it is essentially what the chorus had already said at the beginning of the fourth *stasimon* (976f): "Now there is no hope left for the children's lives. Now there is none. They are walking already to murder." If Zürcher's assertion were correct, that hereby a new motif for the death of the children is introduced, then Medea's words could only have the following meaning: Although at one time I have toyed with the thought of killing my children, it was no absolute decision. But now, when I see them before me, I understand that I cannot do such a thing. I shall let them live—take them with me to Athens, where they will further cheer me. But no, it is too late for that. They have already brought the deadly gifts to the king's daughter and have thereby become murderers in the eyes of the Corinthians. By letting them live I shall only deliver them to the vengeance of my enemies. The deed has inevitably sealed their doom.

Yet such an interpretation of the monologue is certainly false. It is difficult to see why an invocation to the avenging spirits of Hades (1059) should introduce the idea of inevitability, if inevitability does not motivate the vengeance, but is rather an unforeseen accident. More important and decisive is another consideration. We should ask ourselves why the children must necessarily fall into the hands of the Corinthians. Medea had never doubted that she would be able to save herself after carrying out the deed. Her only question, before the appearance of Aegeus, was where she would flee and what would become of her. Here in the monologue she does in fact contemplate taking her children with her to Athens. It is indeed possible to save them, in which case we can speak neither of the "inevitability" of their death, nor of a juxtaposition of two opposing motifs, unless we wish to maintain that Euripides had fused

[7] Philip W. Harsh, "Repetitions of Lines in Euripides," *Hermes,* LXXII (1937), 446f. Cf. also Page's commentary.

two different accounts of the myth. Indeed there did exist a version where
Medea's children were killed by the Corinthians.[8] This variant must have
been the origin of the festival that is mentioned in the *exodos* of the
tragedy (1381ff). Yet it is highly unlikely that Euripides should have
arbitrarily chosen discordant motifs from different traditions.

Actually we are not at all dealing with two separate elements: infanticide as *revenge* and *inevitability*. The death of Medea's children is inevitable because it is a necessary part of her vengeance on Jason, which
is also inevitable because Medea *must* revenge herself, although here it
is better not to speak of a psychological need for vengeance. We cannot
resolve this question by an interpretation of the monologue alone, for
the monologue itself can be fully understood only when viewed in the
larger perspective of the play. Then the objections raised against the
last twenty verses will also disappear.[9]

II

To be able to picture the tragedy in its totality, let us follow Goethe's
advice and start by examining *how* the play is constructed. This question
will be simplified if we consider more closely two things which had
already been noticed and criticized by Aristotle, who twice in the *Poetics*
finds fault with the dramatic technique of the *Medea*. In the first instance (1454 b 1) he deals in general terms with the λύσις, the unraveling
of the plot, and demands that it should follow naturally from the action
of the play. For this reason he considers it improper to resolve the complications of a drama through unexpected external interventions for
which the audience has not been prepared in the course of the action.
This kind of ending he calls λύσις ἀπὸ μηχανῆς, or *deus ex machina* as
we usually term it.[10] As an example of this faulty λύσις ἀπὸ μηχανῆς he
cites the *Medea*. This criticism can refer only to the sun-god's dragon-
chariot, in which the heroine escapes the fury and vengeance of Jason.
It is indeed strange that Aristotle should have chosen this particular play
as an example, for there are many more obvious instances of *deus ex
machina* in Attic tragedy. The intervention of Helios to send his granddaughter the chariot must have appeared especially arbitrary and artificial to him. He must also have had the impression that this kind of
departure was incompatible with the character of Medea as she had

---

[8] Parmeniscus in the gloss on 264.

[9] Cf. Bruno Snell, "Das früheste Zeugnis über Sokrates," *Philologus*, XCVII (1948),
125ff; Gerhard Müller, *Studi Italiani di Filologia Classica*, XXV (1951), 65ff; and
Hans-Dieter Voigtländer, *loc. cit.*

[10] Cf. Andreas Spira, *Untersuchungen zum Deus ex machina bei Sophocles und
Euripides* (Kallmünz/Opf, 1960).

been presented in the course of the dramatic action.[11] But it seems to me even more conspicuous that neither Seneca nor Corneille dispensed with the dragon-chariot, even though in other respects the French drama-tist very clearly improves certain weaknesses of the Euripidean play, especially the appearance of Aegeus, the second scene to which Aristotle also voiced an objection.

This unexpected ending must first of all seem completely superfluous. We have already said that Medea could very well have escaped in a purely human manner, as indeed the messenger who reports the deaths of Creon and Creusa, advises her to do (1122f). She could have killed her children immediately after the monologue and fled. Her safety in itself is therefore no sufficient justification for the λύσις ἀπὸ μηχανῆς. That is certainly correct in itself, but had Medea left in this manner, it would have been a fearful escape. The messenger does in fact say (1122f): "Medea, run for your life, take what you can, a ship to bear you hence or chariot on land!" Yet from the point of view of theatrical effectiveness the flight of Medea was an inappropriate ending. The revenge had to be complete. Who the victor was had to be physically manifest. The lone figure of Jason grieving over the bodies of his sons would not have created this unequivocal impression. True theater demands not a stealthy, but a mighty exit.[12] There had to be a final confrontation in which the contrast between the triumphant Medea, full of derision and scorn, ex-hibits the bodies of her children to completely annihilate Jason, thus creating a lasting impression for the audience. This can only be achieved if the heroine has unusual means at her disposal, for without them she is helplessly exposed to the fury of her husband. Seneca emphasizes this by having Jason appear on stage not alone but in the company of a military escort. Anouilh in his version also supports this point, even though he foregoes the *ex machina* solution. His play also contains a final confrontation, but instead of a triumphal exit he has Medea plunge into the flames of her children's funeral pyre, made from the chariot in which she and Jason had originally fled to Corinth. Anouilh is the great adaptor of Greek tragedy to the contemporary stage, and it is interesting to observe how skilfully he interprets the original before transposing it into a modern idiom. Although a cursory glance at his works may leave the impression that they have little more than the name in common with their ancient models, in reality he is recreating the true essence of

[11] It is interesting that almost all the participants in the conference of the "Fondation Hardt" share Aristotle's dissatisfaction with the ending of the tragedy. See the dis-cussion on the lecture by Kamerbeek, *Entretiens*, pp. 30ff. Cf. N. E. Collinge, "Medea ex machina," *Classical Philology*, LVII (1962), 170ff.

[12] Cf. Hans Diller, *Entretiens*, p. 32.

the Attic art form in a twentieth century mold. The suicide of Medea
may therefore be a correct interpretation of the Euripidean tragedy, but
it represents a mode of expression that is modern rather than Attic.
No doubt Euripides could not have his Medea die in this way, precisely
because she was the granddaughter of Helios. She *had* to depart avenged
and victorious, and by having her go off in the chariot of the sun, Euripides falls back upon the mythical nature of his protagonist, which was
so well known to his audience.[13] In the course of the play he had presented Medea as completely human. She is well aware of her divine
origin, but this merely intensifies her pride and makes her feel even more
keenly the humiliation she has endured. She never speaks of superhuman
faculties, nor does she count on miraculous powers to bring her plans
to fruition. The reference to her knowledge of drugs, φάρμακα (394f),
surely has no such connotation. In the whole play she is merely a
woman, an extraordinary woman to be sure, but still entirely human.
If the poet emphasizes her divine origin only once and near the end of
the play, it must be to achieve a specific theatrical effect. Yet in fact
what he does here differs very little from the common practice of all
Greek writers from Homer onward, who employ a motif when it is called
for, and abandon it whenever it conflicts with a particular poetic intent.[14]

If, however, we wish to justify fully this transgression against Aristotelian canons, we should not be content with seeing it as a mere
striving for theatrical effect. We must realize that the whole structure of
the tragedy not only requires, but is throughout directed to this ending.
But first we must understand the poet's intent. Strohm has pointed out[15]
that the *exodos* of the play corresponds in detail to the second *episode,*
but drew no further conclusions from his discovery. This *episode* presents
their confrontation after Jason had left Medea to marry the daughter
of the king. The actual breach of faith lies outside the beginning of the
play, while the prologue and the first *episode* show the effect of Jason's
infidelity upon Medea. In this confrontation, Jason is master of the
situation and speaks first; in the *exodos* the roles are reversed. The
difference between the characters clearly emerges from the similarity of
the two scenes. Jason is not portrayed as a temperamental man; he does
not come to provoke Medea or to gloat over her misfortune. He is calm,
objective, and completely convinced of the correctness of his action. This
gives him a feeling of confidence and superiority, which unintentionally

[13] Collinge stresses particularly this significance of the dragon-chariot.
[14] W. Schmid, *Geschichte der griechischen Literatur* (Munich, 1929), I, 149.
[15] Hans Strohm, *Euripides: Interpretationen zur dramatischen Form, Zetemata,* 15
(1957), p. 3.

exacerbates Medea's already aroused temper and wounds her still more deeply with its tone of pitying condescension. In both scenes the dialogue is begun by the character who controls—or thinks he controls—the fate of the other (Jason, 446-64, and Medea, 1317-22), and after his exit it is concluded by a passionate outburst on the part of the weaker antagonist (Medea, 623-26, and Jason, 1405-14). In between lies the actual altercation. First the weaker answers the address of his opponent (Medea, 465, and Jason, 1323-50), who in turn tries to refute his arguments (Jason, 522-87, and Medea, 1351-60). Then follows an excited debate in the usual manner of the *agon,* which in the *exodos* consists almost exclusively of short exchanges of dialogue. The correspondence in the structure of the scenes is further stressed by verbal reminiscences: there are the same insults, accusations, and declarations that the opponent's actions have made him an abomination in the eyes of gods and men. They both regret having met each other. All the instances which Medea cites in the second episode to prove her past kindness to Jason and his present ingratitudes are again picked up by Jason in the *exodos,* who sees them as stages in the progress of his misfortune. Euripides certainly wanted us to perceive the relation between these two scenes, and he could only have achieved this effect by using the dragon-chariot, for without it, a final confrontation between Jason and Medea would have been impossible.

This correlation makes the two scenes cardinal points of the whole tragedy. Not only do they form the beginning and end of the dramatic action, but they also contrast as image and its reflection. For the *exodos* represents an exact reversal of the situation in the second *episode.* Between these points we see the gradual transformation of the initial situation into its opposite. This development is decisively influenced by the machinations of Medea, which are further determined by other factors. The second *episode* and the *exodos* provide the framework for this intrigue but are not part of it. In these scenes the protagonists meet in open and unrestrained hostility, and as Strohm has correctly observed,[16] Medea does not make the slightest attempt to deceive her husband in their encounter. The first objection of Aristotle, which directed our attention to the *exodos,* has thus enabled us to establish two stable points of reference and thereby grasp the structure of the entire tragedy. The main action begins at verse 446. All that precedes—the prologue, the *parodos,* the first *episode,* and the first *stasimon*—is a kind of prelude.

[16] *Loc. cit.*

Generally, in Greek tragedy the plot consists of a change from one state to its opposite, or *metabasis* as Aristotle calls it (1452 a 16). This change can be from good fortune to bad or vice versa (1451 a 13f; 1453 a 12ff). Thus in the *Medea* the helpless victim of the decree emerges victorious on all fronts, while the master of the situation, who fancied that he was able to determine the fate of Medea and fulfill all his desires, becomes in the *exodos* a man completely annihilated. On the surface it seems that we actually have a double plot, for two characters whose lives are inextricably bound together experience a change: Jason from prosperity to misery and Medea the reverse. We might even get the impression that Jason is the tragic hero, while Medea, whose *metabasis* is a turn for the good, is lacking in true tragic stature. But such a view is undoubtedly false, for Medea is surely the tragic heroine. A double plot there is, but the concepts of εὐτυχία and δυστυχία [good and bad fortune], which Aristotle must have formulated while thinking of the *Odyssey*, have as little application here as they have to the fortunes of Sophocles' Creon and Antigone.

Nevertheless, an interpretation of the play cannot be content with this rather tentative conclusion, but must try to define more clearly the essence of the tragedy. But the final triumph, for which Euripides introduces the notorious magic chariot, and especially certain expressions in the last speech of the protagonist, present an enormous problem. Jason says to her at the beginning of their heated exchange (1361): "You yourself are grieved and share the pain," to which Medea answers: "That's true, but much less grieved, since you can mock no more." Details like these, as well as the final picture in general, at least tend to diminish the sense of tragedy, and this is surely why objections to the chariot of the sun have been raised time and again.

III

What we have considered up to now has at least provided us with a few points of reference, from which we can follow the plot with greater confidence. Again another aspect criticised by Aristotle is of crucial importance: the appearance of Aegeus in the third *episode*. But to appreciate the significance of the scene, we should first briefly discuss what has preceded.

What we have called the prelude is subdivided into two parts by the entrance of Creon (271): the first part embracing the prologue, the *parodos*, and the first long speech of Medea; the second including the Creon scene and her second speech after his departure. The first *stasimon* is almost a final reflection on this prelude, which it further rounds out by having the second two *strophes* echo themes from the prologue of the nurse.[17] Essentially, the prologue and *parodos* present the condition into which Jason's decision has put Medea and her attendant women. Purely material consequences are also mentioned—for example, the fate of exile which now awaits Medea—but the emphasis is above all on her emotional state. Thus the words of the nurse introduce the essential facts in a rather different manner from the simple, almost dry style of the later Euripidean prologues. She begins with a wish for the impossible that provides the whole initial scene with an emotional undertone, and immediately exposes a motif which will dominate the whole play: the wish to undo the past, the cursing of all ties with Jason, and the remorse for having become completely estranged from her family through crimes she committed on his behalf. From this motif Anouilh fashioned the main theme of his play. There follows in twenty-five verses the equally vivid account of Medea's state of mind. First her despair and deep regret for having left her homeland, then her hatred, which is aimed not directly at Jason but at the children (36): στυγεῖ δὲ παῖδας ["she hates the children"]. This first mention of Medea's offspring is somewhat unexpected after: "From her own misfortune the poor woman has learned how sweet it is not to be cut off from one's country." The nurse then immediately goes on to speak of something else. In Medea's hatred she sees a potential for horrible deeds, but these are unrelated to the children. She can imagine the murder of Creusa or even Creon and Jason, but not the killing of the children. The agitated mode of expression and disconnected train of thought is meant to mirror the nurse's emotional state and thereby increase the tension. To her mind Medea's hatred of the children is associated with the preceding curse on her ties with Jason, of which the children are a constant reminder. The nurse fears that her mistress will be driven to a deed which could only make her situation worse: "She is frightening and anyone who arouses her enmity cannot emerge victorious" (44f). But there is no prophecy of infanticide here. It would also be wrong to conclude from this that the cause of their death is an unnatural hatred their mother bears them. The hate Medea speaks of is directed against her whole life with Jason and against all that reminds her of it. In the lyric passage shortly thereafter Medea curses not only the children and the father, but she even calls herself odious, summing up her feelings with the words: "Let the whole family perish" (114). The unexpected mention

[17] Lines 431f; cf. 1f; 433ff; cf. 34f.

of her children reveals that they are vital to the main theme of the
tragedy. And at this very moment they appear themselves, ingenuous and
naïve, as they return from their games accompanied by their tutor (46).
Here we perceive that the whole plot revolves around Medea's children
and, furthermore, the child in general as well as the relationship of man
and wife to child is a motif which recurs again and again, especially in
the choral odes.[18]

To understand any poetic treatment of a traditional myth, it is important to know the extent of the author's changes and transformations.[19]
A knowledge of the details that have been added, omitted, or especially
stressed can greatly advance our appreciation of a work of art. Unfortunately here we find ourselves in a rather disadvantageous situation. The
information that has primarily come down to us in the scholia is too
scanty for an adequate reconstruction of the Medea story before Euripides.[20] Nor do we know whether the tragedy's crucial motif—Medea's
infanticide—was invented by the poet or was part of the existing traditional material. Lesky comes to the resigned conclusion that we will
probably never be able to resolve this question.[21] Kerényi, however,
maintains that the infanticide was an old traditional ingredient of the
myth.[22] His explanations seem convincing, but rest exclusively on internal evidence. Yet, there is no doubt that in his tragedy Euripides
wished to establish firmly the motif of infanticide, whether he invented
it himself or culled it from tradition.

With Medea's anapests, which are uttered offstage (96ff), a lyric passage
begins in which the emotional stress reaches a climax and then again
gradually subsides with the *antistrophe* of the chorus (173ff), until we
return to the realm of *logos* in the speech of Medea at the beginning
of the first *episode*. What is here presented in lyric form (augmented by
music and dance) is essentially no more than what the nurse had already
told us, and this correspondence may be seen both in the arrangement
of motifs and from verbal reminiscences. For example, the image of
Medea dissolving all her days in a flood of tears (25) is later picked up

[18] See 329, 340ff, 562ff, 669ff, and especially the anapests in 1081ff.

[19] Cf. Günther Zuntz, *Entretiens*, p. 36.

[20] Most of the material is contained primarily in the glosses of Parmeniscus on 9
and 264. Cf. Carl Robert, *Die griechische Heldensage*, III, i, 870ff; Karl Kerényi, *Die
Heroen der Griechen* (Zürich, 1958), 266ff; Karl von Fritz, "Die Entwicklung der
Jason-Medeasage und die Medea des Euripides," *Antike und moderne Tragödie* (Berlin,
1962), especially p. 333.

[21] *Entretiens*, p. 31.

[22] Preface by Karl Kerényi in *Medea: Euripides, Seneca, Corneille, Cherubini, Grill-
parzer, Jahnn, Anouilh, Jeffers, Braun*, ed. by Joachim Schondorff (Munich and Vienna:
Theater der Jahrhunderte, 1963).

in the anapests of the nurse (141) and the choral *strophe* (159). Four
times we hear Medea's voice offstage, and in each case the nurse comments upon it, first alone and then with the chorus. Something new is
introduced with the choral *antistrophe*. The heroine's first utterance is
purely an expression of her despair and a wish to die, her second the
realization of her enormous suffering leading to the curse, which we have
quoted above. After the pause during which the chorus moves into the
orchestra, Medea's third outburst reiterates in more violent form the
curse which she calls down upon herself as well as the wish to find a
release from her hateful life in death. Her last words are somewhat more
specific, for here she unleashes even more violently her rage over Jason's
infidelity and in her hatred wishes death for him and Creon's daughter.
Yet her last outcry returns to the remorse for having left her country
and broken all ties through the murder of her brother.

By repeating in lyric what had already been said in the prologue,
Euripides emphasizes the dominant motifs of the drama: Medea's children, her rootlessness and homelessness, as well as the plight of woman
in general. One could compare the whole scene to an operatic overture,
in which through repetition and variation the themes of the whole com-
position are entwined. There is no action in our sense of the word.
Despair, impotent rage, and remorse would have been the reactions of
any woman under such circumstances, yet among these a very individual
note is struck in the end: "Medea is frightening." She cannot be treated
like this with impunity. She will react. The chorus' wish to speak to
Medea is perfectly natural at this point. The nurse undertakes the
mediation (184ff), and at the beginning of the first *episode* the heroine
appears already somewhat composed, determined to take her own fate
into her hands. The whole situation from the prologue to the *parodos*
can be best summarized by an image which the nurse employs in the
anapests (106ff). She would like to remove the children and she warns
them of their mother's wild temper and feelings of hatred. Then she
speaks of a "cloud of wailing" still forming, but which their mother as
her passion increases will soon inflame with lightning. This part of the
prelude reminds one of the great *parodoi* of the *Persians* or the *Agamemnon,* creating a mood as well as displaying the underlying tensions
which are bound to lead to a storm.

The first speech of Medea adds little that is new. The motifs of the
homelessness of an exile and the plight of woman in the existing social
order occupy most of the space,[23] and only at the end does it become

---

[23] Cf. Hans Diller, "Umwelt und Masse als dramatische Faktoren bei Euripides,"
Entretiens, pp. 89ff.

clear that she is firmly bent on revenge, although its form is still uncertain. Only in very general terms does she say that her husband, Creon,
and Creusa will have to pay the penalty (260). She does not say how this
is going to happen, and the time of her revenge remains likewise indefinite. It is important to realize that the action can only be set in
motion as the result of an external impetus.[24] It is clearly indicated
where the impulse will come from and what it consists of. In speaking
to the nurse the tutor mentions a rumor (70ff) that Creon is thinking of
banishing Medea and her children. This exile is the new development
which swells the heroine's vindictiveness and forces her to carry out her
designs at once, if she will realize them at all.

Such is the content of the Creon scene and the second speech of Medea
which follows it. Furthermore, this scene is of very special significance,
because it contains a small but independent subplot which completes
the picture of Medea's character and also sets the stage for the climax
of the tragedy. Creon wants to remove Medea from Corinth, because, as
he openly admits, he is afraid of her. He justifies his fear from everything
he knows of her. She is σοφή [shrewd] and κακῶν πολλῶν ἴδρις [versed in
many evil arts] (285), she has every reason to be angry, as Creon well understands, and they all know of her threats to destroy the three perpetra-
tors of her misfortune—Jason, Creon, and his daughter. A kind of tragic
irony characteristic of this play lies in the fact that the measures he takes
to assure his own and his family's safety actually increase the danger
and hasten his downfall. Because of this new outrage, Medea is driven
to decisive and swift implementation of her scheme, which is exactly
what Creon wished to avoid. Now he becomes the victim of her first
μηχάνημα [machination]. The king wishes Medea to go at once. He himself will make sure that she crosses the borders as soon as possible, and
he will not return home until he has expelled her (275f). Under such
circumstances Medea does not have the slightest chance of carrying out
her vengeance, and must first of all entreat a postponement. The king
himself unconsciously provides her with the means of luring him into
the trap. When Medea again bewails her lost homeland (328), Creon
replies that *next to his children* he too loves his country most of all. The
children motif reappears, but here its significance goes beyond mere
effect on the audience. Medea uses Creon's revelation in two ways. She
comes to realize how much children mean to a man, and immediately
exploits this, pointing out the distress of her own children in appealing
to Creon's paternal feelings. Thus he grants her a day's grace, even

[24] Cf. Jacqueline de Romilly, *Évolution du pathétique d'Eschyle à Euripide* (Paris,
1961), p. 119.

though he knows all too well that in doing so he is committing a grave error (350). Yet Creon's statement also shows her that she can wound Jason most deeply by killing his children. It is *here* that the thought of infanticide first occurs to her.

Medea's belief that such a revenge is effective and therefore necessary is strengthened in the second *episode,* when Jason declares that the main reason for his action was precisely his concern for the children (562ff). Of course, Jason's children are also hers, and herein lies her own tragedy.

In the speech (364ff) with which the first *episode* ends, she gives free rein to her indignation. She decides to carry out her revenge this very day. It is still the same as in the first speech—a wish to murder the king, his daughter, and her husband, but now she wonders how to do it. Should she openly kill her enemies with a weapon? That would not be a satisfactory revenge, for in so doing she herself might perish and become the laughing-stock of her enemies. She therefore decides to use poison, a method in which she is especially well versed. But she now suddenly interrupts herself. What is going to happen to her when her enemies are dead? She is, after all, without home or shelter. If she cannot find these, she cannot be truly victorious. In that case she might as well die, and it would indeed be better to seize a sword, kill her enemies, and face the consequences of her action. She sets herself a time limit, during which she will try to find some place of refuge. The only consequence of Medea's appearance is that she is now firmly resolved to take vengeance this very day. But what, and above all, how she will do this still remains uncertain. Yet, when she now confronts Jason in the second *episode,* we are fully aware of her predicament.

Her long enumeration of all she has done for Jason rounds out the exposition and completes the account of past events. We actually do not learn anything new about Medea, but her position is now placed in the context of Jason and his world. The *agon* at once brings both situations and the corresponding human attitudes into clearer light, and throws them into relief by means of antithesis. Kurt von Fritz[25] rightly stresses the contrast of the characters and especially the depreciation of one who was formerly a Greek national hero. But here we are not so much interested in the legendary past, as in the role that this character plays within the dramatic framework. It is of course completely erroneous to dismiss Jason's attitude here and in the fourth *episode* as mere cynicism; we may call him a

[25] *Op. cit.,* above, n. 20.

weakling and Lothario who has pulled himself up by the hem of
Medea's skirt to become a hero in the Argonautic expedition. Nevertheless, it is worthwhile to examine the Euripidean Jason more closely. To
understand his relationship with Medea, we must first ignore the stereo-
typed marital conflicts presented in the contemporary cinema. Things
are more complicated here. Jason is not the husband who, tired of his
wife, has fallen in love with another woman and now loses his head. We
may take him at his word when he repeatedly denies his love for Creusa.
In this respect Corneille understands Euripides very well: to present
an unambiguous picture of Jason's sincerity he introduces a special
character, an old friend to whom Jason can speak in confidence and thus
dispel any suspicion of duplicity.[26]

To understand Euripides' Jason we may best begin with a motif
already mentioned, that of an exile's rootlessness. It is important to
note that the fate of homelessness has completely different meanings for
Jason and for Medea. Medea's own situation becomes painful only when
Jason leaves her. With an expression that reminds us of Andromache's
words to Hector, she states that her husband was everything to her (228).
Leaving her country, her mother and father, in fact even murdering her
brother and severing all ties with her family, epitomize the plight of the
woman who relinquishes her entire previous existence to follow her
husband. Medea, however, does not exchange one mode of life for a
similar one. In order to lead a purely human existence with Jason she
separates herself from a family descended from the sun-god and therefore
related to both the divine and heroic worlds. The failure of her relationship will be all the more painful because she has sacrificed so much
for it.

Jason describes the same situation rather differently (551ff): "When I
came here as a fugitive from Iolkos, overcome with countless, inescapable
difficulties, could I possibly have found a better remedy than marrying
the daughter of the king?" He had to flee his own country, and now that
he is in a foreign land, his main concern is to build a new life. But for
him, the son of a king, merely existing is not enough. Even in Corinth
he wants to be what he was, to live ἀξίως δόμων ἐμῶν ["worthy of my ances-
try"] (562), and this means that he, his family, and his descendants must
become firmly rooted in that community. Now he is offered the opportunity to ally himself with the king's family, to make the children of
his first marriage the stepsons of the princess, and one day to ascend
the throne of Corinth. This would be extremely advantageous not only
for him but for his children, and in the end could even benefit Medea,

---

[26] Act I, Scene 1.

if she would only be sensible. He, therefore, seizes the opportunity; he cannot comprehend how someone might reproach him for this and be concerned with such a trifle as the λέχος ["life in bed"]. But it is in this very point, the λέχος of which Jason speaks repeatedly, that the main difference lies. For him marriage and children, indeed, all human ties, are only a means to an end. The value of life depends on social status and its perpetuation in generations to come. That is why children are important for him. It would be most convenient if one could have children without women, for then there would be no annoying complications like his present conflict with Medea. Jason on many occasions speaks of women and the female point of view, which he compares to the male. This antithesis of the male and female world is also a motif which passes through the whole play, above all in the choral odes. Medea herself continually appeals to the feeling of solidarity among the members of her sex. Such an antithesis is nothing new in Greek literature. We think at once of *Iliad* VI, but there we do not find a gulf separating the two realms; Andromache's world differs from Hector's, but does not oppose it. What divides Hector from his family is not a completely different scale of values, but the painful necessity of being brave (ἔμμεναι ἐσθλός). In Euripides, however, the male world is completely dehumanized. Jason is the child of a noble family, whose every effort is directed exclusively toward gaining status, and whose ideal is to live well (οἰκεῖν καλῶς) and to feel no want (καὶ μὴ σπανίζεσθαι, 559f). Opposed to him stands Medea as a woman and as a champion of human values and personal relationships.

IV

We now come to the second dramatic incident to which Aristotle objects: the entrance of Aegeus. The king of Athens chances to pass through Corinth on his journey from Delphi to Troezen. Medea asks and obtains the desired asylum. She now has a harbor for her plans, where she can fasten the cable (769f). The appearance of Aegeus is without a doubt the turning-point of the drama (ἡ εἰς τὸ ἐναντίον τῶν πραττομένων μεταβολή, 1452 a 21f). This fact has only been questioned by modern interpretations that have tried to see the climax in the great monologue, of which we have spoken at the outset. Aristotle thinks that this turning-point is poorly constructed, because the appearance of Aegeus is ἄλογον (1461 b 20f). The appropriate translation here is probably not "irrational" or "silly," but rather "absurd" or "dragged in by the hair."

Corneille in discussing his own Medea deals with the role of Aegeus in considerable detail.[27] He finds two things objectionable. First, that Aegeus lingers at the court of Creon without paying a formal visit, and then that he promises to receive Medea in Athens after she has carried out her plans for revenge, even though he himself is not going directly there. Medea, however, is going to revenge herself on this very day—so Corneille continues—and she will find herself in an extremely awkward position if she will have to wait at Athens for Aegeus to return. Moreover, the waiting period will be very long, for we know that the Athenian will spend a considerable time at the court of Pittheus, fall in love with his daughter, not return to Athens until her pregnancy is well advanced. So much for Corneille. We may completely ignore his first objection, which merely implies that Aegeus behaved in a manner which would have been improper at a French royal court. As for the exact computation of time spent with Pittheus, we may answer Corneille with the words of Goethe's Chiron (*Faust* V. 7426-34):

> I see, the academicians
> Have hoaxed you like themselves with their editions.
> A mythical woman is a special case.
> Poets present her as she seems in place;
> She never grows of age nor old,
> Remains enchanting to behold,
> Is borne off young, is courted still in age;
> Enough, no time can bind the poet's page.
>
> (trans. Louis MacNeice)

In all, Corneille's objections arise from a rather superficial reading of the scene. Euripides clearly lets us know that he is working with a different version of the legend. Aegeus is already married when he meets Medea (673). The very reason for his journey to Troezen, the consultation with Pittheus regarding the Delphic oracle, is eliminated, when as gratitude for his help Medea holds out to him the prospect of being blessed with the offspring he so desires (717f). We can assume that Aegeus abandons the journey, for when he leaves, the chorus utters a conventional blessing in which it speaks of his return home (760).

Aristotle surely had none of these things in mind when he called the scene ἄλογον, nor can he be referring to the fact that Aegeus comes unexpectedly and by chance, because he himself says that a good *peripeteia* occurs contrary to expectation (γίγνεται παρὰ δόξαν 1452 a 4). Perhaps we

[27] *Corneille, Théâtre,* texte préfacé et annoté par Pierre Lièvre, Bibliothèque de la Pléiade (Paris, 1950), I, 610ff.

might better understand Aristotle's objection if we compare the arrival
of Aegeus to the reversal in Sophocles' *Oedipus Rex,* which the philosopher cites as an exemplary *peripeteia.* In this play, when the search
for the murderer of Laius has come to a dead end, a messenger comes
from Corinth and announces the death of Polybus, whom Oedipus believes to be his father. At this point it turns out that the king of Corinth
was only his adoptive father. With this revelation the discovery of the
truth is at once made possible. Yet even here it is a chance happening
and in no way follows from the sequence of events that Polybus will
die at this particular time. It is even less inevitable that the messenger
must be precisely the man who many years ago had received the child
Oedipus with the pierced feet from a herdsman of Laius, and who could
therefore say with every certainty that Oedipus is not a Corinthian.
Nevertheless, there is significant difference from the reversal of the
Medea. Oedipus' ties with the royal house of Corinth are well known; he
himself had just given Jocasta a detailed account of his youth. The
death of Polybus at the appropriate moment is of course not inevitable,
but it is nevertheless in the realm of what is possible and imaginable.
It is also not improbable that the very man who has played such a
special role in the life of Oedipus, and who rejoices that the child of
those days will become king of his city, should be the one to bring
the message. All this then, to turn again to Aristotle, lies not in the
realm of the ἀναγκαῖον [inevitable], but it is surely within the εἰκός
[probable].

In contrast, the arrival of Aegeus in Corinth seems forced, for from
the content of the play we cannot infer the slightest connection between
Medea and Aegeus or Athens. But there is a real relation between the
journey of Aegeus and the Medea plot, though it lies below the surface and is not as easily perceived as in Sophocles' play. Its nature is
purely poetic, for what ties together these seemingly disparate actions
is again the children motif. Childless Aegeus has gone to Delphi to
inquire what he must do to get offspring; from there he journeys to
Troezen, because he does not understand the oracle and needs someone
to interpret it for him. The child, however, as we have already observed
several times, is the central theme of the tragedy. Again a man appears
who desires progeny, and most likely for the same reasons as Creon and
Jason. For the third time Medea sees how important children are to a
man. Just as she had exploited this knowledge with Creon, she now
achieves her goal by promising Aegeus that with her magic arts, she
will help him have children. The meeting with the Athenian king is
the last link in a chain of evidence that proves Jason would be most

vulnerable where his children are concerned. Aegeus' arrival not only marks the reversal which brings about the beginning of the revenge action and the *metabasis,* but it also determines once and for all the specific form of the revenge—infanticide.

After Aegeus' departure, Medea can begin to act, and she does, first of all explaining to the women of the chorus the details of her revenge plan which have now been crystalized. Corneille was very puzzled by this announcement. He thought, quite correctly from his standpoint, that it was highly improbable that none of these many witnesses should have informed the king of Medea's intentions. In Attic tragedy, however, the poet had to accept the presence of the chorus as a convention. Moreover, Corneille has even failed to recognize how very skilfully Euripides employed the constant presence of the chorus, making it a kind of confidant to the protagonist, thereby affecting many variations on the theme of women's solidarity against men. By appealing in the prelude to their common womanly interests which are thwarted in the existing social order, Medea has already asked the chorus at least to help her revenge by keeping silent, and she repeats time and again that it is their duty as women to stand by her.

From the beginning the children play a decisive role in Medea's plan (774ff). Through them she gains access to the royal house, which she must have to achieve her ends. The children are sent on the pretense of asking permission to stay in Corinth. Since this also accords with Jason's wishes, she can count on his support and has him summoned (820), so that in the fourth *episode* she can make him the unsuspecting instrument of her plot. The children will convey wedding gifts to his young bride Creusa, but these will be poisoned and bring death. Here, in contrast to her previous revenge speeches, she mentions neither Creon nor Jason. She says only in very general terms that the girl and anyone who touches her will die a miserable death (788). All attention is focused exclusively on Creusa, who is the prime object of Medea's revenge. Medea kills her not out of jealousy but to prevent her from bearing children to Jason (804f). She then states what she *must* do next: "I shall kill my children" (790ff). It is the first clear revelation of the main theme, and it shocks the chorus immensely. But her *thymos* will not allow her to be made a laughing-stock. And infanticide is the form the revenge must inevitably take, for that alone can cause the supreme agony (793ff).

Medea herself realizes that this revenge will result in her own annihilation as a human being, and yet as she admits in 1013ff: "The gods and I, in a kind of madness, have planned it so." [28] In a sense Euripides' heroine perishes with the children, much the way Anouilh presents it in the final scene of his brilliant version. The granddaughter of Helios may stand in triumph on her dragon-chariot, but Medea the woman is dead.

[28] See Rex Warner's translation of the *Medea* (First published in 1944; reprinted in 1946 by John Lane, The Bodley Head, Ltd., London; also published in 1955 by the University of Chicago Press in the *Complete Greek Drama*, edited by David Grene and Richmond Lattimore) for the following lines: 1040f, 1056f, 1062f, 976f, 1122f, 1013f.

The *Hippolytus* of Euripides

by Bernard M. W. Knox

The usual critical treatment of the *Hippolytus* of Euripides is an
analysis in terms of character, an analysis which, whatever its particular
emphasis, is based on the Aristotelian conception of tragic character and
the relation between character and reversal of fortune. In the case of the
Hippolytus, this analysis, far from arriving at a generally accepted line
of interpretation, has produced nothing but disagreement. Is Hippolytus
the tragic hero, destroyed by an excess of chastity, a fanatical devotion
to the goddess Artemis? Or is Phaedra the tragic heroine, and the conflict
in her soul the tragic conflict of the play? The claims of Theseus should
not be neglected; his part is as long as Phaedra's, and the Aristotelian
word *hamartia* is used to describe his conduct by the goddess Artemis.
Such divergence of views is natural in a play which develops so many
characters so fully; though literary statistics are distasteful, the size of
the parts in this play (an important statistic for the actors, at any rate)
shows how difficult the problem of emphasis is. Hippolytus speaks 271
lines, Phaedra and Theseus 187 apiece, and, surprisingly enough, the
Nurse has more lines than either Phaedra or Theseus, 216. The attempt
to make Phaedra the central figure of the play seems perverse—why
not the Nurse? She too has her conduct described as *hamartia*—and
even Hippolytus is not a central figure on the scale of Medea, who speaks
562 lines in a play of similar length, or Oedipus, who has 698 in the
Oedipus Tyrannus, a play which is a little longer. The search for a
central tragic figure in this play is a blind alley. When the action is so
equably divided between four characters, the unity of the work cannot
depend on any one, but must lie in the nature of the relationship between all four. In the *Hippolytus* the significant relationship between
the characters is the situation in which they are placed. It is exactly the

same situation for each of them, one which imposes a choice between the same alternatives, silence and speech.

And we are shown that their choice is not free. Aristotle's comments on the tragic character assume, to some extent, that the human will is free to choose. But the freedom of the human will and the importance of the human choice are both, in the prologue of the *Hippolytus,* expressly denied. In no other Greek tragedy is the predetermination of human action by an external power made so emphatically clear. In the *Oresteia,* where each word and action is the fulfilment of the will of Zeus, the relation between human action and divine will is presented always in mysterious terms; the will of Zeus is an inscrutable factor in the background which is clearly revealed only at the close of the trilogy. And while Clytemnestra is onstage in the *Agamemnon,* we are not distracted by any feeling that her purpose as a human being is not decisive; in fact, it is the most important thing in the play. Sophocles' Oedipus has fulfilled and is still fulfilling the oracles of Apollo, but it is Oedipus, a human being making human decisions, who commands our undivided attention. And significantly, the prophecy of Apollo is presented as exactly that, a prophecy and not a determining factor; Apollo predicts, but does no more—it is Oedipus who acts. Both the *Oedipus* and the *Agamemnon* may be ultimately, in logical (though not necessarily religious) terms, determinist, but dramatically they emphasize the freedom of the human will. But the *Hippolytus* begins with a powerful presentation of an external force which not only predicts but also determines; Aphrodite tells us not only what will happen but announces her responsibility and explains her motives. It is a complete explanation and one which (even if it were not confirmed in every particular by another goddess at the end of the play) we are bound to accept. Aphrodite is one of the powers which rule the universe; and though what she says may shock us, we must accept it as true.

The play, from this point on, should be simple, the unrolling of an inevitable pattern. But Euripides has a surprise in store. As we watch the human beings of the drama, unconscious of the goddess' purpose, work out her will, we are struck by their apparent freedom. In no other Greek tragedy do so many people change their minds about so many important matters. Here again Euripides is departing sharply from the procedure of his fellow dramatists. Clytemnestra's purpose in the *Agamemnon,* concealed from the chorus and her victim by the resolution of that male-thinking brain, dangerously close to the ironic surface of her speech of welcome, triumphantly achieved when she stands over Agamemnon's body, this inflexible purpose is the straight line along which the whole play moves. Oedipus' determination to know the truth, carried relentlessly to the brink of the abyss and beyond, is the line of development of the greatest plot in Western tragedy. But in the *Hippolytus* the line of development of the characters' purposes is a zigzag. Phaedra resolves to die without revealing her love, and then makes a long speech about it to the chorus. The Nurse urges her to reveal it, regrets her action when she hears her mistress speak, and then returns to urge Phaedra on to further lengths of speech. And Hippolytus, when he learns of Phaedra's passion, first announces his intention to tell Theseus the truth, and then changes his mind and keeps silent.

"In this world, second thoughts are best," says the Nurse. Three of the principal characters have second thoughts (the Nurse, in fact, has not only second but third and fourth thoughts); the play makes an ironic juxtaposition of the maximum dramatic complication of individual choice with a predetermined and announced result. The choice of one alternative then the other, the human mind wavering between moral decisions, accepting and rejecting in a complicated pattern which emphasizes the apparent freedom and unpredictability of the human will— all this is the fulfilment of Aphrodite's purpose.

The choice between speech and silence is the situation which places the four principal characters in significant relationship and makes an artistic unity of the play. But it does much more. The poet has made the alternations and combinations of choice so complicated—Phaedra chooses first silence then speech, the Nurse speech then silence, then speech, then silence, Hippolytus speech then silence, the chorus silence, and Theseus speech—that the resultant pattern seems to represent the exhaustion of the possibilities of the human will. The choice between silence and speech is more than a unifying factor in the play, it is a situation with universal implications; a metaphor for the operation of human free will in all its complicated aspects. And the context in which it is set demonstrates the nonexistence of the human free will, the futility of the moral choice.

The goddess Aphrodite presents the issue and announces the outcome. Her preliminary work is done (πάλαι προκόψασ', 23); the moment has arrived for the consummation of her design, the punishment of Hippolytus (τιμωρήσομαι, 21). But there is still one recalcitrant detail, Phaedra's determination to remain silent. "She, poor woman, is dying in silence. No one in the house shares the secret of her disease."

$$\text{ἡ τάλαιν' ἀπόλλυται}$$
$$\text{σιγῇ· ξύνοιδε δ' οὔτις οἰκετῶν νόσον (39-40).}$$

But this last obstacle will be removed; things will not fall out this way, ἀλλ' οὔτι ταύτῃ τόνδ' ἔρωτα χρὴ πεσεῖν (41). The truth will come out, κἀκφανήσεται (42). And Theseus will kill his son.

In the scene between Phaedra and the Nurse we are shown the first stage of the accomplishment of Aphrodite's purpose—Phaedra's change from silence to speech. Her words are the involuntary speech of delirium, the breakout of her suppressed subconscious desires; but this delirium is also the working of the external force, Aphrodite, who predicted this development and now brings it about before our eyes. Phaedra's wild fantasies make no sense to the Nurse and the chorus; but their meaning is clear to the audience. Her yearning for the poplar and the grassy meadow, for the chase and the taming of colts on the sand, is a hysterical expression of her desire for Hippolytus.

The Nurse calls her outburst madness (μανία, 214), that is, meaningless speech, and Phaedra, when she comes to her senses, calls it madness too (ἐμάνην, 241), but in a different sense, passion. She has revealed nothing, but she has for the first time put her desire into words, and broken her long silence. Her passion (ἐμάνην) has overcome her judgment (γνώμη, 240); in her case the choice between silence and speech is also a choice between judgment and passion. In the next few lines she defines her dilemma, poses the alternatives, and sees a third course open to her.

> τὸ γὰρ ὀρθοῦσθαι γνώμαν ὀδυνᾷ.
> τὸ δὲ μαινόμενον κακόν· ἀλλὰ κρατεῖ
> μὴ γιγνώσκοντ' ἀπολέσθαι (247-49).

To be right in judgment (ὀρθοῦσθαι γνώμαν), that is, in her case, to remain silent, is agony (ὀδυνᾷ); passion (τὸ μαινόμενον), in her case, speech, is evil (κακόν). Better (ἀλλὰ κρατεῖ) to make no choice and perish (μὴ γιγνώσκοντ' ἀπολέσθαι)—to perish unconscious of the alternatives, to abandon judgment and choice, to surrender free will. This is what she comes to in the end, but she has not yet reached such desperate straits. She is still in the no man's land between the alternatives of speech and silence, for her delirious outburst has not revealed her secret to the Nurse. But it has brought her a momentary relief and thus weakened her determination. She is now less able to withstand the final assault on her silence which the Nurse, at the request of the chorus, proceeds to make.

The Nurse has little hope of success; she has tried before and failed—πάντα γὰρ σιγᾷ τάδε (273), "Phaedra keeps silent about it all," she tells the chorus. But she makes a last attempt. The essence of her practical viewpoint can be seen in her reproach to Phaedra when she gets no answer; for her there is no problem which cannot be resolved by speech.

"Well, why are you silent? You should not be silent, child. Either you should refute me, if I say something wrong, or, if I say what is right, you should agree with my words."

> εἶεν· τί σιγᾷς; οὐχ ἐχρῆν σιγᾶν, τέκνον,
> ἀλλ᾽ ἤ μ᾽ ἐλέγχειν, εἴ τι μὴ καλῶς λέγω,
> ἢ τοῖσιν εὖ λεχθεῖσι συγχωρεῖν λόγοις (297-99).

She gets no answer still, and in an angry reminder to Phaedra that she is ruining her children's future, she mentions, without realizing its significance, the name Hippolytus. This fortuitous thrust provokes a cry of agony and a plea for silence. "I beseech you, in future, be silent about this man," τοῦδ᾽ ἀνδρὸς αὖθις λίσσομαι σιγᾶν πέρι (312).

The Nurse does not realize the reason for Phaedra's agitation, but she senses the moment of weakness and presses her advantage. She now makes a frontal attack on Phaedra's silence; throwing herself at her mistress' feet, she seizes her hand and knees. It is the position of the suppliant, the extreme expression of emotional and physical pressure combined, and it is enough to break Phaedra's weakened resolution. "I will grant your request," δώσω (335). "My part is silence now," replies the Nurse, "and yours is speech," σιγῷμ᾽ ἂν ἤδη· σὸς γὰρ οὐντεῦθεν λόγος (336).

Phaedra finds speech difficult. She invokes the names of her mother and sister, examples of unhappy love, and associates herself with them; but she finds it hard to speak plainly. "If only you could say to me what I must say myself," πῶς ἂν σύ μοι λέξειας ἁμὲ χρὴ λέγειν (345). This is her wish, to break silence and yet not speak, and she actually manages to make it come true. In a dialectic maneuver worthy of Socrates himself, she assumes the role of questioner and makes the Nurse supply the answers and repeat the name Hippolytus, this time in a context which leaves no doubt about its significance. "You have said it," she says to the Nurse, "you did not hear it from me," σοῦ τάδ᾽ οὐκ ἐμοῦ κλύεις (352).

This revelation is more than the Nurse had bargained for. She who saw only two attitudes toward speech for Phaedra—rebuttal or agreement—can adopt neither herself; she has no advice to give, no solution to propose. She is reduced to despair and silence; she who reproached Phaedra for wishing to die now resolves on death herself. "I shall find release from life in death. Farewell. I am no longer living."

> ἀπαλλαχθήσομαι
> βίου θανοῦσα. χαίρετ᾽· οὐκέτ᾽ εἴμ᾽ ἐγώ (356-57).

The full meaning of her words to Phaedra is now clear to us and to her.

"My part is silence now," σιγῷμ᾽ ἂν ἤδη. "Speech from this point on is yours," σὸς γὰρ οὐντεῦθεν λόγος.

Speech is Phaedra's part now, and she pours out her heart to the chorus. The relief of speech, which first forced itself on her in a delirious outburst, is now the product of conscious choice. She tells the chorus the path her judgment followed τῆς ἐμῆς γνώμης ὁδόν (391). First of all, to hide her sickness in silence, σιγᾶν τήνδε καὶ κρύπτειν νόσον (394). But this proved insufficient; more was needed, to subdue her passion by self-control, τὴν ἄνοιαν εὖ φέρειν / τῷ σωφρονεῖν νικῶσα (398-99). And when this failed, she resolved on a third course, to die. She is still resolved to die; her change from silence to speech has made no difference to the situation, for she can depend on the silence of the chorus and the Nurse. But she has had the comfort of speech, told her love and despair to a sympathetic audience, and what is more, an admiring one. "Honor? Who hath it? He that died o' Wednesday," says Falstaff, and this is the essence of Phaedra's dilemma too. She has resolved to die in silence to save her honor, to be εὐκλεής; but this very silence means that she cannot enjoy her honor while living, and it will not even be appreciated after her death. No one will ever know the force she overcame and the heroic nature of her decision. Death in silence involved an isolation hard for any human being to bear; and she makes it clear that her desire to be appreciated was one of the forces driving her to speech. "May it be my lot," she says, "not to pass unnoticed when I act nobly, and not to have many witnesses when my acts are disgraceful."

> ἐμοὶ γὰρ εἴη μήτε λανθάνειν καλὰ
> μήτ᾽ αἰσχρὰ δρώσῃ μάρτυρας πολλοὺς ἔχειν (403-4).

Now she can act nobly, die rather than yield to passion, and yet not pass unnoticed. The chorus, the representatives of the women of Troezen, recognize and praise her nobility (431-32). Phaedra can have her cake and eat it too. But it is not destined to end this way, ἀλλ᾽ οὔτι ταύτῃ τόνδ᾽ ἔρωτα χρὴ πεσεῖν, said Aphrodite in the prologue.

For the Nurse now intervenes again. Her passion and despair silenced her and drove her from the scene when she realized the nature of Phaedra's sickness. But she has changed her mind. She has now rejected silence, which abandoned Phaedra to her death, and chosen speech, which is designed to save her life. "In human life," she says, "second thoughts are somehow best."

> κἂν βροτοῖς
> αἱ δεύτεραί πως φροντίδες σοφώτεραι (435-36).

Phaedra's silence was γνώμη, judgment, her speech was, at first, μανία, passion. But in the Nurse's case these relationships are reversed. Her passion, despair, drove her to silence, and her speech now is the product of γνώμη, judgment. It is speech (λόγος) in both senses of the Greek word, speech and reason; the nurse here represents the application of human reason to a human problem.

The "reason" behind the Nurse's lines is one stripped bare of any restraint of morality or religion, though it uses the terms of both. The speech is a masterpiece of sophistic rhetoric, in which each argument points toward the physical consummation of Phaedra's love. But this is a conclusion which the nurse is clever enough not to put into words. She leaves the implied conclusion to work on Phaedra's weakened resolution and contents herself, to conclude her speech, with specific advice in which every phrase is an ambiguity. τόλμα δ' ἐρῶσα (476)—bear your love (as you have so far) or—dare to love; τὴν νόσον καταστρέφου (477), subdue your love (as you have so far) or—make it subject to you, turn it to your own good; ἐπῳδαὶ καὶ λόγοι θελκτήριοι (478), incantations and charmed words, to cure her of her passion or—to make Hippolytus love her. The Nurse is probing to see what effect her speech will have on Phaedra; she does not dare commit herself fully yet.

She gets a violent reaction. These are οἱ καλοὶ λίαν λόγοι (487), too fair-seeming words; Phaedra asks for advice that will save her honor, not please her ears. But she has made an important admission; the Nurse's words did please her ears, τὰ τοῖσιν ὠσὶ τερπνά (488). The Nurse sees the weakness in Phaedra's defense and pushes hard. She speaks bluntly and clearly now. "You need not graceful words [so much for honor] but the man."

> οὐ λόγων εὐσχημόνων
> δεῖ σ' ἀλλὰ τἀνδρός   (490-91).

This is plain speaking, and Phaedra replies with an angry and agonized plea for silence, οὐχὶ συγκλῄσεις στόμα; (498). But the Nurse presses her advantage, and pushes the verbalization of Phaedra's suppressed wishes to a further stage; she has already mentioned "the man," τἀνδρός, and now she invokes "the deed," τοὔργον (501)—the act of adultery itself. This word brings out into the open the consummation which Phaedra rejected with such horror in her speech to the chorus (413-18), but now it is attractive as well as repulsive—like love itself, ἥδιστον . . . ταὐτὸν ἀλγεινόν θ' ἅμα (348)—and Phaedra now reveals that if the Nurse continues to put evil in a fair light, τᾀσχρὰ δ' ἢν λέγῃς καλῶς (505), she will come to it, and be consumed in what she now flees from, εἰς τοῦθ᾽ ὃ φεύγω νῦν ἀναλωθήσομαι (506).

The Nurse is clever enough to return to ambiguities, the love-charms, φίλτρα . . . θελκτήρια (509), which will relieve her sickness without disgrace or damage to the mind. The Nurse thus returns to her original proposal; this is the same circular movement of her earlier interview with Phaedra, in which the name "Hippolytus" was the point of departure and return. And here, as there, the closing of the circle with the repetition makes clear the meaning of the words. Phaedra must know now, after all that has been said, what the Nurse means by "love-charms." But the ambiguous phrasing is a triumph of psychology on the Nurse's part. She remembers how Phaedra tried to evade responsibility by a verbal fiction before—"If only you could say to me what I must say myself" and "You have said it. You did not hear it from me"—and she gives her mistress the same opportunity again. And Phaedra takes it. Her question is not "What will be the effect of this love-charm?" but "Is it an ointment or something to drink?" πότερα δὲ χριστὸν ἢ ποτὸν τὸ φάρμακον (516). She has abandoned her critical intelligence, γιγνώσκειν, γνώμη, surrendered control over her own choice; she is now following the third and most desperate of the three courses she saw before her. "To be right in judgment is agony, passion is evil, best of all is to perish without judgment or choice," μὴ γιγνώσκοντ᾽ ἀπολέσθαι.

That she surrenders control of her actions here is made clear and also plausible by the relationship between Phaedra and the Nurse which the words and tone of the next few lines suggest. She is now a child again, and the Nurse does for the grown woman what she had always done for the child—evades her questions, makes light of her fears, relieves her of responsibility, and decides for her. "I don't know," she says, in answer to Phaedra's question about the nature of the love-charms. "Don't ask questions, child. Just let it do you good," οὐκ οἶδ᾽· ὀνάσθαι μὴ μαθεῖν βούλου, τέκνον (517). To Phaedra's expression of fear that her secret will be revealed to Hippolytus, the nurse replies, "Leave that to me, daughter," ἔασον ὦ παῖ. "I'll take care of that," ταῦτ᾽ ἐγὼ θήσω καλῶς (521). With a prayer to Aphrodite συνεργὸς εἴης (523), "Cooperate with me," and a statement that she will tell her thoughts to "friends within the house," the Nurse goes into the palace. And Phaedra lets her go. She has gone through the cycle of conscious choice, first silence, then speech, and come at last to abandon choice all together and entrust her destiny to another. And the result will be, as she said herself, destruction, μὴ γιγνώσκοντ᾽ ἀπολέσθαι.

For that result she does not have long to wait. "Silence," Σιγήσατ᾽ ὦ γυναῖκες (565), is the word with which she follows the closing line of the choral *stasimon* to open the next scene. She is listening to what is happening inside the house, where Hippolytus is shouting at the Nurse. What Phaedra both feared and longed for has come true; Hippolytus knows of her love.

The opening lines of the ensuing dialogue show Hippolytus in his turn confronted with the same choice, between silence and speech. He must choose between telling Theseus what he has heard, and remaining silent, as he has sworn to do. His first reaction is a passionate announcement that he will speak, an appeal to earth and sun to witness what he has just heard.

> ὦ γαῖα μᾶτερ ἡλίου τ᾽ ἀναπτυχαί
> οἵων λόγων ἄρρητον εἰσήκουσ᾽ ὄπα (601-2).

To the Nurse's plea for silence, σίγησον ὦ παῖ (603), he replies, "Impossible. What I have heard is dreadful. I cannot keep silence," οὐκ ἔστ᾽ ἀκούσας δεῖν᾽ ὅπως σιγήσομαι (504). This impulse to speak is, as in Phaedra's case, passion overriding judgment, but the passion which inspires him is not the same. Behind Phaedra's delirious words and subsequent conscious surrender to the Nurse's questioning, we can see the power of Aphrodite working in her; but Hippolytus' outburst is the shocked and incredulous reaction of the virgin mind, the working of Artemis in him. And in his case, as in Phaedra's, the passionate impulse endangers the chief objective of the conscious mind; Phaedra's speech endangers her honor, that εὔκλεια which is her life's aim, and Hippolytus' speech endangers his highest ambition, reverence, εὐσέβεια, for it involves breaking the oath he swore to the Nurse. Though they make their choices in different order (Phaedra choosing first silence, then speech, Hippolytus first speech, then silence), the parallel is striking. And the agent who brings about the change of mind is in each case the same, the Nurse.

The connection between the two situations is emphasized not only verbally and thematically but also visually. For the Nurse now throws herself at the feet of Hippolytus, as she did at Phaedra's, and clasps his hand and knees, as she did hers. The supreme gesture of supplication is repeated, to meet with the same initial resistance and final compliance. But this time she begs not for speech but for silence.

Hippolytus rejects her request with the same argument she herself had used against Phaedra's silence. "If the matter is good," he says, "it will be better still when published," τά τοι κάλ᾽ ἐν πολλοῖσι κάλλιον λέγειν (610) —a line which recalls what the Nurse had said to Phaedra, "Then you will be even more honored if you tell," οὔκουν λέγουσα τιμιωτέρα φάνῃ (332). Hippolytus launches on his passionate denunciation of women. The violence of his speech relieves the passion which made him ignore his oath, and he ends his speech with a promise to keep silence, σῖγα δ' ἕξομεν στόμα (660). He will respect the oath. "Don't forget this, woman," he says to the Nurse, "it is my reverence which saves you," εὖ δ' ἴσθι τοὐμὸν σ' εὐσεβὲς σῴζει, γύναι (666). Hippolytus too changes his mind; "in this world second thoughts are somehow wiser."

But Phaedra's situation is desperate. She does not believe that the disgust and hatred revealed in Hippolytus' speech will remain under control—"He will speak against us to his father," she says, ἐρεῖ καθ' ἡμῶν πατρί (690)—and even if she could be certain of Hippolytus' silence, she is not the woman to face Theseus with dissimulation. She wondered, in her long speech to the chorus, how the adulteress could look her husband in the face (415-16), and even if she had the necessary hardness, the situation would be made difficult, to say the least, by Hippolytus' announced intention to watch her at it (661-62). Now she must die, as she intended from the first, but she can no longer die in silence. That would no longer be death with honor—τοιγὰρ οὐκέτ' εὐκλεεῖς/θανούμεθ' (687-88). Speech has brought her to this pass, and in order to die and protect her reputation she now needs more speech. "Now I need new words," she says, ἀλλὰ δεῖ με δὴ καινῶν λόγων (688).

"May I not pass unnoticed when I act nobly," she said in the beginning, "nor have many witnesses when I act disgracefully" (403-4). She got the first half of her wish—the chorus was witness to her noble resolution to die in silence—but the second half was not granted. Hippolytus is a witness to her weakness, and he must be silenced. To this motive for action against him is added the hatred of the rejected woman who has heard every word of his ugly speech. The "new words" which she finds, the letter to Theseus accusing Hippolytus of an attempt on her virtue, will save her reputation and satisfy her hatred. They will guarantee the ineffectiveness of Hippolytus' speech, if speak he does, and they will also destroy him.

But there are other witnesses to be silenced too, the chorus. She asks them to hide in silence what they have heard, σιγῇ καλύπτειν ἀνθάδ' εἰσηκούσατε (712), and they agree. They bind themselves to silence by an oath. Thus the chorus, like the three principal characters so far seen, chooses between the same two alternatives, and seals its choice, silence, with speech of the most powerful and binding kind, an oath. The chorus will not change its mind.

The preliminaries are now over and the stage is set for Hippolytus' destruction. Phaedra commits suicide, and Theseus finds her letter. What happens now, whether Aphrodite's purpose will be fulfilled or fail, whether Hippolytus will live or die, depends on whether Theseus chooses silence or speech. He does not keep us waiting long. "I cannot hold it inside the gates of my mouth," he says, τόδε μὲν οὐκέτι στόματος ἐν πύλαις/καθέξω (882-83). But it is not ordinary speech. By the gift conferred on him by his father Poseidon, he can speak, in certain circumstances, with a power that is reserved for gods alone—his wish, expressed in speech, becomes fact. In his mouth, at this moment, speech has the power of life and death. And he uses it to kill his son. "Father Poseidon, you gave me once three curses. With one of these, wipe out my son."

> ἀλλ' ὦ πάτερ Πόσειδον, ἃς ἐμοί ποτε
> ἀρὰς ὑπέσχου τρεῖς, μιᾷ κατέργασαι
> τούτων ἐμὸν παῖδ' . . . (887-89).

Here the last piece of the jigsaw puzzle of free will is fitted into place to complete the picture of Aphrodite's purpose fulfilled. And Theseus' curse is at the same time a demonstration of the futility of the alternative which the second thoughts of Phaedra, Hippolytus, and the Nurse have suggested. "Second thoughts are somehow wiser"—they were not for these three. Perhaps first thoughts are best; μὴ γιγνώσκοντ', as Phaedra said. But Theseus is the one person in the play for whom second thoughts would have been wiser; and he gives himself no time to have them. He acts immediately, without stopping to examine the case or consider alternatives; μὴ γιγνώσκοντ' ἀπολέσθαι, to abandon judgment and perish—Phaedra's last desperate course—is Theseus' first impulsive action.

The alternatives before these human beings, first and second thoughts, passion and judgment, silence and speech, are chosen and rejected in a complicated pattern which shows the independent operation of five separate human wills producing a result desired by none of them, the consummation of Aphrodite's purpose. The fact that the moral alternatives are represented by silence and speech is not merely a brilliant device which connects and contrasts the situations of the different characters, it is also an emphatic statement of the universality of the action. It makes the play an ironical comment on a fundamental idea, the idea that man's power of speech, which distinguishes him from the other animals, is the faculty which gives him the conception and power of moral choice in the first place.

This Greek commonplace is most clearly set forth in a famous passage of Aristotle's *Politics* (I, i, 10). "Man alone of the animals possesses speech (λόγον). Mere voice (φωνή) can, it is true, indicate pain and pleasure, and therefore it is possessed by the other animals as well . . . but speech (λόγος) is designed to indicate the advantageous and the harmful (τὸ συμφέρον καὶ τὸ βλαβερόν) and therefore also the right and the wrong (τὸ δίκαιον καὶ τὸ ἄδικον): for it is the special property of man, in distinction from the other animals, that he alone has perception of good and bad (ἀγαθοῦ καὶ κακοῦ) and right and wrong (δικαίου καὶ ἀδίκου) and other moral qualities (καὶ τῶν ἄλλων)."

It is clear that Euripides was familiar with the idea, for he makes at least one ironical reference to the contrast between man, who has speech, and the animals which do not. Hippolytus, in his furious invective, wishes that women could be provided with dumb animals instead of servants like the Nurse. "Animals with bite instead of voice should be housed with them, so that women could neither speak to anyone nor get speech back in return."

> ἄφθογγα δ' αὐταῖς συγκατοικίζειν δάκη
> θηρῶν, ἵν' εἶχον μήτε προσφωνεῖν τινα
> μήτ' ἐξ ἐκείνων φθέγμα δέξασθαι πάλιν (646-48).

Here he wishes that speaking beings could be made dumb, but in his own moment of trial and agony before Theseus he reverses his wish, and begs an inanimate object, the house, to speak in his defense. "House, if only you could somehow send forth a voice and bear witness . . ."

> ὦ δώματ' εἴθε φθέγμα γηρύσαισθέ μοι
> καὶ μαρτυρήσαιτ' . . . (1074-75).

Speech is what distinguishes man from the other animals. But in the *Hippolytus* its role is not simply to point out the distinction between right and wrong. It is presented not as the instrument which makes possible the conception of moral choice and expresses moral alternatives, but as an explosive force, which, once released, cannot be restrained and which creates universal destruction. Ποῖ προβήσεται λόγος (342). "To what length will speech go?" asks the Nurse, when she has finally succeeded in opening Phaedra's lips. It goes far enough to ruin all of them. It assumes many forms, Phaedra's delirium, the Nurse's cynical argument, Hippolytus' invective, Phaedra's letter, Theseus' curse—and in all of these forms it is the instrument of Aphrodite's will.

The *Hippolytus* is a terrible demonstration of the meaninglessness of the moral choice and its medium, speech. But it is not a mechanical demonstration; the unifying and meaningful situation is the key to the play, but that does not mean that character is unimportant. The demonstration is in fact powerful precisely because the choices and alternations of choice made by the human beings are in each case the natural expres-

sion of the individual character. As has often been remarked, if the prologue were removed, the action would still be plausible. The external
directing force works not against but through the characteristic thoughts
and impulses of the characters involved. But the brilliant delineation of
character in the *Hippolytus* does more than motivate the action plausibly.
The characters, like the situation, have a larger dimension of meaning
than the purely dramatic; they are individual examples which illustrate
the fundamental proposition implied in the situation—the futility of
human choice and action.

The four characters involved are very different; different in purpose,
action, and suffering. But they all go through the same process. Action in
each case, far from fulfilling conscious purpose, brings about the opposite
of that purpose. The individual purpose is the expression of a view of
human life and a way of living it; in each case this view is exposed, by
the individual disaster, as inadequate. And the view of human life implies, in turn, an attitude toward the gods; these attitudes are in each
case proved unsound. The human beings of the world of the *Hippolytus*
live out their lives in the darkness of total ignorance of the nature of
the universe and of the powers which govern it.

Phaedra's purpose and way of life can be summed up in one word, the
word which is so often on her lips, εὐκλεής, "honorable." She has a code
of honor proper for a princess, an aristocratic and unintellectual ideal.
From first to last this is Phaedra's dominant motive, except for the fatal
moment when she surrenders her initiative to the Nurse. It is to preserve
this honor that she takes her original decision to die in silence; to enjoy
appreciation of her honor she indulges in the luxury of speech to the
chorus; and to rescue her honorable reputation from the consequences
she ruins Hippolytus and brings guilt and sorrow on Theseus. But it is
all to no purpose. In the end her conspiracy of silence is a failure and
her honor lost. Hippolytus and the chorus keep the oaths that they have
sworn, and remain silent; the house cannot speak; but the goddess Artemis coldly reveals the truth to Theseus, who learns not only that his wife
had a guilty passion for Hippolytus but also that she has tricked him
into killing his innocent son. Phaedra's attempt to save her honor has
proved an expensive failure.

Not only is her purpose baffled and her code of conduct shown to be
inadequate; her concern for her honor is dismissed by the gods as irrelevant. Both Aphrodite and Artemis treat Phaedra's honor with complete
indifference. "She is honorable—but still, she dies," ἡ δ' εὐκλεὴς μὲν, ἀλλ'
ὅμως ἀπόλλυται (47), says Aphrodite; and when Artemis reveals the truth
to Theseus she makes it clear that she is concerned with the reputation,

not of Phaedra but of Hippolytus. "I have come," she says to Theseus, "to show that his mind was just, so that he may die in honor" ὡς ὑπ' εὐκλείας θάνῃ (1299)—to save his reputation. Phaedra's passion, far from being buried in silence so that she can be honored after death, will be the subject of song in the ritual cult of Hippolytus. "It shall not fall nameless and be silenced, Phaedra's passion for you."

> κοὐκ ἀνώνυμος πεσών
> ἔρως ὁ Φαίδρας ἐς σὲ σιγηθήσεται (1429-30).

Phaedra's purpose, to save her honor, is one consistent with her ideal of conduct and her life as she has lived it so far. It is characteristic of the Nurse that her purpose has nothing to do with ideals; it is specific and practical, she wishes to save not Phaedra's honor but her life, and to that end she will use any means which promise success. Her love for Phaedra is the motive for her actions from first to last. But in the end she succeeds only in destroying Phaedra's honor and her life as well; and hears herself rejected utterly and cursed by the person to whom she has devoted her entire life and whose well-being is her only objective.

The Nurse has no aristocratic code of conduct. Her word is not honorable, εὐκλεής, but λόγος, speech, reason, argument. She believes in, and tries to effect, the settlement of human problems by human reason, λόγος, expressed in speech, λόγος, which influences others as argument, λόγος. This is in fact not an aristocratic attitude but a democratic one, and the Nurse has another quality characteristic of Athenian democracy, flexibility. She can adapt herself quickly to new situations, seize a new ground of argument—a capacity illustrated by the fact that she shifts her ground in the play not once, like Phaedra and Hippolytus, but three times. She is in fact so flexible that her attitude is not a consistent moral code at all, but merely a series of practical approaches to different problems. It is natural therefore that the Nurse should be made to speak in terms that clearly associate her with the contemporary sophists, who, like her, had a secular and confident approach to human problems, the rhetorical skill to present their solution convincingly, and a relativism, which, expressed as the doctrine of expediency, enabled them to shift their ground, as the Nurse does, from one position to another.

For the Nurse, when she first talks to Phaedra, the choice between speech and silence is meaningless. She believes only in the choice between speech and speech. "You should not be silent, child. But either refute me if I speak badly, or agree if I speak well" (297-99). This implies her basic confidence that no problem is beyond the power of human reason, but when she hears the first hints of what is wrong with Phaedra (337-42), her confidence begins to falter. Ποῖ προβήσεται λόγος; "to what lengths will speech go?" she asks. And when she understands the truth, she tries to stop Phaedra's speech, οἴμοι τί λέξεις; (353) "Oh. What will you say?" She abandons hope of saving Phaedra's life, and consequently has no further use for her own. She goes off to die.

She comes back with her confidence renewed. She is now ashamed of her emotional reaction, her inadequacy, νῦν δ᾽ ἐννοοῦμαι φαῦλος οὖσα (435). Second thoughts are best. What has happened to Phaedra is not ἔξω λόγου (437), not something beyond the powers of reason and speech.

The powerful speech into which she now launches is easily recognizable as contemporary sophistic rhetoric at its cleverest and worst; it is a fine example of "making the worse appear the better cause." It is the devil quoting scripture; she cynically accuses Phaedra of ὕβρις (474), insolence and pride toward the gods. She uses the stock sophistic argument to justify immoral conduct, the misdemeanors of the gods in the myths. And she reveals, in her description of the way of the world—the husbands who conceal their wives' infidelities, the fathers who connive at their sons' adulteries—a cynicism which is the well-known result of sophistic teaching, the cynicism of a Cleon, a Thrasymachus. Only a hardened cynic, in fact, could fancy that Hippolytus could be corrupted. And the Nurse's argument takes this for granted. Speech is all that is needed, λόγοι θελκτήριοι, winning words, and in a double sense—the love-charms and also her pleading the cause of love which will charm Hippolytus into compliance.

When we next see her she is begging for silence. Ποῖ προβήσεται λόγος; was a prophetic question. Speech has unloosed forces beyond her control —ἔξω λόγου, and she now persuades Hippolytus to remain silent. But Phaedra has overheard their interview, and now resumes control of the situation. She pours out on the Nurse all the fury and hatred which Hippolytus' terrible denunciation has aroused in her. She uses the verbal loophole the Nurse so cleverly left her; "Did I not tell you to be silent?" οὐκ εἶπον . . . σιγᾶν; (685-86), and curses her terribly, calling on Zeus to blast her with fire and destroy her root and branch.

Ζεύς σε γεννήτωρ ἐμὸς
πρόρριζον ἐκτρίψειεν οὐτάσας πυρί (683-84).

But the nurse is still not silenced. "I can make a reply to this, if you will listen," ἔχω δὲ κἀγὼ πρός τάδ᾽, εἰ δέξῃ, λέγειν (697), she says, and she maintains her practical unprincipled viewpoint—"If I had succeeded, I would be one of the clever ones," εἰ δ᾽ εὖ γ᾽ ἔπραξα κάρτ᾽ ἂν ἐν σοφοῖσιν ἦ (700). And desperate though the situation is, she still has a way out. "There is a way to save you, even from this situation, my child," ἀλλ' ἔστι κἀκ τῶνδ' ὥστε σωθῆναι, τέκνον (705). But the Nurse, her way out, and the whole concept of λόγος, reason and speech, for which she stands, are rejected by Phaedra in one biting phrase—παῦσαι λέγουσα, "Stop talking" (706). And we hear no more of the Nurse.

The worldly, practical approach to the problem has proved no more successful than Phaedra's simple code of honor. The Nurse's one purpose, to save Phaedra's life, has, when translated into action, ensured her death. And the Nurse's outlook implies a view of the gods, a skeptical view, which is ironically developed in a play which has begun with the appearance of the goddess Aphrodite in person. The Nurse reveals her basic skepticism in her opening speech (176-97), in which she dismisses speculation about future life as unprofitable. Life as we know it is painful, she says (189-90), but as for some other thing, dearer than life, darkness enfolds it and hides it in clouds (192-93). There is no revelation of what lies beneath the earth, κοὐκ ἀπόδειξιν τῶν ὑπὸ γαίας (196). Later, when she recognizes the power of Aphrodite, she still expresses her belief in "scientific" agnostic terms. "Cypris was no god, then, but something greater, whatever it may be, than a god."

> Κύπρις οὐκ ἀρ' ἦν θεός
> ἀλλ' εἴ τι μεῖζον ἄλλο γίγνεται θεοῦ (359-60).

This rationalism of hers is the most unsound of all the views of the order of the universe expressed or implied by human beings in the play, and by a supreme irony this representative of skeptical thought is chosen to be the most important link in the chain of events which Aphrodite has forged. The Nurse's "reason" is the driving force in the process which brings Phaedra and Hippolytus to their deaths.

Hippolytus' purpose and his ideal is put before us early in the play; it is to live a life of piety and devotion to the virgin goddess Artemis. "I am in your company, and exchange speech with you," he says to the statue of Artemis. "I hear your voice though I may not see your face. May I round the final mark of the course of my life even as I have begun."

> σοὶ καὶ ξύνειμι καὶ λόγοις ἀμείβομαι,
> κλύων μὲν αὐδήν, ὄμμα δ' οὐχ ὁρῶν τὸ σόν·
> τέλος δὲ κάμψαιμ' ὥσπερ ἠρξάμην βίου. (85-87)

He hopes to round the final mark, to run the full course of a life of reverence and piety; but his prayer is to be ironically fulfilled this very day. At the end of the play he hears Artemis' voice though he cannot see her face, and exchanges speech with her as he lies dying, but he has

been cut off in full career, his chariot wrecked. And before that he will
have suffered the spiritual agony of seeing his father condemn and curse
him as a hypocritical adulterer, a man whom it would be a mockery to
associate with Artemis.

Like Phaedra, he is an aristocratic figure; in fact most of the commonplaces of the aristocratic attitude are put into his mouth in the course of
the play. But he is also an intellectual and a religious mystic. His principles, unlike Phaedra's, are clearly and consistently formulated; for him
the most important thing in life is εὐσέβεια, reverence toward the gods. "I
know first of all how to treat the gods with reverence," ἐπίσταμαι γὰρ
πρῶτα μὲν θεοὺς σέβειν (996), he says when defending himself against his
father's attack. Except for the moment of passion when he threatens to
break his oath and speak, he is guided in every thought and action by
his εὐσέβεια. And when he finally decides for silence and his oath, he
emphasizes this motive; "Know this, woman, it is my reverence which
saves you," εὖ δ' ἴσθι τοὐμὸν σ' εὐσεβὲς σῴζει, γύναι (656), he says to the Nurse.
He might have said, "It is my reverence which destroys me," for all
through his father's bitter onslaught he stands by his principles, respects
his oath, and keeps silent about Phaedra's part in the affair. As was the
case with Phaedra and the Nurse, it is the central concept of his whole
life and character which destroys him.

And, like them, he represents an attitude toward the gods. It is a
religious position which is intellectual as well as mystic. His reverence
for the gods manifests itself mainly in the worship of one goddess, Artemis; and he completely rejects another, Aphrodite. The position is logical;
on the intellectual plane the worship of Artemis is clearly incompatible
with the worship of Aphrodite, and acceptance of the one does constitute
rejection of the other. The mass of humanity can ignore the contradiction, as the old servant does in the opening scene, just as most Christians
manage to serve Mammon as well as God, but for the man who has
dedicated his life to God, or to a goddess, there can be no compromise.
Hippolytus must choose one or the other: "Man must choose among the
gods as the gods choose among men," ἄλλοισιν ἄλλος θεῶν τε κἀνθρώπων μέλει
(104), he says to the servant. And Hippolytus has chosen Artemis. It does
not save him. He dies in agony in the prime of youth, and before he dies
he has to go through the mental agony of hearing himself, the virgin
soul, παρθένον ψυχὴν ἔχων (1006), treated by his father as a lustful hypocrite. And he sees himself in the end as a man who has spent his life in
vain, ἄλλως; "In vain have I toiled at labors of reverence before mankind," μόχθους δ' ἄλλως/τῆς εὐσεβίας εἰς ἀνθρώπους ἐπόνησα (1367-69). He even
goes so far as to wish that human beings could curse the gods, and though

he is reproached by Artemis for this sentiment, he shows his disillusion in his farewell to her. "This great companionship of ours, you find it easy to leave," μακρὰν δὲ λείπεις ῥᾳδίως ὁμιλίαν (1441). His reverence is inadequate not merely as a way of life but also as a religious belief; it cannot stand unmoved in the face of reality—the knowledge that his privileged association with Artemis made him not a man to be envied but a pitiful victim and that all the goddess can do for him is promise to kill another human being to avenge him.

Theseus is an early Attic king, but with the customary anachronism of Athenian tragedy, he is presented as a fifth century statesman. His characteristic expression of thought and feeling is that of the man in the public eye, the man who is always conscious of his audience. When he states the charge against his son and invokes Poseidon's curse, he calls on the city to hear, ἰὼ πόλις (884), making it an official act. Even in his mourning for Phaedra he is conscious of his public stature, ἔπαθον ὦ πόλις (817), and in his tirade against Hippolytus he speaks to the audience as often as he does to his son, σκέψασθ᾽ ἐς τόνδε (943), προφωνῶ πᾶσι (956). And he supports his action by an appeal to his reputation; if he is worsted by Hippolytus, the monsters he conquered in his heroic youth will no longer serve as proof that he is harsh to evildoers (976-80). His life is devoted to the maintenance of a reputation; even in his private sorrow he never forgets that the eyes of Athens are upon him.

He is a statesman, but not, like his son, an intellectual. He is the man of action; and this point is emphasized by his impulsive act, his appeal to his heroic past and his contempt for speech (λόγος). This appears clearly in his attack on his son; he describes Hippolytus as one who pursues evil with "pious words," σεμνοῖς λόγοισιν (957). "What words," he says, "can argue more effectively than this woman's corpse?" κρείσσονες τίνες λόγοι τῆσδ᾽ ἂν γένοιντ᾽ ἄν; (960-61). "Why do I try to compete with you in words on this matter?" τί ταῦτα σοῖς ἁμιλλῶμαι λόγοις; (971). He follows this last remark with action, the proclamation of banishment; he is a man not of words but of deeds. When he called Poseidon's curse on his son he did not wait, as Artemis reminds him later, for proof or prophecy or cross-examination, but followed his impulse. He is like another Athenian statesman, Themistocles, who, says Thucydides, was best at intuitive action in an emergency, κράτιστος . . . αὐτοσχεδιάζειν τὰ δέοντα, and the best man to decide immediate issues with the least deliberation, τῶν . . . παραχρῆμα δι᾽ ἐλαχίστης βουλῆς κράτιστος γνώμων (I, 138); Theseus acts with the swift decision of a Themistocles, an Oedipus. But he is wrong. And his mistake destroys the thing to which he has devoted his life. It is a mistake he can never live down, his public reputation is gone, as Artemis coldly tells him; "Hide yourself in shame below the depths of the earth, or take wing into the sky . . . among good men there is now no portion you can call your own" (1290-95).

Theseus, too, has a distinct religious attitude. His is the religion of the politician, vocal, formal, and skin deep, verbal acceptance but limited belief. He first appears on stage wearing the wreath of the θεωρός, the state visitor to an oracle, and he can roundly recite the names of the gods in public proclamation or prayer—"Hippolytus . . . has dishonored the awful eye of Zeus," τὸ σεμνὸν Ζηνὸς ὄμμ' ἀτιμάσας (886), but he only half believes in all this. He prays to Poseidon to kill his son, and before the day is out; but when the chorus begs him to recall his prayer he replies: "No. And in addition, I shall exile him from this land," καὶ πρός γ' ἐξελῶ σφε τῆσδε γῆς (893). That revealing phrase "in addition" is expanded in the succeeding lines. "Of these two destinies he will be struck by one or the other," δυοῖν δὲ μοίραιν θατέρᾳ πεπλήξεται (894). Either Poseidon will strike him down or he will live out a miserable life in exile. The hint of skepticism is broadened when the messenger arrives to announce the disaster. He claims that his news is of serious import (μερίμνης ἄξιον [1157]) to Theseus and all the citizens of Athens, but Theseus' first thought is of political news. "Has some disaster overtaken the neighboring cities?" (1160-61) Informed that Hippolytus is near death he asks, "Who did it? Did he get into trouble with someone else whose wife he raped, as he did his father's?" (1164-65) And only when the messenger reminds him of his curse does he realize the truth. "O gods, Poseidon, then you really were my father, you listened to my curses" (1169-70). It is a revelation which proves the unsoundness of his skepticism, and he accepts it with joy. But he will live to regret it and wish his prayer unspoken. "Would that it had never come into my mouth," ὡς μήποτ' ἐλθεῖν ὤφελ' ἐς τοὐμὸν στόμα (1412).

Theseus has gone through the same cycle as the other characters of the play. All four of the characters live, and two of them die, in a world in which purpose frustrates itself, choice is meaningless, moral codes and political attitudes ineffective, and human conceptions of the nature of the gods erroneous. But two of them learn, at the end of the play, the truth which we have known from the beginning, the nature of the world in which they live. They learn it from the lips of Artemis, as we have already heard it from the lips of Aphrodite. Artemis comes, like Aphrodite, to reveal (ἐκδεῖξαι [1298], δείξω [9]); she confirms, expands, and explains the process of divine government of which the prologue was our first glimpse.

These two goddesses are powers locked in an eternal war, a war in which the human tragedy we have just witnessed is merely one engagement. In this particular operation Aphrodite was the active agent and Artemis the passive; but Artemis now informs us that these roles will be reversed—there will be a return made for this in which Artemis will assume the active role and Aphrodite the passive. The terms in which she explains her passivity in this case to Theseus make clear that this is permanent war; an eternal struggle in which the only losses are human lives.

"This is law and custom for the gods," she says, θεοῖσι δ' ὧδ' ἔχει νόμος (1328). "No one wishes to stand hostile against the energy of a god who has a desire—we stand aside always."

> οὐδεὶς ἀπαντᾶν βούλεται προθυμίᾳ
> τῇ τοῦ θέλοντος ἀλλ' ἀφιστάμεσθ' ἀεί (1329-30).

The authority for this law and custom, as Artemis makes clear, is Zeus himself; but for her fear of Zeus, she says, she would not have allowed Hippolytus to die. What has happened, then, is no anomaly, but the working of the system of divine government of the universe, an eternal pattern of alternate aggression and retreat. And we can see from what Artemis says that when she has the active instead of the passive role, she will be as ruthless as Aphrodite was in this case.

The words which describe Aphrodite's direction of human affairs are thus equally applicable to Artemis; they constitute a description of the function of divine government as a whole. And there are two words, repeated throughout the play at crucial moments and in significant contexts which characterize the nature of the government of the universe. One of these words, σφάλλειν, describes the action characteristic of the gods, and the other, ἄλλως, describes the human condition which results from that action.

Σφάλλειν, to trip, throw, cast down. It is Aphrodite's own word for her action in the play. "I throw down those who despise me," σφάλλω δ' ὅσοι φρονοῦσιν εἰς ἡμᾶς μέγα (6). The literal accomplishment of this metaphorical threat comes when the bull from the sea "throws" the horses of Hippolytus' chariot, ἔσφηλε κἀνεχαίτισεν (1232). But this action is not confined to Hippolytus. The word recurs in connection with all the principal characters of the play. "You are quickly thrown," ταχὺ γὰρ σφάλλῃ (183), says the Nurse to Phaedra in her opening speech. She is referring to Phaedra's sudden changes of mind, the capriciousness of the sick woman who vacillates between staying indoors or out, but the words have a terrible significance in the light of what happens later when Phaedra changes her mind about something more important. Speaking of her own love for Phaedra and wishing, for her own peace of mind, that she did not love her so much, the Nurse laments the fact that "consistent conduct in life," βιότου δ' ἀτρεκεῖς ἐπιτηδεύσεις (261), "brings, so they say, not pleasure but overthrow," φασὶ σφάλλειν πλέον ἢ τέρπειν (262). It is true enough; the one consistent attitude in her, her love for Phaedra, brings her to ruin, and the words describe more exactly still the attitude and practice of Hippolytus, who is as consistent as the Nurse is flexible, as single-minded as the Nurse is versatile. Phaedra, after she has heard Hippolytus denounce her and all her sex, sees herself as "thrown," σφαλεῖσθαι (671). As Theseus reads the fatal letter the chorus prays to an unnamed god, ὦ δαῖμον, not to throw the house, μὴ σφήλῃς δόμους (871). And when Theseus explains to Hippolytus how he could curse and con-demn him, he uses the same word; "I was tripped and thrown in my opinion by the gods," δόξης γὰρ ἦμεν πρὸς θεῶν ἐσφαλμένοι (1414). It is this remark of his which provokes Hippolytus' wish that the human race could curse the gods.

The goddess trips, throws, leads astray, frustrates—all these are mean-ings of σφάλλειν, and the word which describes the operation of the human will in these circumstances is ἄλλως—otherwise, differently, wrongly, in vain. This adverb is used to describe the operation of human will throughout the tragedy; the character's actions produce results op-posite to their purpose, things turn out "otherwise." "Our labor is all in vain," ἄλλως τούσδε μοχθοῦμεν πόνους (301), says the Nurse of her efforts to make Phaedra speak, the word has a double sense here, for the Nurse succeeds in her final attempt, but the results are not what she intended. "Vainly," says Phaedra to the chorus, "have I pondered in the long watches of the night, seeking to understand how human life is ruined."

> ἤδη ποτ' ἄλλως νυκτὸς ἐν μακρῷ χρόνῳ
> θνητῶν ἐφρόντισ' ᾗ διέφθαρται βίος (375-76).

This understanding she never attains, but it is given in all its fullness to Theseus and Hippolytus at the end of the play. "In vain, in vain," chants the chorus, "does the land of Greece increase sacrifice of oxen to Zeus and Apollo. . . ."

> ἄλλως ἄλλως παρά τ' Ἀλφεῷ
> Φοίβου τ' ἐπὶ Πυθίοις τεράμνοις
> βούταν φόνον Ἑλλὰς ⟨αἴ'⟩ ἀέξει (535-37).

"In vain," says Hippolytus in his agony, "have I performed labors of reverence before mankind."

μόχθους δ' ἄλλως
τῆς εὐσεβίας
εἰς ἀνθρώπους ἐπόνησα (1367-69).

And the Nurse, speaking specifically of humanity's ignorance of anything beyond this life, characterizes the whole human situation with the
same word. Μύθοις δ' ἄλλως φερόμεσθα (197), "We are carried off our course,
led astray, supported vainly, by myths." In the context it is of course a
rationalist criticism of popular beliefs, but the verbal pattern of the
whole poem invests it with a deeper meaning. We are borne astray,
carried to a destination we did not intend, by myths, myths in which
the Nurse does not believe, but which the appearance and actions of the
two goddesses in the play prove to be not myths in the Nurse's sense, but
the stuff of reality. The underlying meaning of the Nurse's words is
brought out by the emphatic manner in which both goddesses are made
to emphasize their connection with myth; myth, μῦθος, is the word they
use of their own speech. "I will quickly reveal the truth of these words
[myths]," δείξω δὲ μύθων τῶνδ' ἀλήθειαν τάχα (9), says Aphrodite; and Artemis, after telling Theseus the truth, asks him cruelly, "Does my word
[story, myth] pain you?" δάκνει σε Θησεῦ μῦθος (1313). Human beings are
indeed borne astray by myths, the goddesses who trip their heels and
thwart their purpose. Humanity is merely the "baser nature" which
"comes between the pass and fell-incensed points of mighty opposites."

Of the nature and meaning of Aphrodite and Artemis in this play
much has been written, and there is little to add. They have many aspects;
they are anthropomorphic goddesses, myths, dramatic personalities with
motives and hostile purposes, and they are also impersonal, incompatible
forces of nature. They are indeed "mighty opposites," and that opposition may be expressed in many terms—positive and negative, giving and
denying, increase and decrease, indulgence and abstinence—but what
Euripides has been at some pains to emphasize is not their opposition,
but their likeness. The play is full of emphatic suggestions that there is
a close correspondence between them.

When Hippolytus describes the meadow sacred to Artemis from which
he has made the wreath he offers to her statue, he mentions the bee,
μέλισσα (77), which goes through the uncut grass in spring. It is an appropriate detail, for the name μέλισσα, bee, was given to priestesses of
Artemis, and the bee is in many contexts associated with virginity. But
some five hundred lines later the chorus compares Aphrodite to a bee,
"She hovers like a bee," μέλισσα δ' οἷά τις πεπόταται (562-63). This trans-
ference of symbol from the appropriate goddess to the inappropriate one

is strange, and it is reinforced by another striking correspondence. The
chorus, early in the play, describes Artemis, under one of her many titles,
Dictynna. "She ranges through the marsh waters, over the land and over
the sea, in the eddies of the salt water."

> φοιτᾷ γὰρ καὶ διὰ λίμνας
> χέρσον θ' ὑπὲρ πελάγους
> δίναις ἐν νοτίαις ἄλμας (148-50).

And later, the Nurse, describing the power of Aphrodite to Phaedra,
uses similar language; "She ranges through the air, and she is in the
wave of the sea."

> φοιτᾷ δ' ἀν' αἰθέρ', ἔστι δ' ἐν θαλασσίῳ
> κλύδωνι (447-48).

The function of these surprising echoes is to prepare us for an extraordinary feature of Artemis' concluding speeches; she repeats word after
word and phrase after phrase of Aphrodite's prologue. These two polar
opposites express themselves in the same terms. "I gained a start on the
road long ago," πάλαι προκόψασ' (23), says Aphrodite, and Artemis uses the
same unusual metaphor—"And yet I shall gain nothing, and only give you
pain," καίτοι προκόψω γ' οὐδέν, ἀλγυνῶ δέ σε (1297), she says to Theseus. "I
shall reveal," δείξω (6), says Aphrodite; and Artemis says that she comes
"to reveal," ἐκδεῖξαι (1298). "I am not unnamed," κοὐκ ἀνώνυμος (1), says
Aphrodite, and Artemis takes up the phrase: "not unnamed (κοὐκ
ἀνώνυμος) shall Phaedra's love for you fall and be silenced." Both of
them claim, in similar words and with opposite meanings, that they
reward the reverent and punish the wrongdoer (5-6 and 1339-41), and
each of them, with the same characteristic word, τιμωρήσομαι (21 and 1422),
announces her decision to kill the other's human protégé.

They are opposites, but considered as divinities directing human
affairs they are exactly alike. The repetitions emphasize the fact that
the activity of Aphrodite and the passivity of Artemis are roles which
will be easily reversed. And the mechanical repetition of Aphrodite's
phrases by Artemis depersonalizes both of them; we become aware of
them as impersonal forces which act in a repetitive pattern, an eternal
ordered dance of action and reaction, equal and opposite. From the law
which governs their advance and retreat there can be no deviation;
Artemis cannot break the pattern of movement to save Hippolytus, nor
can she forgive Aphrodite. Forgiveness is in fact unthinkable in such a
context; it is possible only for human beings. These gods are, in both
the literal and metaphorical senses of the word, inhuman.

Artemis does indeed tell Hippolytus not to hate his father, πατέρα μὴ στυγεῖν (1435). But this merely emphasizes the gulf between god and man. She does not, on her plane, forgive Aphrodite; rather she announces a repetition of the terrible events we have just witnessed, a new human victim is to die to pay for the loss of her favorite. "The anger of Cypris shall not swoop down on your body unavenged. For I shall punish another man, with my own hand, whoever chances to be most loved by her of mortals, with these inescapable arrows."

> ἐγὼ γὰρ αὐτῆς ἄλλον ἐξ ἐμῆς χερὸς
> ὃς ἂν μάλιστα φίλτατος κυρῇ βροτῶν
> τόξοις ἀφύκτοις τοῖσδε τιμωρήσομαι (1420-22).

This, together with the promise that his memory will be the myth of a virgin cult, is the consolation she offers Hippolytus for the fact that she stood aside and allowed him to be destroyed. She cannot weep for him, that is the law which governs the nature of gods (κατ' ὄσσων δ' οὐ θέμις βαλεῖν δάκρυ [1396]); nor can she stay by him as he dies. "It is not lawful for me to see the dead and defile my eye with their dying breath."

> ἐμοὶ γὰρ οὐ θέμις φθιτοὺς ὁρᾶν
> οὐδ' ὄμμα χραίνειν θανασίμοισιν ἐκπνοαῖς (1437-38).

And she withdraws, leaving father and son alone.

It has often been remarked that this disturbing play ends on a note of serenity. Méridier's comment is typical: "le dénouement s'achève, grâce à la présence d'Artémis, dans un rayonnement de transfiguration. Et cette scène finale, où la tristesse déchirante s'épure peu à peu et s'apaise dans une sérénité céleste. . . ." The ending is serene, but the serenity has nothing to do with Artemis, who throughout her scene with Hippolytus coldly and insistently disassociates herself from him, so that he bids her farewell with a reproach. The serenity comes not from the goddess but from the two broken men who are left onstage after she withdraws.

Hippolytus forgives his father. To err is human, as Artemis says to Theseus,

> ἀνθρώποισι δὲ
> θεῶν διδόντων εἰκὸς ἐξαμαρτάνειν (1434);

but to forgive is not divine. It is an action possible only for man, an act by which man can distinguish himself from and rise above the inexorable laws of the universe in which he is placed. And though Hippolytus recognizes that he is following Artemis' advice, he shows too that he is fully conscious of the fact that in forgiving he is doing what she cannot do. As he forgives his father he calls to witness his sincerity "Artemis of the conquering arrow," τὴν τοξόδαμνον Ἄρτεμιν μαρτύρομαι

(1451). The epithet is not ornamental; it recalls vividly Artemis' announcement of her intention to repay, twenty-five lines before—"with these inescapable arrows (τόξοις ἀφύκτοις) I shall punish another." Hippolytus calls to witness his act of forgiveness the goddess who cannot herself forgive.

It is significant that Artemis leaves the stage before the end of the play; her exit closes the circle which began with Aphrodite's entrance. Within its circumference, the human beings of the play fulfilled through all the multiple complications of choice an external purpose of which they were ignorant. But Aphrodite's purpose is now fulfilled, she has no further use for these creatures, and Artemis has gone. The play ends with a human act which is at last a free and meaningful choice, a choice made for the first time in full knowledge of the nature of human life and divine government, an act which does not frustrate its purpose. It is an act of forgiveness, something possible only for human beings, not for gods but for their tragic victims. It is man's noblest declaration of independence, and it is made possible by man's tragic position in the world. Hippolytus' forgiveness of his father is an affirmation of purely human values in an inhuman universe.

Watching the *Trojan Women*

by Eric A. Havelock

At the beginning of the drama, the audience looks down on the
dancing floor and sees two actors, one a woman prostrate upon the
ground, the other a god, tall, remote, and aloof, standing back. They
have nothing to say to each other; the woman indeed says nothing at
all. The god is speaking over her head and addressing his remarks to
us. But there is a third presence, that of the city of Troy, partly destroyed,
smoking, but still standing. Behind the prostrate woman we see the city
gates and in the foreground to either side the tents and huts of the
Greek army, which has just sacked the city and killed all its male
inhabitants.

Poseidon identifies himself: I have just arrived, he says, from the
crystalline depths of the Aegean, the dancing floor of the sea nymphs.
We became aware that he now confronts another dancing floor, a scene
of a very different celebration. Yes, it is to Troy, smashed and smoking,
that I am paying this visit—Troy always a favorite city of mine from the
days when I helped to build her—but now she has been captured, as I
shall tell you. And he proceeds to speak his piece, to place in our hands
the theater playbill which his oral statement must supply, and acquaint
us with the details of the situation past and present in which the drama
is to be acted out. The Greek device of the Wooden Horse had ended
the ten years' war; the city was taken and Priam himself cut down at the
altar of Trojan Zeus; the Greeks, their purposes accomplished, are now
leaving at last for home. "Nothing remains for me but to abandon my
shrines and altars in this city; the purposes of Hera and Athene, bitter
enemies of Troy, have prevailed."

Here under these roofs, he continues, still wait certain women survivors, special cases, reserved for the captains of the Greek host. The
public slaves have already been distributed. The present group, of
course, includes Helen, now a prisoner (at the pronunciation of her

"Watching the *Trojan Women*" by Eric A. Havelock. Written for this collection.
Copyright © 1968 by Prentice-Hall, Inc.

name we perhaps lean forward in our seats; but her entrance is to be postponed). Here recumbent is Hecuba, Priam's queen, one of whose daughters, Polyxena, has already been secretly dispatched by the Greeks as an offering to the tomb of Achilles. Another, Cassandra, once the virgin priestess of Apollo, is now allotted as concubine to Agamemnon, the commander-in-chief. "Oh Troy, farewell, the goddess Athene has destroyed you." And so his monologue ends. The situation is defined almost as a nonsituation. Troy is finished, there is nothing to be done about it, and we wonder what else is now left for act or word to accomplish.

Of course, there are the Greeks, victorious, glutted, and perhaps a little weary. They at least represent something achieved, something to identify with. Or do they? Athene will settle with them. Poseidon no sooner pronounces the name of this formidable goddess than she enters and joins him, addressing him with serene formality, and proceeds to open up a fresh page of history: she would like to restore friendly relations with Poseidon and enter into partnership with him in a matter connected with Troy. The god wonders perhaps if her past hatred has at last yielded to compassion. She is careful not to disillusion him until she has made him promise to act with her. Then she shows her hand; hate and hate alone remains the mainspring of her intentions. She now proposes to turn against the Greeks; had they not committed impieties against her worship during the sack of the city, including the attempt to ravish Cassandra? At any rate, catastrophe for the Trojans requires a matching catastrophe visited upon the Greeks; Zeus has granted her the loan of the thunderbolt. With Poseidon's help a hurricane at sea can be raised to wreck the Greek fleet on its way home, and the coasts of the Cyclades will be strewn with drowned men. Poseidon readily agrees. Turning from her to face the amphitheater, he closes with an apostrophe upon the folly of all men who sack and destroy cities.

So ends the prologue to whatever drama may still ensue. Aside from the narrated facts, what have we already learned from it? Surely that there is a control over the universe exercised by powers who are indeed powerful, and capable of some affection, but an affection which never prevails over their enmities. They can receive worship, and expect it, but men may expect no return for this. What men must guard against is offense. One thing that can involve a divinity with its human worshipers is a feeling of offended dignity. Hecuba, we remember, is still lying on the ground, but the two gods remain serenely aloof from her, meanwhile defining for us the course of history past—the capture and sack of the city—and of history future—the fate of the Greek victors. Their joint statements provide a fixed frame, determined in time, within the limits of which a few persons will speak their parts and then leave.

The deities withdraw and do not return; the divine dispositions, or the historical necessities, have now been stated as a kind of verbal backdrop against which, as it is retained in our memory, we now are asked to place the contemplation of the human scenes that are to follow.

There is a pause and the recumbent figure rouses itself. The flutes take over and she begins to sing. The human action, if it be called such, begins as opera, and it is vital to an understanding of the tonalities of this drama to remember the fact. First Hecuba sings a song of her own, a monody. Her opening words are a summons to courage: the worst can be faced and we shall still survive. Troy and my royalty belong to the past; better to yield to the gale of misfortune and let one's ship drive before it. This, however, is the hour for lamentation, so let me lament the loss of land and children and husband—a great tradition which now vanishes. "Oh how hard this bed of earth on which lie my aching limbs." (The language is harsh, and physically explicit). But even in affliction the muse can sing, though there is nothing to dance about— and she presents, in lyric narrative, a song of how the Greeks joyfully mustered and sailed to Troy and moored in her harbors. It was Helen they came for, that disaster to Sparta, that killer of Priam and my own destroyer. Here now let me mourn my present condition, a slave on the ground, before the Greek camp.

But come, she now cries, addressing the chorus, let us all lament; I will lead the funeral dirge for Troy as I once led the dance in Troy's palaces. The chorus emerges, responding to her invitation, in two groups of semi-choruses, one after the other. The first group says that they have heard her cry and are fearful. What is it? She makes formal announcement to them: the hour of departure is at hand. I hope, she adds, that my Cassandra will not be included; she is delirious and a dishonor to her captors. And having said this, Hecuba raises the ululation over Troy. The second group then emerges from the Greek camp. They are terrified: are we going to be killed? No. The queen resumes her role as announcer. The hour of departure, she repeats, is at hand, and then she joins with the two groups in a duet of lamentation. While she mourns her present servitude and misery they sing a farewell to their past lives: no more weaving at the domestic loom—goodbye to my children—a new mating with new men and a curse on it—a new duty of drawing the well water from a Greek spring. What shall be my destination, I wonder? If only I could go to Athens the lovely. But God forbid it be Sparta, that nurse of the accursed Helen, and of Menelaus our destroyer. After Athens my second choice would be Thessaly—a happy country, they say—or Sicily or south Italy—a wonderful people, and a happy countryside—so they say.

Their song is ended. So far the survivors, these Trojan women, have been allotted the ritual role of the formal lament, the grieving, the keening, with which Greek custom came to terms with disaster in order to mitigate, to comfort, to manage a farewell to the dead; a performance which should make it possible to come to terms with grief and go on living. The scene is reminiscent of, and is modeled upon, the formal laments which conclude the action of the *Iliad,* as Hector is brought home for burial. They recall with equal force the lament of Thetis for her son—she, like Hecuba, summoned her choir in order to lead them in musical farewell.

So far then, the grim prologue being concluded, a certain serenity of acceptance, a beauty of utterance has taken over the mood of the drama. The first shattering interruption to this is prepared in the last cadences of the song. They descry the arrival of the herald Talthybius, who now confronts the queen with the formal announcement of the dispositions made both for her and for the chorus. He tersely reports that the lots have been drawn and individual assignments completed. Hecuba's first question reverts to her daughter Cassandra and she is answered: Cassandra has not been exempted. She is to be assigned to the household of Agamemnon. Hecuba at first infers that her status will be that of a domestic servant of the wife Clytemnestra: she clutches at straws. No, explains the herald, she is to be a concubine, the object of Agamemnon's erotic passion. "Dash down your keys of consecration, rip the garlands from your hair!" exclaims the mother. The first shock has been registered; Cassandra's previous virginal and sanctified status is to be violated.

What have you done with my other daughter, Polyxena? We, the audience, have been told already by Poseidon. But the herald veils the truth from the mother by replying evasively: she is now the servant of Achilles' tomb. "Congratulate her, she is beyond tribulation." His words are spoken as an epitaph and are not understood, and Hecuba's failure to grasp his full meaning indicates the kind of person she is and the kind of response she is capable of making to the characters who, as the drama proceeds, successively confront her. She next learns that Andromache is to pass to the son of Achilles as a prize, and she offers no comment on this. Such a fate in itself does not disturb her. But as for herself, she has been assigned, she learns, to Odysseus, and the revelation provokes an astonishingly vehement invective against that monster of deceit and hatred. She protests her allotment to him as a bitter degradation; it is almost as though she spoke with prescience of the frightful consequences of Odysseus' policies as these are later to be revealed. But her protest is still sung lyrically, as have been her responsions throughout the dialogue. Talthybius, by contrast, has offered his phlegmatic announcements in iambics. The antithesis deliberately underlines the harsh intrusion through his presence of the reality represented by the Greek army and its purposes.

And now the character for whose fate we have already been partially prepared emerges before us. The herald, commanding that she be produced for her assignment to the commander-in-chief, is forestalled by flames issuing from one of the buildings into which the women have been herded. He at first concludes that the women intend suicide. The freeborn take it hard when they are enslaved, is his clinical observation. But this threatens a loss of valuable property to his masters which he intends to prevent. No, says Hecuba to him—and it is one of her very few moments of ascendancy—you don't understand. It is my daughter Cassandra, frenzied and inspired, who performs her ecstatic dance. And as Hecuba speaks Cassandra emerges whirling from the doorway that has concealed her, waving above her head a ceremonial and smoking torch. She has been the virgin votary of Apollo, sharing the god's gift of prophecy though fated not to be believed, and she remains faithful to her part— horribly so. For her present performance conceals one more prediction —the final one of her career.

She waves her torch to illuminate the temple of her consecration—the temple that is the desert strand before the smoking walls—and calls upon the god who presides over this scene—not Apollo, but Hymen, the god of marriage. Blessed the bridegroom Agamemnon, blessed the bride Cassandra who now duly celebrates her coming consummation as a maiden should. Lead the dance, Apollo. So she mocks her erstwhile patron god. Join the dance, mother, yes, swing, swing with me while the maids of Troy in chorus hail the bridegroom fit for his bride.

This is a terrible parody, but it is also the beginning of a terrible prophecy. We begin to realize that Hecuba has not got it quite right: Cassandra knows what she is doing, but as always is condemned to be misunderstood. Her mother thinks she is genuinely beside herself, unaware of her actions, and she would gently take her torch away and lead her off. How could she view her union with Agamemnon in this light? Whereupon Cassandra gives up the song and dance, and in plain unvarnished iambics shows the reality behind her masquerade: Mother, let me explain. The marriage I am celebrating is really going to be a murder; the house of Atreus is going to be destroyed. I can foresee my own killing, and then the murdering mother killed in turn by her own son—

but never mind the details. The victim of history, the luckless recipient of catastrophe, is not Troy, but Greece. Have the Greeks not already killed Iphigenia and as aggressors, unprovoked, suffered myriad casualties on the Trojan plain, and endured bitter separation from home, wives, and children? (I could reveal worse things, but refrain.)

Contrast the Trojans, Mother: it is they who have won epic glory, their sacrifice is defensive and patriotic, their lives while they lived them were domestic and civilized. The Hector for whom you are grieving was able to prove himself on the battlefield, and only Greek aggression made this possible; otherwise his life would have been obscure. The Paris for whom you lament made a wonderful marriage to a daughter of the gods; without it, he too would have died obscure. I grant it is prudent to avoid war if one can; but if it comes, then a city offering noble resistance and meeting with a noble defeat can win a crown in history. So why mourn Troy, or for that matter, my marriage? After all, I am going to destroy the enemy that has destroyed us.

Here is sanity indeed, and cynicism profound. The chorus well exclaims: "For you calamity becomes an occasion for gleeful laughter. Your oracles, however, are likely to remain obscure." The herald justifies this comment by contemptuously dismissing both the polemics against the Greeks and the eulogy of Troy, though he adds with a slight shiver: Agamemnon must be crazy to want to marry a girl like you. The threat behind her speech is vaguely felt. However, he continues, please follow me to Agamemnon's quarters; it will be your turn next, Hecuba. His shrug of the shoulders, his distance from the tragic intensity of her insight, provokes Cassandra to a bitter tirade against the role and character of all heralds, lackeys of their masters, and stupid at that. You can assign Hecuba to Odysseus, she says to him, but do you think she will ever serve in his household? And she then predicts the toils and dangers of the return of Odysseus, summarizing the plot of the *Odyssey* and the bitter homecoming of the hero as she had previously resumed the plot of the *Iliad*. The dramatist does not forget Cassandra's traditional role as the prophetess whose audience must remain unconvinced until it is too late. So she scores again by indirection over the Greeks, and incidentally completes the historical information supplied in the prologue. We now have been reminded not only of the disasters that are to descend upon Odysseus, but of the fate of Agamemnon and all his house.

This fate she now explicitly defines, breaking into brisk trochaic tetrameters: "Let us get on with it. I am a bride—but a bride of death; here are your garlands, Apollo." And she flings them figuratively in his face. "Goodbye, everybody, I go to join the dead—my kindred dead beneath the ground. But I will destroy the house of Atreus first."

Hecuba's response is to collapse in a dead faint; thus nature renders her the normal and necessary relief. Indeed, she embodies throughout the drama the normal value scheme of a distressed victim who has been schooled to meet disaster with appropriate sentiments and appropriate grief. Not for her to reread the lessons of history or reverse the judgments which tradition has approved. Confronting first Cassandra, and then Andromache, she faces two women of a younger generation—a postwar generation we might say—who have seen through to the bottom and found only sound and fury signifying nothing. Cassandra's parody of marriage turned to murder is followed by her parody of the *Iliad* turned from a Greek victory into a Greek defeat. So she undercuts and explodes the entire heroic scheme of things. For the Ajax of Sophocles, the heroic was still a standard to live by in defeat; for Cassandra it is a perverse and ingenious lie.

Hecuba restored prefers to remain prostrate and seeks both sorrow and consolation in memory. Propriety, she adds characteristically, demands that I invoke heaven in my calamities, even if heaven seems to be of no help; let me sing a song of my past good fortune and of my present miseries. And she proceeds to recall her matriarchate in Troy, when Troy was the capital of a kingdom, and then the collapse of all dynastic and family hopes: husband and sons dead, one daughter united to an alien, and myself, the mother of Hector, a domestic slave—and all because of that accursed Helen. It is thus that she corrects, according to her lights, those perversions of history that she has heard from her daughter's mouth. As for that daughter, it is her loss of priestly status against which her mother now protests. What touches her is Cassandra's situation, not the insights which Cassandra has offered; these have not reached her. Where is my other daughter Polyxena? she exclaims, almost querulously. "I need her. I am all alone. Oh, let me die." But of course she does not die. Her sentiments and emotions are appropriate to her mind, the mind of a conventional woman now in deep distress, and using the resources of her conventions to achieve that level of understanding which is open to her. Of its kind, it is noble, but the other women in the play have no part in it.

At this point the chorus takes over and we hear their melodies and watch the choreography which engages the dancing floor. Their song reminds us that this play is about women: O Muse, sing a new song—a lament for Troy and my own captivity. And they tell in lyric narrative of the wooden horse and the people flocking to the gate to drag it in as a present to the temple of the goddess Athena—the Trojan Athena. Then the night-long celebration, the parties and the dances, as the siege seemed lifted, and then, as sleep descends the cry of the enemy released to kill, a cry heard in the very heart of the city: death for all our men, and for ourselves concubinage with Greeks, to breed more Greeks.

It is precisely this woman's problem—the tragic problem of the chattel childbearer assigned a role which seems to make personal integrity impossible—which is then to be focused before our smarting sensibilities as Andromache enters the arena.

She is, in fact, towed in on a wagon heaped with captured spoils, sitting on them, holding her boy, Hector's heir, to her breast. Indeed, she is sitting on Hector's erstwhile property. She knows, and we know, that she is appropriately assigned to the son of Hector's enemy, the man who killed her husband, and who has left an heir who will now take her, while Hector's heir, fruit of her body, will be summarily disposed of. But this is not yet revealed.

The two women first unite in a duet, a threnody for their dead: Hector was the son of one and the husband of the other, and the two women exchange sentiments appropriate to these two relationships; nor are Priam or Troy forgotten in their song. The performance is often misunderstood. Of its kind it is appropriate and moving, but essentially the expression of a convention, as was that initial threnody with which Hecuba and the chorus opened the play and announced their roles.

As the lament ends, the two women exchange information: Cassandra has just been taken from me; yes, and Polyxena, your other daughter, has been murdered. To Hecuba's cry of anguish, Andromache then replies with a clinical exposure of her own situation: I would rather be Polyxena. You mustn't say that, replies Hecuba, reverting to those standards of the commonplace that we have learned to expect from her: "while there's life there's hope." No, says her erstwhile daughter-in-law, your Polyxena now enjoys total insensibility, but look at my dilemma: I was Hector's devoted wife; my domesticity and decorum and service to his interests were a byword. I was the embodiment of a woman's loyalty to her man. It is precisely this reputation which has now undone me; it became talked about among the Greeks, and made me the desired and appropriate prize of the son of Achilles. Am I now to employ consistency and practice toward him, my new master, the same loyalties? One night of physical union, they say, can effectively divorce a woman from her previous allegiance; I despise such women who can lightly forget the old embrace; even a dumb animal resists a new yoke-fellow, and we are

human beings, aren't we? And she then passionately invokes the memory
and image of her dead husband: "we were matched so perfectly and now
you are dead, while I am dispatched to Greece to be yoked as slave to
another man." Implicit in her cry of bitter grief is a plea for forgiveness
—for she will indeed mate and marry again, even if perforce. It is her
nature to identify with the man to whom she is assigned: I have no hope
left, she concludes, and no claim to delude myself that I am going to
do something moral and good—yet we all need to think that we do. The
chorus can only ruefully comment that she has indeed voiced their own
problem: her dilemma as a woman of mating age is going to be theirs.

Translators of the play have sought here occasion for a squeamish
shudder. On the contrary, the bitterness of the moral dilemma is stated
with clear-eyed and dispassionate clarity and realism. Given a woman's
function, biological, emotional, and social, given her role in the heroic
world as male property, how can she possibly retain her own heroic
integrity?

Hecuba's response is predictable: better to bend like the reed than
resist like the oak (her simile is in fact different, of a ship riding out the
gale; it is the second time she has used it). Honor your new mate, she
advises, completely insensible to Andromache's personal dilemma, then
you will conciliate him, and be able to raise my grandson to be a second
bulwark of Troy, who in turn will beget new Trojans and restore the
city. Hecuba's value scheme in fact is identical with that of those whom
Andromache would defy and would identify with the opposition.
Hecuba's thoughts are wholly of status and of dynasty, and of what a
woman can do to maintain these institutions. These, after all, constitute
her own creation and achievement, her own claim on history. She is a
queen mother, not a lover or a private person. And may she not be right?
Is not this the level of reality that can survive and be salvaged even when
personal identities are destroyed?

Whereupon Talthybius enters almost as though Hecuba had spoken
the prompting lines. He has a fresh announcement to make; he has to
swallow several times to get it out; he is not enjoying his mission. But
the fact is that the boy, this grandson, by a political decision of
the Greeks—reinforced by the urgings of Odysseus—is to be taken and
thrown from the battlements and so removed from future history. His
present duty is to take the boy from Andromache's protecting arms. In
reply to her wild gesture of protest, he can only recall her to the reality
that is hers. You have no recourse whatever, you are utterly helpless.
There is literally nothing you can do, *nothing*. Accept the fact that you
are defeated. And as if to underline her reduction to nullity, he adds a

further warning: don't indulge in the last consolation of a solemn curse against the Greeks, the slayers of your son. You can do this of course, but in that case your son will be denied burial. In fact, he is reminding her that her situation is one in which not only must she surrender her little boy to be murdered, but she can be blackmailed into accepting this without protest.

She, like Cassandra, has now seen to the bottom of things, and for her, as for Cassandra, the normal world has been stood on its head. She can see this quite clearly as it applies not only to her own situation, but to that of her child. Just as her previous loyalty now becomes the direct cause of compulsion to disloyalty, so the child's proud patrimony as Hector's son, his noble birth and lineage and status now become the direct agents of an ignoble and pitiable death. A father—such is the truth behind the words in which she now expresses herself—a father by his very importance can function as the murderer of his own son.

Meanwhile the child has clung to her in fright. For a few more lines, twenty-five in all, she is allowed, or allows herself, the emotional privilege of an outburst of total grief. Her affliction is unmeasured precisely because a child should normally expect the protection of its mother, and it is precisely this that she cannot give him, nor can the father in his grave avail. Her last moments with the child are harrowing beyond belief and leave no crumb of consolation either to her or to us, except one: she vehemently inveighs against Helen as the fatal curse and cause of all. This she can safely do, for Helen's status is ambiguous. Is she Greek or Trojan? But even this, Andromache's last verbal resort, is in the conclusion to be rendered null and void. Before the play ends we also learn how totally ineffective the imprecation is to prove. The curses have already been spoken by Hecuba and the chorus, and are repeated throughout the drama, but it turns out that Helen is the one personality whose life and integrity, such as they are, survive.

"Here, take the child and kill him quick." Her despair is total. So also had Cassandra briskly departed to her doom. This is the one response remaining for those who had seen the reduction of their own lives and purposes to nullity. "As for me, bundle me off to the ship for my bridal." Thus she predicts and accepts her inevitable role. The chorus can only reiterate the curse already pronounced on Helen. It is Talthybius, a man of common clay, who, taking the boy, breaks down and in moving lyrics pronounces the final lament for him. The mother has departed dry-eyed to her new destiny. She has survived even the illusions of grief.

It remains for Hecuba to close the scene, and if possible by conventional lament to draw a veil over the brutal realities revealed. She beats her breast on the stage in traditional gesture as she had in Homer's *Iliad*. Characteristically, it is for herself that she even now chiefly laments.

To view the *Trojan Women* as a protest against man's inhumanity to man is to indulge in a half-truth. Nowhere does the play exploit the spectacle of cruelty directly applied in act or word; nowhere is the heel of oppression placed directly upon the neck of the oppressed. The emissary of the Greek conquerors is perhaps the most humane character in the play, a reluctant minister of policies that he dislikes. Rather, it is as though the world into which the victors and vanquished have survived has grown tired, and in the general lassitude the meanings expressed in our normal common humanity have been exhausted. When Astyanax is taken away, emotionally speaking, the worst has happened. Episodes still to come contain nothing more "tragic" in the conventional sense of that term than what we have now witnessed. But if it is possible, they do manage to carry disillusionment one stage further and expose the sheer vacuity of normal moral pretensions.

This occurs in the presentation of Helen, confronting Menelaus, her husband and lover—or judge and executioner. It is of the essence of the moral ambiguity of the scene that to the very end we are not sure which he is. But first comes another choric interlude, the second *stasimon*. Beautiful as it is, it has been misjudged as an occasion for sheer emotional relief, an escape from the intolerable situation of the drama. It is in fact woven more closely than this into the web of the plot. The opening stanza recalls how long ago the first Troy was destroyed by Telamon, who joined Hercules to accomplish this bloody task in requital against Laomedon king of Troy, who had cheated them of their wages for building its walls. The stanza is notable for its evocation of Athens, the beautiful, the blessed, and the happy, the city of the olive crown that fronts on Salamis where Telamon was king. The contrast between the city of light and the city of destruction is unmistakable. In the dramatist's imagination, his own Athens becomes that symbol of those values of security, prosperity, and peace which Troy is denied. She is lifted up above the hazards of this life; in an earlier song the chorus had expressed their longing that in their distress and helplessness Athens might receive them. The present stanza is succeeded by two others which recall the honors that Troy once received when the gods loved her sons. Two of her princes were snatched up to heaven, Ganymede to be the favorite of Zeus and his cupbearer, and Tithonus to lie forever in the arms of the Dawn. These princes of the house of Troy, do they now turn their faces to look upon our city in its smoking ruin? If so, they do so with total serenity, unmoved while they continue to smile upon the company that they keep, the company of the immortals. What then has Eros, that divine passion, done for Troy, the Eros that has flamed in the very hearts of the gods? The answer is: *nothing*.

As the song concludes, we await the entrance of that embodiment of Eros, Helen. We shall see exposed on the dancing floor the human counterpart to that divine principle. At first we see only the aggrieved husband, a pompous little man, savoring his present advantage as Helen's captor, though in fact she is his as he admits, only by decision of the Greek army. He is a cold fish, and protests to the chorus that his motive in coming to Troy was not to get Helen back. (Euripides is here contradicting the traditional story, as presented, for example, by Herodotus.) He has come to punish Troy and Paris, and this he has done. Now I have her as my prisoner; the Greeks have handed her over to me—to kill her or to take her back home. I have decided to forget about killing her here. I will sail back home with her and then, of course, kill her in compensation for my friends who have died here in Troy.

The patent ambiguities of the professions he thus makes hide a basic confusion, not to say insincerity, in his purposes. If he wants to use her death to appease the dead in Troy, then Troy is the place where she should die. He has in fact no ultimate intention of killing her at all. Is he not historically committed to that sequence of events narrated in the *Odyssey?* Everyone knew how Helen, of all the women concerned, got home to survive and to preside with serenity over Menelaus' household. Indeed, through the mouth of Cassandra earlier in the drama Euripides had already explicitly alerted us that the version of events narrated in the *Odyssey* is canonical and that he is following it. Helen will enjoy her divine inheritance, and what is it if not the power to remain physically beautiful and erotically attractive, the embodiment of passion conceived as the object. It is this and not the moralities, the compassion, the duties, and the loyalties, not Apollo's gardens or the altars of Zeus—not these, but Eros the unmoral and the destructive which alone prevails and survives, and departs unscathed from this scene of wreckage where normal hopes and expectations have been blasted, and where gods, family, and pieties have been denied.

Her triumph in confrontation with Hecuba constitutes the queen's last and most complete defeat. Hecuba's scheme of things has not stood up before Cassandra and Andromache; still less can it stand up to this. At first she rightly warns Menelaus not to confront Helen. She knows what men are, she knows that a cold fish can respond to a certain level of stimulus. But then as husband and wife meet, and Helen asks a last word, a chance to defend her role in history and herself as a personality,

Hecuba savagely and confidently urges Menelaus to grant due process: "Listen to her provided he let me reply." So sure she is of the issues of the argument as she sees them, an argument in which the stake is Helen's life or death, and the issue is now the basic framework of justice among gods and among men, the traditional moral sanctions which support human life and decision and make sense of them.

We can guess the outcome of the argument when it has scarce begun. Helen, with serene self-confidence, turns first to her husband and assumes the intimate posture of a wife, talking to her man and seeking to reassure him that she does not really dislike him. They have some differences, to be sure, to patch up between themselves, she says, but they exist on both sides. Thus the dramatist allows her completely to reverse the relationship which both Menelaus and Hecuba had assumed to be inevitable and proper: instead of the grovelling suppliant, the smiling courtesan who knows how to manage things.

Before the debate began, Hecuba, in a last gesture of affirmation, had addressed a prayer of thanks to that Mind or Reason which in default of the traditional gods must be assumed to rule the universe and assure its justice. Confident that Helen will be executed, she sees in this execution a final meaning which would still make sense of all her sorrows. But this last confidence is undercut as completely as the previous assurances in which she had sought refuge. As the play draws to its end, she is preparing the body of her grandson for burial. It lies in her arms like a broken doll, a plaything which the Greeks have carelessly hurled over the battlements. The messages which the three younger women have striven to communicate to her have finally prevailed. Hecuba looks at last into the heart of things and announces to the chorus that she has indeed looked there and found—*nothing.*

Why the *Trojan Women?*

by Jean-Paul Sartre

Contrary to the popular conception, Greek tragedy is not a theater of wildness. We imagine actors leaping forth, roaring and writhing onstage, victims of prophetic trances. But these actors speak through masks, and they walk on buskins. The tragic play, performed under conditions as artificial as they are rigorous, is first of all a *ceremony,* which certainly aims to impress the viewer, but not to activate him. Horror here becomes majestic, and cruelty solemn. This is true of Aeschylus, writing for a public who still believes in the great legends and the mysterious power of the gods. But it is even more true of Euripides, who marks the end of the tragic cycle and the transition to another form of play: Menander's "new" comedy. For at the time Euripides writes the *Trojan Women,* the beliefs have become more or less dubious myths. As yet unable to overturn the old idols, the Athenians' critical spirit is already able to contest them. The play has retained its ritual value. But the audience is interested more in the manner of speaking than in what is said. Thus the traditional virtuoso selections, which they appreciate as connoisseurs, take on new meaning. Tragedy then becomes an implicit conversation about commonplaces. The expressions which Euripides uses appear to be the same as those of his predecessors. But because the audience no longer believes them, or believes them less, they sound different, they say something else. Think of Beckett or Ionesco, who offer the same phenomenon. It consists in using the commonplace in order to destroy it from within, and naturally the demonstration will be all the more effective the more completely—and glaringly—the commonplace is presented. The Athenian public "received" the *Trojan Women* the way the middle-class public now receives *Godot* or *The Bald Soprano:* delighted to hear commonplaces, but aware as well that they were also witnessing their disintegration.

"Why the *Trojan Women?*" (French title: "Pourquoi *Les Troyennes?*") by Jean-Paul Sartre. Introduction to Sartre's adaptation of the *Trojan Women.* Copyright © 1965 by Éditions Gallimard. Reprinted by permission of Alfred A. Knopf, Inc., owners of the American rights. Translated by Jeffrey Mehlman.

The result is a serious difficulty for the translator. If I am faithful to the letter and speak of "white-winged dawn" or Athens "shiny as oil," I shall appear to be adopting the language of the eighteenth century, I shall be saying the commonplace. But the French viewer of 1965, unable to guess what this means—because the religious and cultural context it evokes no longer exists for him—will take it literally. This is the failure of the otherwise excellent translation of the Budé edition; the banal is affirmed instead of destroyed. In four or five centuries actors who want to perform Beckett or Ionesco will be faced with the same problem: how to indicate the distance separating public and text.

Between Euripides' tragedy and fifth century Athenian society an implicit relationship exists which we can now see only from the outside. Hence if I want to revive this relationship, I cannot be satisfied with a translation of the play; I have to *adapt* it.

Purely imitative speech was excluded as was transposition into modern spoken French, since the text ought as well to keep its distance from us. I thus chose a poetic language which preserves the text's ceremonial aspect and ritual value—but modifies the accent. Speaking allusively to an audience whose experience he shares, and who, though no longer believing in the beautiful legends, still loves to be told them, Euripides can afford humorous and precious effects. It seemed to me that in order to obtain the same effects, I should use less destructive language. First let the audience take the legends seriously; then we will be able to demonstrate their ineffectiveness. We accept Euripides' underlying humor in the case of Talthybius because Talthybius, after all, is the "good soldier Schweik," the average man overwhelmed by events, or, in the case of Helen, because of Offenbach. Everywhere else it risked destroying not only the commonplaces but the play itself. Hence I could only recapture it at a distance, obliging the viewer to step back somewhat from the drama.

But there is not only the problem of language. There is also a cultural problem. Euripides' text contains numerous allusions which the Athenian public understood immediately, but to which we no longer respond because we have forgotten the legends. I have eliminated some and developed others. Thus the Greeks did not require of Cassandra a lengthy explanation of Hecuba's ultimate fate. They knew very well that having been transformed into a bitch, she would mount the mast of the ship that should have taken her away and fall into the sea. But when, at the play's end, we see Hecuba leave with her companions, we might suppose that she will follow them to Greece. The real ending, however, is much stronger. It means that all of Cassandra's predictions will come true.

Odysseus will spend ten years before finding his homeland; the Greek fleet will perish in a shipwreck; Hecuba will not leave Trojan soil. That is why I added Poseidon's final monologue.

Similarly the Athenian viewer knew that Menelaus, after having rejected Helen, would eventually give in and take her away on his ship. Moreover, the chorus in Euripides alludes discreetly to this. But nothing allows the French viewer, who has heard the vows of Menelaus, to imagine this reversal. He has to be shown, hence the indignant complaint by the chorus attending the ship's departure of the reconciled couple.

Other changes involve the general style of the play. It is not a tragedy like the *Antigone,* but an oratorio. I have tried to "dramatize" it by developing the oppositions which remain implicit in Euripides: the conflict between Andromache and Hecuba; Hecuba's dual attitude, alternately abandoning herself to her grief and calling for justice; the change in Andromache, that "petite bourgeoise, "who appears first as wife, then as mother; the erotic fascination of Cassandra, who rushes into Agamemnon's bed knowing all the while that she will perish with him.

All this, you may reply, does not justify the choice of the play. I must then say a word about the contents. The *Trojan Women* was presented during the Algerian war in a very faithful translation by Jacqueline Moatti. I was struck by the success the play received from a public favorable to negotiating with the National Liberation Front. It was evidently this aspect which interested me at first. As you know, even in Euripides' day the play had a precise political meaning. It was a condemnation of war in general and colonial expeditions in particular.

We know today what war means; an atomic war will leave neither victors nor vanquished. And that is precisely what the play demonstrates. The Greeks have destroyed Troy, but they shall not enjoy any of the spoils of this victory, since the vengeance of the gods will destroy them all. It was not even necessary to say that "every reasonable man ought to avoid war," as Cassandra affirms; the situation of every single one of them offers ample evidence. I chose to reserve the last word for Poseidon: "It'll kill the whole lot of you."

The colonial wars are the only element of the text I have allowed myself to accentuate somewhat. I speak a few times of "Europe." The idea is modern, but corresponds to the ancient opposition between Greeks and barbarians, between Greater Greece, which was developing its civilization toward the Mediterranean, and the establishments of Asia Minor, where Athenian colonial imperialism reigned with a ferocity Euripides denounces pitilessly. And if the expression "filthy war" (*sale guerre*) takes on a very precise meaning for us, look at the Greek text. You will find its close equivalent there.

Finally there are the gods, the other interesting aspect of the play. Here I believe I have followed Euripides very faithfully. But in order to render intelligible the critique of a religion totally foreign to us, it was still necessary to keep a certain distance. The gods who appear in the *Trojan Women* are at once powerful and ridiculous. On the one hand they control the world; the Trojan War is their work. But seen close up they behave no differently than human beings and, like them, are motivated by petty vanities and grudges. "The gods have broad shoulders," says Hecuba when Helen projects the responsibility for her own bad conduct onto Athena. Moreover, the prologue demonstrates that the goddess is capable of betraying her own allies for the slightest offence. Why wouldn't she have sold her sanctuary in order to obtain a beauty prize? Since he uses commonplaces only the better to destroy them, Euripides employs the legend—without ever insisting, merely by confronting the myths one with another—to indicate the difficulties of a polytheism his audience already no longer believes in. Does monotheism escape this condemnation? Hecuba's moving prayer to Zeus, which astonishes Menelaus—and implies a Renan-like[1] sort of religiosity, according to which history, in the last analysis, would obey supreme Reason—might lead one to think so for a moment. But Zeus is no better than his wife or daughter. He will do nothing to save the Trojans from an unjust fate, and, by a curious paradox, it is the folly of all the gods together that will avenge the Trojans.

The play thus ends in total nihilism. What the Greeks felt as a subtle contradiction, the contradiction of the world in which they had to live, appears to us who see the play from the outside as a negation, a refusal. I have tried to indicate that difference. Hecuba's final despair, which I have emphasized, answers the terrible words of Poseidon. The gods are killed with the men, and that common death is the lesson of the tragedy.

[1] Ernest Renan, nineteenth century French historian and Biblical critic—ED.

Orestes

by Christian Wolff

The plot of *Orestes* is Euripides' invention. It comes like a parenthesis between two well-known stories, one of Orestes' return to avenge his father and reclaim his house and rule (the subject of Aeschylus' *Choephoroi* and the *Electras* of Sophocles and Euripides), the other, its sequel, of Orestes' purgation, trial, and acquittal in Athens (the subject of Aeschylus' *Eumenides*). But though its action is new and without mythical precedent, the play is filled with echoes of these familiar stories. Thus Euripides partly repeats his own *Electra*. As in that play there had been a plot to kill Clytemnestra, so in *Orestes* a plot is hatched to kill Tyndareus' other daughter, Helen (cf. 1421ff, 1588, *Electra* 976). The famous call to the dead Agamemnon to assist his children in their vengeance (*Electra* 677ff, already an adaptation of *Choephoroi* 479ff) reechoes when Orestes, Electra, and Pylades ask for help in their plot against Helen (1225ff). Then, as Clytemnestra had been lured off to her death by Electra (*Electra* 1128ff), so Electra now draws Helen's daughter Hermione into the palace to be held hostage and possibly killed (1123ff). Finally, drawing on Sophocles, the scene in which Helen cries out offstage as though she were being killed while Electra onstage shouts her rejoicing (*Orestes* 1301ff) recalls the latter's exultation when Clytemnestra is killed in the older poet's *Electra* (1409ff).

Each of these echoes, however, creates effects of dislocation. Not an aging, corrupt queen, killer of her husband, but the young and innocent Hermione is now victim. Invoking Agamemnon's help is far less relevant in a plot on Helen than it had been in enacting vengeance on the wife who murdered him. Here, in fact, this traditional motif directly contradicts an earlier moment in the play where Orestes imagines that, had he asked his father whether or not to kill Clytemnestra, Agamemnon would have supplicated him on his knees not to do it (288ff). What appears at first to be a formal repetition, somewhat misplaced, sets off a characteristically Euripidean dissonance, and then marks the contradic-

"*Orestes*" by Christian Wolff. Written for this collection. Copyright © 1968 by Prentice-Hall, Inc.

tions of his protagonist's motives. Orestes' remorse for one killing is
wiped out by the project of another. More generally, the new sense of
the plot of *Orestes*, set into relief by echoes of *Electra*, has been well
outlined by one commentator as follows: "the former crime [that is,
killing Clytemnestra], at divine behest [Apollo's command; cf. *Orestes*
1665], is accomplished by human agency; the latter crime [killing Helen],
at human behest [it is Pylades' idea, 1105], is blocked by divine agency
[the final reappearance of Apollo]." [1] In *Electra* Orestes had committed
a crime under divine compulsion; now he sets out spontaneously to
commit another whose necessity is doubtful. Clytemnestra had been a
guilty victim. Helen has her guilt, but nothing makes it clear that Orestes
should be her punisher; and Hermione, another prospective victim, is
an innocent bystander. Set against *Electra*, the action of *Orestes* appears
to be motivated by a kind of gratuitous self-indulgence.

But the play not only recalls a past story, it also anticipates its traditional sequel, and again there are shifts of meaning. Orestes' trial for
murder, forecast at the end of *Electra* and represented in Aeschylus'
Eumenides, becomes in this play a trial before the public assembly of the
citizens of Argos. Yet where Orestes had been acquitted at his traditional
trial, he is now condemned; not on grounds of justice, but for patently
political reasons. Euripides has, in fact, represented the trial at Argos
with transparently contemporary features—notably two speakers typi-
fying, respectively, an Athenian demagogue (903ff), such as Cleophon (as
the scholiast suggests), and the politician of adaptability (888ff) perhaps
a caricature of Theramenes (cf. Aristophanes, *Frogs* 538ff). Apollo, ap-
pearing at the end of the play, will finally forecast the old trial at Athens,
assuring justice and Orestes' acquital; the jury will be made up of gods
(1650), not men as in the tradition represented by Aeschylus. But where,
a spectator in the Athens of 408 might have asked himself, are the gods
or such an administration of justice as would give a man fair trial in his
city at such a time? Juxtaposing his new plot with the old myth,
Euripides now lays bare the gap betwen everyday reality and the ancient
story. It is a familiar way with him, but never does he take it quite
so far. This new plot moves as far from its traditional conclusions as
possible. Orestes, condemned to death, unregenerate, abandoned by
whatever gods had led him on, reaches the point of killing Hermione,
setting his ancestral house on fire, and destroying himself, Electra, and
Pylades. Then Apollo appears and turns the action about to force its
traditional conclusion. The torches are stayed (they might recall the

[1] N. A. Greenberg, "Euripides' *Orestes*: An Interpretation," *Harvard Studies in Classical Philology*, LXVI (1962), 162.

torches carried in celebration at the end of the *Eumenides*). Orestes
will be purified and given new trial, and he will marry Hermione at
whose neck he holds his sword.

One might suppose Euripides, as he is so often accused of doing,
means to negate the myth completely. Yet not only does *Orestes,* for all
the novelty of its plot, parallel parts of a traditional story, but it is also
filled with reminiscences of other tragedies and the sound of legendary
names—Glaukos the sea-god, Ganymede, Oiax the brother of Palamedes,
Odysseus, Telemachus, the Achaian herald Talthybius, the hero Dio-
medes, Hector, Leda, and the Dioscuri. And, most notably, we never
cease hearing about the mythical background of Orestes' race, the
names and stories of Tantalus, Pelops, Atreus, Thyestes, Aerope, Agamemnon, and Iphigenia; and of Troy and Helen. The old stories weigh
heavily on this new one, conjuring up an endlessly oppressive past, a
weight accompanying Orestes' own crime (cf. 28ff, 164ff, 192ff, 289ff, 374f,
392ff, 505ff, 526ff, 546ff, 819ff, 1587ff, 1648ff).

The plot of *Orestes,* then, stands in a twofold relation to the myth.
As it is new and seems to depart from the familiar mythical tradition,
it represents a break with the past. But, as it is dense with references to
that past, this break effects no release. The past has no more viable connection to the present, but is still a burden on it. This burden is so
great that the present—the plot of the play—appears to lose its substance, to lead nowhere, to achieve nothing. The new story, in terms
of the traditional continuity of the myth to which the play returns in the
end, might just as well not have taken place. Euripides dramatizes a
sense of emptiness and superfluousness, something, one suspects, of the
contemporary mood in Athens, and perhaps something of a more general
sadness.

The action itself, to consider it more closely, falls into two parts. In
the first Orestes, Electra, and then Pylades are together in a situation
that is desperate but begins by holding some hope, in Menelaus' help
and possibly a reasonable decision from the Argive assembly. That hope
is shown, in a series of encounters, to be vain. Orestes and his sister are
condemned to death and prepare to take their own lives. Then, suddenly, they decide instead to plot revenge on Menelaus for his treachery,
a project that takes up the latter half of the play. The procedure from
one part to the other, like that of the play throughout, is by abrupt,
unexpected (but carefully devised) shifts. These are reflected in the
central figure of Orestes, in his unpredictable oscillations between sanity
and madness, and in the contradictions of his mood and purposes.

As the play opens his situation is critical twice over. Outwardly he faces a trial for murder before a hostile city which holds him completely captive. Inwardly he appears overcome by guilt, the effects of which erupt in a physical illness resembling epilepsy. His inner disturbance in turn is given two definitions. In accordance with the tradition, it is represented as the work of the furies (37, 317ff; cf. 408, 410, 423). But then, when Menelaus asks, "what disease destroys you?" (395f), Orestes answers, ἡ σύνεσις, ὅτι σύνοιδα δείν᾽ εἰργασμένος ("the intelligence—that I am conscious of my terrible deeds"). A psychological abstraction articulates an inner condition which before had been called, in the language of myth, the work of the furies. In the same spirit Orestes recognizes that "it is not my appearance"—his haggard and unkempt looks—"but my deeds [erga, which can have the sense of "reality," as in Trojan Women 1232] that torment me" (388); and that "my body is gone, but the name has not left me" (390; cf. 398f). The characteristic Greek habit of antithesis here serves to give rational formulation to an internal state, and so breaks through the surface of the myth.

But, in the characteristically Euripidean way, rational articulation is not commensurate with larger circumstances or human character. Orestes, having expressed this kind of insight into his own condition, straightway forgets it. He needs to be saved from both his madness and the outward circumstances of Argos' hostility. To Menelaus he can appeal for help only in the latter case; there is no human help for madness. But he does not consider what help would save him if the madness continues. Orestes forgets the question of his guilt. Although we have seen him haunted to distraction by the memory of his deeds, he can be equally ready to shift the blame for them to Apollo (276, 285f, 591ff; cf. 416). This contradiction is then accompanied by another. Exhausted by his conscience, Orestes is indifferent to whether he lives or dies, and yet again he is anxious only to live and argues passionately for it (644ff, 677ff; cf. 382f). Menelaus turns out to be no help. The Argives convict Orestes, and again he is resigned simply to die (1023f).

Here, having gone through a cycle of suffering, reaction, and final defeat, the first part of the play's action ends. That the protagonists have exhausted all their hopes and resources will underline the sense of irrational and gratuitous action that follows, the second half of the play. Just as they are ready to die the thought of revenge sparks a new plot. Menelaus' betrayal will be avenged by killing Helen. And as that plot is elaborated, hope for survival is once more raised (1172ff; cf. 1152); Electra suggests holding Hermione hostage to force Menelaus to help. Orestes is passive, originating neither of these proposals, though he then pursues both with enthusiasm. He exemplifies how susceptible for any action whatever a man may be who has nothing to lose. Thus, in turn, neither he nor Electra nor Pylades notices either the practical or the moral contradictions in their plans. They do not consider how Menelaus could in fact help them, locked in as they are on all sides (430), surrounded by armed guards (444, 761ff), and objects of all Argos' hostility (cf. 1530). Menelaus seems to be as powerless as he claims (688ff). He has had to bring in Helen secretly by night for lack of means to protect her against the anger of the citizens (57ff). He might have helped by speaking for Orestes at his trial, as he promised (704ff), and did not. But that time is past; now Menelaus is no use. In moral terms, the condemned trio do not reconcile their claim to go down fighting in a noble death (cf. 781, 1093, 1152) and the ignoble object of that fight— killing a woman and using an innocent girl as hostage. (The question of what is noble, *kalon,* was raised already with Clytemnestra's death [194; cf. 417] and reduced to a paradoxical formulation, *to kalon ou kalon,* "the noble [beautiful, proper] [which is] not noble" [819], by which the word, and value, lose their simple sense [cf. 610, 891, 1106, 1131, 1213, 1316, 1614].)

As these contrary motives are revealed, the original uncertainty about whether or not to accept death persists. The ideals of facing death nobly and of suicidal recklessness alternate with an intense desire to survive. Having said he would "freely" give up his life to be avenged on Menelaus (1170ff), Orestes indulges immediately the hope of survival: "would that an unhoped-for salvation befall those that kill and die not —that is my prayer; what I wish is sweet—even by speech to delight the mind cheaply with winged fables" (1173-76). When the conspirators pray to Agamemnon, it is first that they be saved (1234, 1238), and then that they meet with success, without specifying survival or vengeance (cf. 1243 and 1172), and closing with the vague epigram, "we are bound, all of us, either to live or die" (1245), which catches one of the play's refrains, the protagonists' always wavering purpose: "to live or die" (758, 848, 1152; cf. 1174).

Electra deceives Hermione by asking her to plead with Helen for their lives (1334ff). But Orestes tells the girl when he has captured her that she will be "a salvation to us, not yourself" (1348). Electra next looks forward only to revenge (1350ff). The action that follows and the report of it by a Phrygian slave concerns itself only with that, the attempted killing of Helen. Then, as the Phrygian is cornered by Orestes and grovels at his feet begging to be left alive, the pursuit of life reemerges in a grotesquely comic light. "To live," the Phrygian pleads," is everywhere more sweet than to die for those who are sensible" (1509). "Sweet" echoes Orestes' earlier sudden hope of survival (1175f), though he had also called "sweetest" a death in common with Electra (1054). ("Those who are sensible [sane, shrewd]," *tois sōphrosin,* recalls, if it were necessary, that Orestes is probably mad [cf. 254, 502].) When he asks shortly after, "as a slave do you fear Hades which will free you from ills?" (1522), he echoes his own words of appeal to Menelaus for "escape from ills" (448). The Phrygian answers that every man, even a slave, looks on the light "with pleasure" (1523). Orestes approves: "well spoken; your intelligence saves you" (1524); and he calls the fawning of the slave frantic for his life by the same name, *synesis,* he had earlier given his consciousness of guilt, on whose account he was ready to die (395ff). Now he appears willing to spare the wretch's life (1524f), yet he shifts once more: "but I shall change my mind" (1526). Finally the slave runs off, and Orestes, before going after him, announces that he had no intention of killing him in the first place, for he—this killer of women—does not consider a eunuch slave, neither man nor woman, worth killing (1527f).

This brief scene recapitulates the play. Orestes plays viciously at an indecision with which he is himself really afflicted. The slave in turn is a distorted reflection of the Orestes who had cried out for his life (644ff, 677ff), and whatever pathos those cries had expressed is now grotesque ridicule. And the cause of that ridicule is Orestes himself. He taunts the slave, dangling the lure of life before him, as he himself has been taunted, bedeviled, and harassed—by circumstances, gods, men, and the impulses of his own mind. Orestes in his dejection had said to Menelaus that "we are enslaved to the gods, whatever the gods are" (418). He now acts out divine arbitrariness upon another slave, his own image.

There follows the second confrontation of Menelaus and Orestes, which should represent the consummation of the plot for survival. But Orestes first threatens to destroy Menelaus—whom he had planned to make his means of safety—Hermione, and the palace, "house of his fathers," by fire (1594ff), which would kill himself, Electra, and Pylades as well. The matter of rescue comes up just at the end of the scene. First Orestes bypasses it, asserting his right, not simply to live, but to rule in Argos (1600ff). Then Menelaus, no longer able to endure the threats to his daughter's life, cries out, "what shall I do?" (1610; cf. 596) Persuade the Argives not to kill us, says Orestes. But that is evidently impossible; it is much too late for any persuasion. Menelaus simply admits his helplessness: "you have me" (1617). That had been the object of the plot for survival, and now it is Orestes' cue to call for the palace to be set on fire (1618ff). Irrationally grounded, the pursuit of life turns into a suicidal holocaust.

The *Orestes* begins by suggesting a moral conflict made internal, turning on its protagonist's sense of guilt, but that issue, mostly under the pressure of outward circumstances, is dissipated. (There is one brief reminder of it in the last scene, when Menelaus claims he is at least pure "in hands," that is, free of ritual pollution, to which Orestes rejoins, "but not in mind" [1604].) The plot turns outward to revenge and survival. But as the presuppositions of these are at cross purposes, the actions that result negate themselves. The play opens with Orestes' desperate situation; the first part of it ends with the exhausting of all hope; and the latter part reaches once more its point of departure, Orestes' imminent death. Apollo's final appearance, then, breaks the cycle and restores the myth's traditional conclusion, that Orestes is saved. But returning to the myth is a further negation of human actions. Orestes' plan of revenge, for which he had, finally, been willing to lay down his life, is canceled. Insofar as that plan was criminal, Apollo's appearance and the return to the myth are providential—but that point we shall consider later. Thus far we have noticed a disjunction between the mythical elements and the immediate action of the play, which suggests a sense of the superfluous or gratuitous. This sense now appears as well in the bafflement of human purpose which that action demonstrates.

"Change in all things is sweet," Electra says to Orestes, restless in his sickness (234). "Yes," he answers, "for it give the illusion [*doxa*] of health, and seeming [*to dokein*] is better, even if there is no truth" (235-36). Illusion and seeming in every form dominate the play. The project for survival, we saw, was born out of wishful thinking (1173ff). Euripides represents a world whose real substance has become elusive and men who shy from realities too hard to bear, preferring hope in illusion. But delusion and madness can follow. "Even though you may not be sick," Electra tells her brother, "but only imagine you are, it is an affliction and perplexity for mortals" (314-15). "You see nothing of what you imagine you know clearly," she assures him (259). Orestes responds by recoiling from his sister's embrace, thinking her a fury (264f). At the end of the play, finally, Orestes tells Apollo, recalling the god's command to kill Clytemnestra, "the fear came upon me that I was imagining the voice of some demon [*alastôr*] and not yours" (1668-69; cf. *Electra* 979). We are made to look back on the possibility that the basis of the whole action, Orestes' matricide, was inspired by a delusion.

This inner doubt of Orestes, in turn, is dramatized by action that is often baffling. The play deludes its audience about what is happening. Euripides' noted flair for the theatrical here creates effects not only spectacular and surprising, but deceptive and illusory as well. They are climaxed in the representation of the plot against Helen. Orestes and Pylades have gone into the palace, while Electra stands watch outside with the chorus. The chorus leader imagines that someone—a country-man—has come up and is lurking about the house (1269), only to decide that it was no one, "contrary to what you [Electra] imagined" (1274). Shortly after, a cry is heard from inside, ". . . I am wretchedly perishing" (1296), and the chorus tentatively identifies Helen's voice, "so one might conjecture" (1298). She cries out again, "Menelaus, I am dying" (1301). Such cries of victims from offstage are frequent in tragedy (e.g., Aeschylus' *Agamemnon* 1343ff, *Choephoroi* 870ff, Sophocles' *Electra* 1404ff, Euripides' *Hecuba* 1035ff, *Electra* 1165f). Nor is there any doubt that those who utter them are in fact being killed. Here Euripides first diverts our attention with the appearance of Hermione, whom Electra lures into the palace—which has become strangely silent (1301-52). Then the chorus shouts to cover, they say, the groaning inside, so that no help might come "before I really see the bloody corpse of Helen . . . or hear an account from one of the servants, for I know some of the things that happened, but about others I know not clearly" (1357-60).

We are led explicitly to expect one of two regular features of a Greek tragedy, either the opening of house doors to reveal those who have been killed inside or a messenger speech telling what has happened offstage. The doors remain shut. We probably (our text is uncertain; cf. 1631-32) will not see Helen again. And the messenger speech seems to be put off by another interruption, the entrance of a Phrygian slave who somehow crawls out from under the palace roof and leaps down to the stage in panic flight from Orestes and Pylades (1369ff). He wails out his fear almost incoherently in a kind of virtuoso aria, a monody in free sequences of lyric meters. The chorus breaks in with single, spoken lines, trying to elicit from him what has happened. He must be our messenger, in the place of the usual dispassionate and orderly narrator. Euripides' theater cannot be more surprising.

The Phrygian's account works its effect by both the events he reports and the manner in which he reports them. He describes a piece of duplicity and its attendant confusion and disorder. There is an illusory quality in things, and men set out to delude one another as well. So far we have seen Menelaus' duplicity toward Orestes and Electra's deceiving of Hermione. The play also shows another kind of deception in hypocrisy, especially Helen's (126ff; cf. 1122f), and in flattery, as in Orestes' appeal to Menelaus (670ff) and his suspicion of the Phrygian: "you please with a coward's tongue, but these are not your thoughts within" (1514). Now Orestes and Pylades are described deceiving Helen by claiming they are her suppliants for their life (1414ff). But in part they really are suppliants for their life, though they sometimes forget it. They are as much deceived as deceiving.

The manner of the slave's report is partly accountable because, unlike the usual messenger, he is directly affected by the play's action. Thus when he calls out "where can I escape, flying to the bright air or sea . . . ?" (1376f) he echoes numerous Euripidean heroes in distress (cf. *Hippolytus* 732ff, 1290ff, *Heracles* 1157f, *Ion* 796f, 1238ff, *Andromache* 861ff). There is probably an element of self-parody here (anticipating Aristophanes' *Frogs* 1352f), but Euripides also gets an effect of dislocation similar to the one described earlier with the repetitions of the *Electra* and other tragedies in the *Orestes*. An incidental figure, a foreign slave, expresses feelings usually reserved for aristocratic Greek heroes. The world has become so disordered that anyone may occupy the stage's center. Further, that not only an affected party but also a foreigner should be our informant indicates how an event may be obscured as it is communicated and suggests an effect of relativity. As the Phrygian appears outlandish to a Greek, so he tells what he has seen with the amazement of an outsider.

After his cry for escape, the Phrygian invokes Ilium and recalls its downfall on Helen's account (1381ff), and again different spheres of reference clash. As cowering slave he is a familiar type, the degenerate oriental, proverbial for cowardice (cf. Aristophanes' *Birds* 1244). Yet now we hear he saw Ajax at Troy (1480) and remembers Odysseus (1404), and he reminds us that the valiant Hector was also a Phrygian (1480). When he describes Helen, whom the play has shown with unsparing realism as vain, unfeeling, self-interested, and insignificant, he uses language reminiscent of the sinister and beautiful figure in Aeschylus' *Agamemnon* (cf. 1386ff and *Agamemnon* 681ff, 742). His actual narrative begins with a Homeric image, "Hellenes, two twin lions . . ." (1401; cf. *Iliad* V, 548, X, 297), also used by Aeschylus (*Choephoroi* 937) and Sophocles (*Philoctetes* 1436). And he echoes Homeric similes when he compares Orestes and Pylades to mountain boars (1459; cf. *Iliad* XI, 324, XII, 42, XVII, 282). But their actions do not match these epic descriptions. The "twin lions" fall in simulated tears at Helen's feet (1410f), the "mountain boars" only stand "facing the woman" (1460). Furthermore, these epic figures are out of harmony with the references to animals, preying and hunting, found elsewhere in the play. To the Phrygian, Pylades is also a "murderous serpent" (1406; cf. *Iliad* XXII, 93ff) and Orestes "a serpent, slayer of his mother" (1424), a phrase already used by Tyndareus (479). Menelaus will exclaim over the horrors committed by "twin lions—I shall not call them men" (1555). The Phrygian's poetic periphrase now describes irrational savagery, what Tyndareus, referring to lawless revenge, had called "bestiality," *to thêriôdes* (524).

Doubt and disorder attend these disparities. The Phrygian next describes Helen's confused attendants, his fellow slaves, scattered and routed. A stock joke about cowardly Phrygians (cf. 1448) is played out, and the various fates of the anonymous slaves are ticked off in comic catalogues (1448ff, 1475ff, 1486ff). The confusion of the scene is represented by continuous and abrupt shifts of style. Aside from the pathetic Euripidean manner, as in the cry for escape, the epic features, and the echoes of other tragedies already noticed, there are extravagant exaggerations of Euripides' own lyric style, such as the constant use of repeated words, sound patterns, anaphoric sequences, invocations, and a variety of metrical effects. Frantic outbursts, narrative, commentary, and genre scenes, such as Helen at her weaving (1473ff), flash by for our distraction. The whole monody is 147 lines long. At the end of it we hear that Helen has "vanished" (1495), and "what followed," the slave says, "I know not" (1498). The messenger cannot report what should have been a foregone conclusion, Helen's death and the manner of it. He ends by remarking on futility—Menelaus' untold trouble and suffering to regain Helen from Troy has gone for nothing (1500f).

Like the short scene noticed earlier between the Phrygian and Orestes, the monody is a mirror—a distorting mirror—of the play's moods and themes. Its opening cry for escape voices a longing shared by all the actors (cf. 598 and 1376). The slave's abject fear recalls Tantalus' terror in punishment (6), Orestes' fear of the furies (38, 270, 312), Clytemnestra's terror before death (825), Helen's fears before the Argives (102, 104, 118) and before death (1296, 1301, 1465), Electra's and Pylades' fears for Orestes (757, 859; cf. 1255), and it looks forward to the chorus' fear, finally, of Orestes' actions (1537f; cf. 1324) and Menelaus' for his daughter's life (1598, 1609). When the Phrygian laments the fall of his city, Ilium, whereby he was made a slave (1381ff), his recollection of a doomed city—of which we are reminded throughout the play—is like the reiterated laments for the fall of a great house (332ff, 807ff, 960ff, 1537ff), backdrop for the downfall of Orestes, its last scion (cf. 664, 673). More generally, the monody reflects the contradictory movements within the play as a whole and the doubtful and suspended action that results;

the punishment of Tantalus (5ff, 982ff) is everyone's inheritance. And the frustration of the actors is dramatized by the expectations which are denied their audience. We still do not know what has happened—the success of Orestes' plot and the fate of Helen. (The latter will not be resolved until Apollo's final appearance; Menelaus is certain she is dead and will not believe a rumor that she has escaped [1556ff], though Orestes repeatedly insists she is alive [1580, 1586, 1614], having, however, also spoken as though she were dead [1512, 1534].)

This lack of knowledge of course heightens the play's sense of excitement—a sense which Euripides effects by inventing a plot previously unknown to his audience. But thus he must lose some of the advantages that the use of a familiar story allows, notably occasions for tragic irony and a sense of inevitability. In their place there is some room for comedy, as in the figure of the Phrygian, and decorative elaborations and archaisms of form and style, as well as stylistic experiments such as the Phrygian's monody and its earlier counterpart, Electra's finely wrought lyric solo (982-1012)—both probably vehicles for the same virtuoso performer. And since its characters are more corrupt than virtuous, and sometimes simply mad, *Orestes* lacks some of the commonly accepted qualifications for a tragedy. Commentators often call it a melodrama. But that should not distract us from its underlying seriousness. It is too systematic in its elaborations of disorder to be taken lightly. Its action has too much of the nightmare about it, a nightmare dreamed by an uncertain world, oppressed by fear and guilt and a memory which longs for release of terrible things that have been done (cf. 213-16, 325-27). It is possible that *Orestes*, like *Trojan Women* (both plays about the aftermath of a famous catastrophe), is a kind of indictment of public conscience.

The moving force of the whole story is revenge. Orestes' initial misfortunes are the result of it. His way out is to pursue it yet again. Revenge is what both the myth and Euripides' invented plot have in common. As it is related to justice, and so more than a private matter— the "wild kind of justice," Francis Bacon called it—it raises questions about political order. The theme of revenge makes us see Orestes' world as it claims to administer justice; and, more remotely, it might make us think of the gods as they are said to show men justice.

In Euripides' *Electra* Agamemnon was avenged, but under circumstances of doubt (*Electra* 966ff), and remorse followed (1190ff). Yet the vengeance was ordered by Apollo, though other divinities, the Dioscuri, say that he acted unjustly and unwisely (1254ff, 1302). But "where Apollo is a fool," Electra remarks, "who is wise?" (972) Justice has its claims and Clytemnestra deserved punishment, as her brothers (the Dioscuri) and her father Tyndareus agree (1244, *Orestes* 499, 505, 538). But the conditions under which that claim has to be made are obscure, an obscurity indicated by calling Apollo unwise. The Dioscuri, in turn, say that, because of "necessity," they could do nothing themselves (*Electra* 1301; cf. 1247f). The problem of justice involved in avenging Agamemnon, as far as gods are concerned, has reached an impasse, which is where *Orestes* begins.

Before he comes to trial Orestes faces the private indictment of his grandfather Tyndareus, who most clearly defines his injustice: he should not himself have exacted vengeance but should have prosecuted Clytemnestra by the procedures of civil law (500ff); though the deed, killing Clytemnestra, was just, the doer of it was not (538f). (The same argument, of course, applies to Orestes' attempted killing of Helen.) Orestes cannot answer this. And yet, as many have observed, Euripides makes the indictment possible by a violent anachronism. The old story takes place before civil justice existed. Aeschylus used the myth to show how that form of justice must emerge from and supersede an older familial system of vengeance. Sophocles in his *Electra* confines the plot completely within the myth, where no public justice exists. But Euripides confronts the myth with contemporary circumstances: Tyndareus refers to homicide laws [512ff] which were reinscribed within the year before the production of the *Orestes*. And so Orestes' injustice can be defined in rational terms, but somehow not adequately, because the displacement of an action out of the old story into a contemporary context is irrational. One might think Euripides means again to discredit the myth, revealing the barbarity of the old story when it is set in a civilized context. But the myth is not so much discredited as simply given. In fact, it recoils on that civilized context which might first have appeared to discredit it.

Tyndareus' accusation actually rests on a specious argument. "His championing of legal process is not so much anachronistic as futile. The law could not be invoked against the reigning queen, and the old man conveniently forgets that Orestes was a child at his father's death. The legal customs he extols had not in fact been invoked by anyone." [2] Furthermore, he first praises laws that call for exile, rather than death, as a punishment (515), and then goes on to urge that Orestes, and Electra as well, be executed (536, 613ff, 915f). For the rest, his character is distinguished by an attempt to blackmail Menelaus into supporting the

[2] G. M. A. Grube, *The Drama of Euripides* (London, 1941), p. 384.

conviction of Orestes (536f, 623ff) and by a concern only for outward forms. He assumes that "fair and unfair are evident to all" (492) and that Orestes, therefore, by his wretched appearance alone, must be guilty (533). He is the only person in the play to take seriously Orestes' pollution and the interdict against speaking to him (481), and yet, carried away by his accusations, he addresses him anyway (526ff). Tyndareus begins by expressing an ideal of justice and leaves in a fury of vindictiveness (609ff).

After the private accusation comes the public trial before the assembly of Argos. Like the other main event in the play, the plot against Helen, we are allowed to see it only through the eyes of a messenger, at one remove. The Phrygian's account is colored by his fear and overelaborate to the point of distraction. The messenger who reports Orestes' trial is partial, a retainer of Agamemnon's family (868ff), and his account is as schematic and truncated as the Phrygian's is overlong. The issues of the trial, at least as we hear them, are oversimplified and thus obscured. The words "just" or "justice" occur nowhere in the account (contrast *Eumenides* 511ff, 675, 699f). Orestes does not plead the command of Apollo in his defense. The countryman who alone supports him passes over the fact that it was not just "a woman" Orestes killed (925), but his mother. The demagogue who carries the assembly with his recommendation of the death penalty offers, in the report, no argued prosecution at all. The only reasonable proposal, exile (512ff), is passed over. Violence of speech (903ff) alone persuades the crowd, which allows itself to be moved by the private interests of a few—the friends of the usurper Aegisthus (894) and Tyndareus, who is not even an Argive (915). There is no rational functioning of justice in the public sphere. The myth of revenge might have seemed barbarous in the civilized world, but in fact it reveals the barbarity of civil justice debased. Orestes is part of a world as flawed as he is.

His injustice in the killing of Clytemnestra, to which he explicitly admits (646f), is, like the myth, given, a kind of legacy. The question of blame and responsibility comes from the past. Thus one might say that the more pressing question which the play sets is, given injustice, what is there to be done? Orestes indicates that dilemma when he says to Tyndareus, "do not say this deed [taking vengeance on Clytemnestra] was wrong [*ouk eu*], but that we the doers of it acted to our misfortune [*ouk eudaimonôs*]" (600f; cf. the sophistic defense of Helen that claims she "did no wrong" [*êdikêsen*] but "suffered misfortune" [*êtuchêsen*], Gorgias, *Helen* 15). He tries to shift attention from past injustice to present release, and at the same time he implies a shift from a criterion of virtue to one of happiness, from a judgment of wrong action to a freedom for well-being. But, as the myth is reasserted at the play's end and cancels its action, so there is no escape from this past.

In the present, justice can only be distorted. Orestes pleads with Menelaus: "I am unjust; in exchange for this evil I ought to receive from you an injustice; for unjustly did my father Agamemnon assemble Greece and come to Ilium . . . to heal the unjust wrong of your wife" (646-50). By this grotesque and obsessive logic the principle of reciprocity substitutes for that of justice. Agamemnon, argues Orestes, gave ten years to get Helen back: Menelaus should give him one day; Agamemnon sacrificed his daughter Iphigenia: Orestes will not require Menelaus to kill Hermione (656ff). He asks, then, for what he thinks his due, a return for what Menelaus has received (643; cf. 244, 452f). The play refers to a number of debts or favors owed. Hermione owes Clytemnestra her upbringing in Helen's absence (64, 109); Orestes owes his to Tyndareus (460ff), and he uses for a part of his defense a claim that he owed his existence more to his father than his mother (555ff; cf. *Eumenides* 658ff). But rendering what is due, *apodidonai* (cf. 643, 652, 1075, 1585), is countered by violation of favor, betrayal, *prodidonai* (cf. 575, 722, 1057, 1087, 1165, 1236, 1463, 1588). The intense loyalties of Electra, Pylades, and Orestes, the countryman at the trial, and the messenger are offset by the betrayals of Clytemnestra and Menelaus. And where betrayal may result from calculating self-interest, loyalty as the play describes it is passionate beyond reason. Its intensity is easily shifted to the pursuit of vengeance.

And that is everywhere. The avenging spirits, first of his father (581ff), then of his mother, hounded Orestes. Oiax wants to avenge his brother Palamedes (433f); Tyndareus his daughter; Aegisthus' friends seek revenge for him (cf. 894). And then Orestes would have vengeance on Menelaus, while Pylades justifies killing Helen as vengeance for Greece (1133ff). Finally, Menelaus will want revenge of Orestes (cf. 1534). Orestes' pursuit of vengeance appears as only an extreme instance of a universal impulse, originating, like his first killing, in pressures from the past, and then, like his second attempt, continuing spontaneously, or rather because of a corrupting habit ingrained by causes that have become irrelevant. The old story of revenge, with its continual reversals, reflects its contemporary context—the constant shifts and revisions of power, climaxed in the years just before this play by the oligarchic revolution of June, 411, followed by the government of the Five Thousand in September of that year, and a return to the democracy by June, 410; and in their wake cycle upon cycle of vengeance and reprisals,

probably the greatest evil of Athenian political life. Earlier in the
century Cleon, according to Thucydides, had argued for swift reprisals
against Mytilene as "the injured party proceeds against the offender with
the edge of his anger too blunted, but the requital that follows most
closely upon the injury best matches its vengeance" (III, 38, 1). Anger,
orgê, and passion, *thumos*, feelings that pervade the *Orestes*, are taken
for guides in the place of rational calculation. In a famous passage
Thucydides notes "the enormity of revenges" under the pressure of civil
disorders; that "to get revenge on someone" was thought more of than
not to have suffered injury in the first place; and that "the leading men
dared the most terrible deeds and executed revenges even more awful
. . . limiting them only by their momentary pleasure" (III, 82, 3-8). And
two years after the production of *Orestes*, Aristophanes' chorus still
appeals for mildness after changes of party and government, calling on
the Athenians to rid themselves of "terror" and give up "anger," *orgê*
(*Frogs* 688, 700); to end reprisals and temper the urge to vengeance.
As in *Orestes*, the political life of the city depends, in some measure,
on a solution of the problem of revenge.

"Passion [*thumos*]," says Aristotle, "has in it a certain pleasure, for
it is combined with hope for revenge" (*Eud. Ethics* 1229 b 32f). There
is, finally, a hedonistic, self-indulgent quality in the impulse to vengeance,
proverbially sweet (cf. Thucydides VII, 68, 1-2). The characters in *Orestes*
are all carried only by the tides of their feelings—whether Orestes at
one extreme, or the nervous Menelaus at the other—which, in a kind
of vacuum, cut off from traditional and public supports, acquire an
extreme intensity that must somehow be satisfied. The loyalty and devotion between Electra, Orestes, and Pylades is one such satisfaction.
But as Orestes' situation becomes utterly hopeless, and nothing more
can be done for him, devotion is frustrated and the feelings thus released
turn outward and look for gratification in vengeance. Both the particular
spur of that vengeance and its general context is betrayal. We have
noticed the disjointedness of the play. In every way it presents divisions
and discontinuities—between the traditional myth and the immediate
action, between the past and present, between impulses to life and to
death, between intention and achievement, between nobility and madness, between justice and politics, between fact and delusion, and—in
style—between an almost naturalistic realism and lyric extravagance.
Orestes' sense of betrayal at the hands of Menelaus is the specific cause
for his plot of vengeance, but Menelaus' seems only a particular
instance of a more general betrayal, which is represented by this dis-
jointed nature of the world. Revenge, then, becomes an irrational

response to the world's failure to render what one imagines is his due. It could be an attempt to force repayment on the loss between what seems and what is. And it is an exasperated explosion of feeling after all human intentions are denied. Until his last-minute appearance, Apollo is the mythical representation of this betrayal in things. When Electra assures Orestes, "I shall not let you go," *outoi methêsô* (262), she is made to echo Apollo's promise to him in Aeschylus' *Eumenides*, "I shall not give you up," *outoi prodôsô* (64). Human loyalty would take the place of divine. But it is far from sufficient. Apollo finally appears.

He comes to restore a mythical conclusion to a situation that has moved as far as seems possible from its mythical basis. His appearance is abrupt, but only the last in a series of surprising entrances: Tyndareus', Pylades', and the Phrygian's. When Orestes reappears to corner the slave, the chorus acknowledges the pattern: "Look, here is a novelty succeeding novelties" (1503). The god had been mentioned only twice since Orestes last blamed him for his misfortune (597f), once, after the trial, as author of Orestes' ruin (955f) and once, in passing, as the builder of Troy's walls now fallen (1388). As the plot moves away from the myth, the god is forgotten. And yet there are a few indications he might return. "He delays," says Orestes, in answer to a question about the god's help, "such is the nature of the divine" (419f). Orestes' last words about Apollo indicate his helplessness without the god: "where might one still escape if he who gave the command [to kill Clytemnestra] will not keep me from death?" (598f) And all the ensuing action bears him out. There is no human solution. The chorus, then, prepare for the possibility of Apollo's coming by turning back to the myth and a traditional statement of the gods' overruling power: "A deity holds the end [*telos*] for mortals, the end, wherever he wishes. It is a great power. By an avenging demon this house has fallen, fallen, by blood, by Myrtilus' fall from the chariot" (1545ff; cf. *Ion* 1615, Aeschylus *Agamemnon* 1487). But they only look backward to a former crime, and see ruin before them now.

Apollo's appearance, surprising and yet somehow expected, appropriately concludes the play. It marks the most violent break in the continuity of the action thus far, yet it alters nothing of what the play had shown about human helplessness. *Orestes* includes an indictment of human character and the political world. Apollo bypasses both. He will "set things right" in Argos (1664), ignoring the city's hostility to Orestes and the decision of its assembly. He announces the deification of Helen, who will become a "salvation" for those at sea (1637), the same Helen whose character we had seen so harshly exposed, and who, the god himself recalls, had been a cause of so many deaths (1641). We noticed earlier the reconciliation he brings about between Menelaus, Orestes, and Hermione. The play had raised a question about human survival. The god solves it by ignoring the terms in which it was set, the substance of the play's action.

It was remarked that insofar as the plot of *Orestes* diverged from the myth it lost a sense of inevitability. The most fantastic possibility might then be realized, one, for instance, which Orestes puts forward as un-thinkable—namely, that Hermione should be killed as Iphigenia was killed (658f). But before the play is over Hermione is almost killed. She is saved only by a still more fantastic possibility, the last-instant inter-ference of a god. Apollo's appearance is thus a sign of the extreme range of life's possible reversals. His coming suggests how fantastic it is that we survive at all.[3] And yet this god had originally ordered Orestes' crime, as he himself reminds us (1665), and so represents also the obscurity and pressure of the past. He shows that these are still present and, by his prophecies (e.g., 1654ff), that they continue into the future as well. The arbitrariness of his interference is the most disturbing demonstra-tion yet of the simply irrational course of things. It recalls Orestes' arbitrariness with the Phrygian slave, differing only as the god has more power and uses it now to restore a traditional order. The plot which Euripides invented for the action of this play moves in cycles which show how futile human action is, coming always back to its starting point, a desperate and helpless strait, and how thus, without achieve-ment, it was insubstantial and empty of all but passionate feelings. For this condition Apollo has no cure. Euripides shows us human beings who cannot save themselves. But the way the god saves them denies their humanity, or rather, finally, isolates it. The break betwen the new plot —"human beings as they are"—and the myth—the received, poetic vision of order—is beyond healing. What is remarkable is the unflinch-ing steadiness with which Euripides can look at this segment of humanity he has chosen to represent, in all its degenerate and criminal nature. And, rather than overwhelm us with the bitter and scornful judgment he must make, he mourns, behind a façade of theatrical virtuosity. *Orestes* has no substantial resolution or catharsis. Apollo sees to that. Thus it is not in the usual sense a tragedy. In fact, it curiously antici-pates the themes of Aristophanes' *Frogs,* that serious comedy—the down-

---

[3] Greenberg, *op. cit.,* pp. 189f.

fall of a city and political life because of a deficiency and degeneration of human virtue; the vindictiveness of human feeling; and the death of tragedy. The *Orestes* is filled with innovations which may surprise, but also disappoint, the expectations which traditional tragedy fulfilled. Part of its peculiar "tragedy" is that true tragedy is no longer possible, as Euripides suggests by turning to one of tragedy's most used myths for his most experimental play.

Tragedy and Religion: The *Bacchae*

by *Thomas G. Rosenmeyer*

I

The *Bacchae* is not intrinsically a religious drama. This flies in the face of certain critical assumptions which have recently gained currency. It has been suggested that Euripides' chief object in writing the drama was to give a clinical portrayal of what Dionysiac religion, hence Dionysus, does to men. According to this view, the *Bacchae* is a more or less realistic document, perhaps an anthropological account of an outburst of manic behavior, of a psychosis analogous to certain phenomena reported from the Middle Ages and not unknown in our own troubled times. The play has even been compared with a modern imaginative treatment of mass psychosis, Van Wyck Brooks' *Oxbow Incident*. I feel that this is mistaken, and for a very simple and obvious reason. Whatever one may say about the ancient tragedians, about the extravagant character of many of the plots, about the implausibility of much that is said and done, the fact remains that the writers are interested in what is typical, in the generic, or, as Aristotle has it, in the universal. To attribute to Euripides a study in abnormality is to indulge in an anachronism. Euripides is not the kind of dramatist, like Sartre, whose poetic urge is stimulated by small grievances rather than catholic insight. Nor is Euripides a scientific observer of sickness; he does not record, he creates. His material is ritual and mythical, and some of it clinical; but the product is something entirely different.

Pindar once uses the tale of Perseus cutting off the head of the Medusa as an image symbolizing the act of poetic creation: living ugliness is violently refashioned into sculptured beauty. The ferocity of the *Bacchae* is to be seen in the same light. By an act of literary exorcism the cruelty and the ugliness of a living experience are transmuted into the beauty of a large vision, a vision which is not without its own horror, but a horror entirely unlike that felt at the approach of the god. It is the kind of horror which Plato touches on in the *Symposium* and the *Theaetetus,* the sudden weakness and awe which get hold of the philosophic soul at the moment when she comes face to face with a like-minded soul and jointly ventures to explore the ultimate. Dionysus is only a means to an end; Euripides exploits the Dionysiac revels to produce a dramatic action which helps the spectators to consider the mystery and the precariousness of their own existence.

Aeschylus, notably in his *Agamemnon* but also in some of his other extant plays, appeals to the audience with an interplay of sounds and sights. With Aeschylus, language is not an instrument but an entity, a vibrant self-sufficient thing, working in close harmony with the brilliant objects filling the stage of the *Oresteia.* The word textures pronounced by the chorus, like the sentence patterns of the actors' speeches, stir the audience as violently as the sight of a crimson tapestry or the vision of evil Furies on the roof. Behind this sumptuous drapery of color and sound, personality takes second place. The characters are largely the carriers of images and speech. Sophocles introduces the personal life, the *bios,* into drama. Now a man is no longer largely the pronouncer of words, the proposer of ideas and emotions, but an independent structure involving a past and a future, a point of intersection for ominous antecedents and awful prospects. This emergence of the organic character, of the heroic life as the nucleus of drama, was a fateful step in the history of literature. Aeschylus also, in some of his later plays, adopted the new structuring for his own purposes.

Euripides goes further. He rejects the autonomy of speech as he rejects the autonomy of the personal life; instead he attempts to combine the two in an organic mixture of his own. In the *Ion* he gives us a parody of the pure *bios* form; mythology is squeezed into a biographical mold, with unexpectedly humiliating consequences for the great hero. In the *Bacchae,* on the other hand, it is in the end not the persons who count, nor the words or sound patterns though the play may well be the most lyrical of all Euripidean works, but the ideas. The *Bacchae,* in spite of its contrived brutality and its lyricism, is a forerunner of the Platonic dialogues. The smiling god is another Socrates, bullying his listeners into a painful reconsideration of their thinking and their values. That is not to say that we have here an intellectual argument, an academic inquiry into logical relations. Rather, the *Bacchae* constitutes a poet's attempt to give shape to a question, to a complex of uncertainties and puzzles which do not lend themselves to discursive treatment. There is no

clear separation of thesis and antithesis, of initial delusion and liberating
doubt, nor is there anything like a final statement or a solution. Nevertheless the poem is cast in the philosophical mode. Sophocles, in the
Oedipus Rex or the *Ajax*, takes a heroic life and fashions its tragic nexus
to the world around it or to itself. Euripides, in the *Bacchae*, takes an
abstract issue and constructs a system of personal relations and responses
to activate the issue. He builds his lives into the issue, instead of letting
the life speak for itself as Sophocles does.

The issue derives from a question which is simple and raw: What is
man? As Dionysus remarks to Pentheus (506),

> Your life, your deeds, your Being are unknown
> to you.

For Plato, the human soul is a compound of the divine and the perish-
able, a meeting place of the eternal beyond and the passionate here. In
the *Phaedrus* he puts the question more concretely. Socrates suggests that
it is idle to criticize or allegorize mythology if one has not yet, as he himself has not, come to a satisfactory conclusion about his own nature and
being (230A):

> I try to analyze myself, wondering whether I am some kind of beast more
> heterogeneous and protean and furious than Typhon, or whether I am a
> gentler and simpler sort of creature, blessed with a heavenly unfurious
> nature.

The word that I have translated as "creature" is the same that appears in
Aristotle's famous definition of man as a "political creature," or rather,
as "a creature that lives in a polis." "Political animal," the usual translation, is unfortunate, for in his definition Aristotle clearly throws the
weight of his authority behind the second alternative of Plato's question.
Man is not a ravaging beast, but a gentler being. But perhaps Aristotle is
not as fully sensitive as Plato to the difficulty posed by the alternative. Is
man closer to the gods or to the beasts?

Another question which is linked to the uncertainty about the status
of the human soul is: What is knowledge? Or, to put it differently: How
much in this world is subject to man's insight and control? Greek philosophical realism, beginning with the Eleatics and reaching its greatest
height with Plato, taught that reality is unchanging, static, difficult of
access, and that in general men come to experience it only through the
veil of ever-changing patterns of sensory impulses. There is an inexorable
friction between total Being and partial Appearance. Man is constrained
to deal with the appearances, but at his best he comes to sense—or, according to Plato, to know—the reality behind the phenomena. The

breakthrough to the reality is a painful process; it can be achieved only at the cost of injuring and mutilating the ordinary cognitive faculties. The perfectionists, including Plato in the *Phaedo,* submit that the breakthrough becomes complete only with the complete surrender of the senses whose activity stands in the way of the vision of reality. That is to say, the perceptual blindness and the phenomenal friction cannot be resolved except by disembodiment and death.

Now if this, or something like it, is the philosophical issue which Euripides is trying to dramatize, he is at once faced with a grave artistic difficulty. How is he, as a dramatist, to convey the universal scope of Reality and the beguiling contradictoriness of Appearance, without rendering the formulation banal or bloodless or both? The statement "Dionysus is all" would be worse than meaningless. It should be emphasized again that Euripides is not trying to say poetically what could also, and better, be said discursively. What does a poet-metaphysician do to clothe the range of abstract issues in the living and self-authenticating flesh of poetry? Is it possible for a dramatist to convey ideas without having his characters preach them ex cathedra, which is by and large the situation we find in the *Prometheus Bound?* Can a philosophical idea which is refracted by a process of poetic mutation continue to score as a factor in a metaphysical argument?

To begin with, the Greek writer has an advantage over his modern colleagues. The ancient conventions of tragedy stipulate that the dramatic nucleus be essayed from a spectrum of approaches. From prologue to chorus to characters to epilogue, each constitutive part of the drama contributes its specific orientation. In the end the various perspectives coalesce into one and invite a unified though never simple audience response. This is the desired effect; sometimes the merging of the lines of coordination is not complete, and the spectators are left without a certain key to gauge their participation. Goethe's *Faust* is, perhaps, once again a fair example of such a case on the modern stage. The author is saying something profound about man and reality, but for various reasons the play leaves us with the impression of partial statements instead of a total imagining, because of the vast scope of the action, because Goethe has inserted certain curious elements of diffusion and fragmentation, and because he tries to play off one culture against another in an attempt to universalize the compass of the theme. Any Greek play is likely to be more successful on this score. The traditional spectrum of perspectives is offset by an extreme succinctness of speech and thought, by a narrow conformity to Greek ways, by an economy of character, and, last but not least, by the condensatory effect of hereditary myth. Myth is itself a condensation of many experiences of different degrees of concreteness. Greek drama simply carries forward the business begun by myth.

Dionysus, who is Euripides' embodiment of universal vitality, is described variously by chorus, herdsman, commoners, and princes. The descriptions do not tally, for the god cannot be defined. He can perhaps be totaled but the sum is never definitive; further inspection adds new features to the old. If a definition is at all possible it is a definition by negation or cancellation. For one thing, Dionysus appears to be neither woman nor man; or better, he presents himself as woman-in-man, or man-in-woman, the unlimited personality (235):

> With perfumes wafted from his flaxen locks
> and Aphrodite's wine-flushed graces in
> his eyes . . .

No wonder Pentheus calls him (353) "the woman-shaped stranger," and scoffs at the unmanly whiteness of his complexion (457). In the person of the god strength mingles with softness, majestic terror with coquettish glances. To follow him or to comprehend him we must ourselves give up our precariously controlled, socially desirable sexual limitations. The being of the god transcends the protective fixtures of decency and sexual pride.

Again, Dionysus is both a citizen, born of Semele, and a Greek from another state, for he was raised in Crete, like the Zeus of the mysteries—surely this is the implication of lines 120ff—*and* a barbarian from Phrygia or Lydia or Syria or India, at any rate from beyond the pale of Greek society. It is not as if the conflicting pieces of information had to be gathered laboriously from various widely separated passages in the play. All of them are to be found in the entrance song of the chorus. After the introductory epiphany of the god himself, the women of the chorus begin to assemble their picture of Dionysus, and it is indicative of what Euripides means him to be that even these first few pointers should cancel out one another. It happens to be true historically that Dionysus is both Greek and non-Greek; recently discovered Mycenean texts have shown that the god's name was known to the Greeks of the Mycenean period. It now appears that the foreign extraction of Dionysus may have been a pious fiction of Apollonian partisans. Dionysus the popular god, the god of mysteries, the emblem of surging life in its crudest form, of regeneration and animal passion and sex, was endangering the vested interests of Apollo, grown refined and squeamish in the hands of the gentry and the intellectual elite. One of the defense measures, and there were many, was to declare Dionysus a foreigner, a divinity whose ways, so the propaganda went, offended the true instincts of the Greek. There was some apparent justification for this. The genuinely foreign deities who were being imported into Greece often were kindred in spirit to Dionysus. At any rate the propaganda took hold. At the end of the fifth century all Greeks tended to believe that Dionysus came from abroad; and yet they considered him one of their own, a powerful member of the Olympian pantheon. Euripides exploits the discrepancy to the advantage of his purpose; he uses it to emphasize the unbounded, the unfragmented nature of the ultimate substance. But the arrival from foreign lands signifies a special truth; it highlights the violently intrusive character of the Dionysiac life, of the unlimited thrusting itself into the limited and exploding its stale equilibrium, which is a favorite theme of Pythagorean and Greek popular thought.

But all this would be bloodless metaphysics, dry-as-dust allegory, were it not for Euripides' grasp of the essential irony enunciated in the passage of the *Phaedrus* and skirted in Aristotle's aphorism. Man is both beast and god, both savage and civilized, and ultimate knowledge may come to him on either plane, depending on the manner in which the totality communicates itself. It is as an animal, as a beast close to the soil and free of the restrictions of culture and city life, that man must know Dionysus. But that means that in embracing Dionysus man surrenders that other half of himself, the spark of the gentle and celestial nature which, the philosophers hope, constitutes the salvageable part of man's equipment. The incongruity of the two planes, the political and the animal, becomes the engrossing puzzle and the energizing thesis of the play. The double nature of man is what the play is really about; the ambivalence of Dionysus is pressed into service largely in order to illumine the ambivalence of human cognition reaching out for its object, for the elusive pageant of truth.

II

In the *Bacchae* men are identified with animals, not as in Aesop where the beasts aspire to be men and become moral agents, but as in a Gothic tale where intelligence and social grace and responsibility are renounced and the irrational, the instinct of blood and steaming compulsion, take their place. Characteristically this way of looking at life paralyzes value judgment. The gulf between men and animals is erased, but whether this is a good thing or not is by no means clear. When the women of the chorus, for example, call Pentheus a beast they do not mean to

flatter him. He is the son of Echion, who was sprung from dragon's teeth,
and there is dragon blood in his veins (1155). He is said to be a fierce
monster (542) whose acts make one suspect that he was born of a lioness
or a Libyan Gorgon. His mother also in her moment of visionary bliss
sees him as a lion rather than as a man. For her, however, this is not a
matter of disparagement; if anything, embracing a lion seems to her
to offer a glimpse of perfection. Not so the chorus; in the passages cited
they show an incongruous pride in human shape and human achievement. But in the fourth choral ode, as they reach their highest pitch of
passion and frenzied insight, they issue their call (1017):

> Appear, in the shape of a bull or a many-headed
> serpent, or a lion breathing fire!

In their first ode also they refer to Dionysus as the bull-horned god
wreathed in snakes (100f). The god Dionysus, the stranger-citizen, the
hermaphrodite, at once superman and subman, is a beast, for which the
chorus praises him. This is the sacred dogma. Even Pentheus, once he
has fallen under the spell of the god, acknowledges him as a bull (920):

> And now, leading me on, I see you as
> a bull, with horns impacted in your head.
> Were you a beast before? I should not wonder.

And Dionysus answers:

> Yes, now you see what is for you to see.

But what of Pentheus' own beast-likeness? Are the women suggesting
that human beastliness is a mere parody of divine beastliness, and therefore to be condemned? Or have the ladies of the chorus not yet traveled
the full length of the Dionysiac conversion, and retain a vestige of
civilized values? Their abuse of Pentheus is couched in terms which
expose them as imperfect Maenads. Contrast that other chorus, the band
of Bacchantes hidden from our sight, whose mysterious acts of strength
are reported to us in the messenger speeches. From them rather than
from their more civilized sisters on the stage we expect the pure lesson
of the new faith. And in fact they preserve no trace of a false pride in
human separateness. They carry the tokens of animal life on their backs
and entertain the beasts as equal partners (695):

> And first they shook their hair free to their shoulders
> and tucked up their fawnskins . . .
>   . . . their spotted pelts
> they girt with serpents licking at their cheeks.

> And some clasped in their arms a doe or wild
> wolf cubs and gave them milk . . .

Under the aegis of Dionysus, men and animals are as one, with no questions asked. The philosophical message is tolerably clear. But the vestigial bias of the pseudo-Maenads onstage is more than a temporary deviation from the orthodox Bacchic faith. In the interest of the message it would have been wiser to abuse Pentheus as a man, incapable of going beyond the limitations of his anthropomorphism. The beast imagery in the choral condemnation of Pentheus is cumulative and emphatic. The praise of Dionysus does not blot it from our memory. It is, in fact, intended to serve as a counterpoint. The animal shape rules supreme; but when all parties have been heard it is not at all clear whether one ought to approve or not. The judgment is suspended and values are held in abeyance.

It is a mistake to consider the Dionysiac ecstasy a perversion of social life, an impasse, a negative situation. The *Bacchae* does not tell a story of maladjustment or aberration. It is a portrayal of life exploding beyond its narrow everyday confines, of reality bursting into the artificiality of social conventions and genteel restrictions. Waking and sleeping are deprived of their ordinary cognitive connotations; who is to say that sleeping, the drunken stupor which succeeds the rite, does not expand one's vision beyond its commonplace scope? In the *Ion* the premium is on wakefulness; in the *Bacchae* we are invited to rest in a gray no man's land which is halfway between waking and sleep, where man shelves the tools of reason and social compact and abandons himself to instinct and natural law (862ff, trans. Phillip Vellacott):

> O for long nights of worship, gay
> With the pale gleam of dancing feet,
> With head tossed high to the dewy air—
> Pleasure mysterious and sweet!
> O for the joy of a fawn at play
> In the fragrant meadow's green delight,
> Who has leapt out free from the woven snare,
> Away from the terror of chase and flight,
> And the huntsman's shout, and the straining pack,
> And skims the sand by the river's brim
> With the speed of wind in each aching limb,
> To the blessed lonely forest where
> The soil's unmarked by a human track,
> And leaves hang thick and the shades are dim.

This is the *strophe* of a choral ode; in the *antistrophe* the chorus invokes
the divine order of things—*physis,* nature—which will assert itself eventually in spite of men (884)

> who honor ignorance and refuse
> to enthrone divinity . . .

The verses cited picture the pleasure and the awe of identification with
nonhuman nature, with the life of the fawn bounding free of the snare
but never quite eluding the hunter, a life of liberty which is yet not
free. The animal senses the sway of natural law even more strongly than
the man. *Strophe* and *antistrophe,* the vision of animal escape and the
address to natural compulsion, are part of the same complex. But in the
text they do not follow one upon the other; they are separated by that
rare thing in Greek poetry, a refrain which is repeated once more iden-
tically, at the end of the *antistrophe.* Refrains in Greek tragedy always
have a solemn ring; they are felt to be echoes of ritual hymns. The fixed
severity of the repetition is something foreign within the headlong flow
of the dramatic current. The mind accustomed to pressing on after the
determined advance of ideas and plot is abruptly stopped in its tracks;
time ceases for a while and the cold chill of monotony reveals a glimpse
of Being beyond the Becoming of the human scene.

Here is an attempt to translate the refrain as literally as the sense
allows (877, 897):

> What is wisdom? Or what is more beautiful,
> a finer gift from the gods among men,
> than to extend a hand victorious
> over the enemy's crown? But beauty
> is every man's personal claim.

Wisdom equals tyranny, beauty equals vengeance. The hunted and the
hunter have their own jealous notions of wisdom and beauty, but their
pretensions are drowned in the vast offering of the gods, the dispensation
of natural law, and the survival of the strongest. This is what the refrain
seems to say; the message agrees well with the propositions of *strophe*
and *antistrophe.* But note the didactic quality of the speech, the question
and answer, and particularly the academic formulation of the last line,
which in the Greek consists of only four words: "Whatever beautiful,
always personal." It is a line which might have come straight from the
pages of Aristotle; better yet, it reminds us of a similarly scholastic
passage in a poem by Sappho in which she contemplates various standards of beauty and preference and concludes: "I [think that the most
beautiful thing is] that with which a person is in love." The poetess

speaks of a "thing," using the neuter gender, and of "a person," any person, desiring the thing. Like a good teacher she starts her discussion with a universal premise. Then, as the poem draws to its conclusion, she discards the generality and focuses on the living girl and on the I, the specific poles of her love whose reality constitutes the authority for the writing of the poem. But the philosophic mode of the earlier formulation remains important; it reminds us that the specific poles of her present love are at the same time representatives of a universal rhythm. In Euripides' ode, also, it is this universal rhythm which comes into view through the hieratic stillness of the refrain and particularly through its last line. The words are almost the same as those of Sappho; the difference is that between a vision intent upon the small joys and sufferings of love, and a vision which comprehends man in the sum total of his powers and feebleness. The refrain may well be the closest approach to poetry shedding its disguise and showing itself as metaphysics pure and simple.

But the glimpse is short-lived, and the clarity immediately obscured. Again it is the chorus itself which is the chief agent of confounding the analysis. It does so by combining in the Dionysiac prospects of its songs the two sides, the real and the ideal, which are inevitably connected in the experience. Both ritual and hope, slaughter and bliss, dance and dream, the cruelty of the present and the calm of the release, are joined together as one. The paradise of milk and honey and the orgy of bloody dismemberment merge in a poetic synthesis which defies rational classification. Of this creative insight into the contradictoriness of things I have already spoken. To complicate the picture even further, Bacchic sentiments are superimposed on traditional choric maxims. In an earlier ode which begins with a condemnation of Pentheus' words and an appeal to the goddess Piety, the women sing (386, 397):

> Of unbridled mouths
> and of lawless extravagance
> the end is disaster . . .
>
> . . . .
> Life is brief; if a man,
> not heeding this, pursues vast things
> his gain slips from his hands.
> These are the ways, I believe,
> of madmen, or of
> injudicious fools.

We recognize the familiar adage of "nothing in excess," the motto of bourgeois timidity and sane moderation, at opposite poles from the

Dionysiac moral of vengeance and expansiveness and the bestialization of man. The injunctions of moderation and knowing one's limits run counter to the hopes of those who worship Dionysus. The two people who live up to the injunctions, Tiresias and Cadmus, come very close to being comic characters, as we shall see directly. Why, then, does Euripides put the pious precept into the mouth of a chorus whose primary artistic function is to communicate precisely what it is condemning, the spirit of unbridled mouths and lawless extravagance? It may be noted that such injunctions in Greek tragedy are often illusory. Setting off as they do a heroic imbalance or a cosmic disturbance, they underscore the poignancy of the action. But in this particular instance the use of the Delphic motto is even more startling than usual. The direction of the metaphysical impact is rudely deflected and the opacity of the poem enhanced by this conventional reminder of irrelevant quietist values.

While the Theban women are away celebrating, the foreign votaries are in Thebes. This is a mechanical displacement necessitated by what Greek tragedy permits; for the Dionysiac revels must be reported rather than seen, and so the true Maenads are offstage. But that puts the chorus in an anomalous position. They are worshipers of Dionysus, but they must not behave like worshipers. Few Euripidean choruses are less intimately engaged in the action and in fact less necessary to the action. It is the chorus offstage that counts. Hence the curious mixture of half-hearted participation and distant moralizing, as if the poet were not entirely comfortable with the choral requirements. This may account for the perplexing admixture of Apollonian preaching which I have just mentioned. It may account also for the remarkable poetic color of many of the choral utterances. The poet, making a virtue of the necessity, calls attention to the detachment of the chorus from the heart of the plot—though not from the heart of the philosophical issue—by giving it some of the finest lyrics ever sounded in the Attic theater. This is not the place for a close appreciation of the poetry; that can be done only in the original. The analysis of ancient poetry is a difficult thing; there are few men who combine the necessary scholarly equipment with an understanding of what poetry is about. Further, some of the clues to such an understanding which in modern poetry are furnished by the experience of living speech are missing for the Greek. Nevertheless few readers can expose themselves to the choral odes of the *Bacchae* without realizing that this is poetry of the highest order. Imagery has little to do with it; in this as in most Euripidean plays the choral poetry is even less dependent on metaphor and simile than the dialogue. There is some pondering of myth, to be sure. But perhaps the most important thing about the odes is the wonderful mixture of simplicity and excitement. The women do not beat around the bush; their interest in life is single-minded, and they declare themselves with all the fervor of a unitary vision. This does not, of course, say anything about the poetry as poetry, but it may explain why the lyrics of the *Bacchae* touch us so powerfully.

There is one image, however, or rather a class of images, which ought to be mentioned: the container filled to the bursting point. In their first ode the chorus uses the trope three times. They sing of Dionysus stuffed into the thigh of Zeus, golden clasps blocking the exit until such time as the young man may be born (94ff). They call on Thebes, nurse of Semele, to (107)

> teem, teem with verdant
> bryony, bright-berried;

the city is to be filled to the rooftops with vegetation, as a sign of the presence of the god. For illustration we should compare the famous vase painting of Exekias in which Dionysus reveals himself in his ship to the accompaniment of a burst of vegetation. Finally the women caution each other to be careful in their handling of the thyrsus, the staff of the god (113):

> Handle the staffs respectfully;
> there is *hybris* in them.

In all three instances it is the fullness of the container which is stressed, not the spilling over. But as the play advances, containment proves inadequate. At the precise moment when the stranger is apprehended by Pentheus' men, the Maenads who had been imprisoned earlier are set free (447):

> All by themselves the bonds dropped off their feet;
> keys unlocked doors, without a man's hand to turn them.

Their liberation is as real as the binding of the stranger is false.

The most striking *mise en scène* of the inadequacy of the container is the so-called palace miracle. Like that of the other passages, its function is symbolic rather than dramaturgical; after it has happened it is never mentioned again. It is not necessary to the progress of the plot, only to the effect and the meaning of the poem. We need not worry much whether the stage director engineered the collapse of a column or a pediment, or whether the spectators were challenged to use their own creative imaginations, though I am inclined to assume the latter. At any

rate, the vision of the palace shaking and tumbling is the most explicit
and the most extended of a series of images pointing to the explosion
of a force idly and wrongfully compressed. Eventually this concept con-
verges on what I have called the friction between total Being and frag-
mentary Appearance, the friction which is worked out also through a
series of antinomies: the brute wildness of the thyrsus versus the spindles
abandoned in the hall, the fawnskins versus the royal armor, the civic
proclamation versus the bleating shout, the beating of tambourines versus
the steady clicking of the loom. Dionysus disrupts the settled life, he
cracks the shell of civic contentment and isolation. Probably the most
important word in the play, as a recent critic has well pointed out, is
"*hybris*." It occurs throughout, and always in a key position. But it is
not the *hybris* of which the tragic poets usually speak, the *hybris* which
figures also in the legal documents, the thoughtless insolence which
comes from too much social or political power. In the *Bacchae, hybris*
is quite literally the "going beyond," the explosion of the unlimited
across the barricades which a blind civilization has erected in the vain
hope of keeping shut out what it does not wish to understand. That is
not to say that the word is not used also in its more conventional sense,
especially with reference to the campaign of Pentheus. As a result, the
efforts of Pentheus take on the aspect of a parody of Dionysiac impulsive-
ness.

Similarly the hunt is a principal symbol because it catches the futility
of organized, circumscribed life. From the vantage point of the larger
reality, all worldly activity appears both hunt and escape. Hunting and
being hunted are the physical and psychological manifestations of
Appearance, the monotonous jolts of the process of generation and decay.
Agave cries when approached by the herdsman (731):

> Run to it, my hounds!
> Behold the men who hunt us! Follow me,
> brandish your thyrsus and pursue them!

The Maenads are resting; they are communing with the god and slough-
ing off the sense of separateness when they are violently pulled back into
the world of Appearance and resume their game of hunting and being
hunted. In this case it is Appearance which causes the disruption; Being
and Appearance are so related that one as well as the other may be the
cause of disturbance and dislocation. There is a perpetual pull between
them which never allows either to win a lasting victory. Without the
constant friction there would be no tragedy; without the violent disruption of one by the other there would be no dismemberment. *Sparagmos,*

the sacred dismemberment of the Dionysiac rites, is both a means to an ✓
end and an autonomous fact. As a means to an end it supplies the
frenzied exercise which terminates in the drugged sleep. The explosion
of energy, the tearing and mutilation of a once living body, leaves the
worshiper exhausted and readies the soul, through a numb tranquility,
for the mystic union with the god. But the dismemberment operates also
as a self-validating event. Through it, symbolically, the world of Appearance with its contradictions and insufficiencies is made to show itself as
it really is. The destruction of Pentheus, then, is not simply a sardonic
twist of an unspeakable bloody rite, but a fitting summation of the lesson
of the play. The limited vessel is made to burst asunder, refuting the
pretensions of those who oppose Dionysus, of the partisans of unreality.

III

Who is Pentheus, and why is it he who dies rather than one of the
other Thebans? When the stranger raises the question whether the king
knows who he really is, he answers (507):

> Pentheus, the son of Agave and of Echion.

Thus Pentheus identifies himself as a member of the ruling house, as
an officer of the State. He bears a name which establishes his position
within the hereditary political structure of his city. Even at the moment
of death he throws off the leveling disguise of the ministrant and cries
(1118):

> Mother, it is I, your son
> Pentheus, the child you bore in Echion's house.

In the judgment of Dionysus this pride in the house, the emphasis on
the limited life, is ignorance. But is it commensurate with the punishment which Pentheus receives? Is there not something about him as a
person which is more likely to justify the violence of his undoing? To
ask the obvious question: Does Pentheus not exhibit an arrogance which
cries out for retribution?

Here we must step gingerly. It is to be remembered that the action
of the *Bacchae* is not primarily borne or promoted by the characters.
Euripides does not in this play operate with idiosyncrasies but with lives.
Suffering is constructed as the measurable content of a life, not as the
unique unquantifiable experience of a specific irrational soul. And the
lives, also, are largely catalysts for the release of social complications.
These complications have nothing to do with the arbitrary contours of

individual dispositions, but answer directly to the needs of the author's metaphysical purpose. The personal relations brought into play are devised chiefly as one of the means for the author to invoke his philosophical riddle. In the *Alcestis* character is all; in the *Bacchae* it counts for very little. It is sometimes said that the tragedy of Pentheus is not that he tried to do what was wrong but that he was the wrong man to do it—that he was, in fact, not a political strongman but precisely the unbalanced, excitable type of person who most easily falls a victim to the allurements of the Dionysiac indulgence. In other words, the character of Pentheus is too Dionysiac to allow him to oppose Dionysus successfully. But this argument will not stand up. Pentheus is no more and no less excitable or unstable than most of the heroes of Greek tragedy. An Odysseus, or a Socrates, is no more fit to stand at the center of a high tragedy than a Pecksniff or a Tanner. Odysseus is not a whole man, as Helen is not a whole woman; they are exponents of a partial aspect of the human range: intelligence in the case of Odysseus, love in the case of Helen. But Pentheus is a whole man, precisely as Oedipus is, or as Antigone is a whole woman. And because he is whole he is vulnerable, more vulnerable than the men and women who are weighted in one direction or another.

Of course he is not a moderate. His order to smash the workshop of Tiresias (346ff) is not well considered. He happens to be right; Tiresias appears to have turned disloyal to Apollo, and so will no longer need his oracle seat. Under the democratic spell of Dionysus, everybody will do his own prophesying. But even if Pentheus were unjustified in his harshness toward Tiresias, his lack of moderation, or, to put it more fairly, his capacity for anger, does not necessarily discredit him. Stability, self-control, discretion smack too much of asceticism and puritan artifice to provide a solid basis for tragic action. Pentheus is a whole man, with none of his vitality curtailed or held in check. But he is also a king, a perfect representative of the humanistic Greek ideal of the ordered life, a political being rather than a lawless beast. Being Aristotle's "creature living in a polis," he is destined to ask the wrong sort of question, a political question, when faced with the reality of religion. His query (473),

> What profit do the celebrants draw from it?

shows the political or educational frame of his thinking. The twentieth century, unlike the eighteenth, is once more inclined to the view that the question of usefulness when applied to religion misses the point, that religion cannot be adjusted to a system of utilitarian relations. But where did Euripides and his contemporaries stand on this issue? In all probability Pentheus' question did not strike the audience as irrelevant; it may, in fact, have impressed them as noble and responsible. At the end of the fifth century, as we can see in the *History* of Thucydides, the preservation of social and political institutions and traditions had become the overriding topic of discussion to which all other values tended to be subordinated. The *Bacchae* demonstrates that this sort of nobility, the exaltation of the political and educational thesis, is as nothing before the primary currents of life. But a nobility which goes under is not the less noble for its defeat. Pentheus dies, and the nature of his death, particularly of the preparations which lead to his death, is deplorable. But the fact remains that his stand, and only his, can be measured in positive moral terms. Clearly the force which kills him eludes ethical analysis.

Because Pentheus is a king he offers a larger area to be affected by the deity. His responses differ from those of other men less in their specific quality than in their intensity. As a king he suffers for the group; his name, as Dionysus reminds him (508), means "man of sorrow." But there is nothing Christlike about him. He proposes to live as a rational man, to leave everything nonrational, everything that might remind us of man's original condition, behind him. Love and faith, the Christian antidotes of the dispassionate intellect, have not yet been formulated. In Plato, characteristically, it is love and reason together, or love-in-reason, which refines man and weakens the animal in him. Nonreason, in the fifth century B.C., is neither love nor hatred but religious ecstasy. This Pentheus means to fight, for he knows it is wrong. Pentheus is not a romantic hero, he does not search for a hidden truth. The same thing is true of the others; both the characters and the chorus are, each of them, convinced that they know best and that their way of life is best. For Pentheus the best is Form, the tested and stable limits of responsibility, law, and control. Against the chorus, which espouses the cause of excitement, of formlessness and instability, Pentheus is the champion of permanence and stability. Neither his anger nor his defeat are valid arguments against the merits of this championship. Like Ajax, Pentheus is identified with armor (781, 809); like Ajax, the armed Pentheus, confined in the panoply of embattled civil life, turns against the forces which are wrecking his fragile cause. As a functionary he represents order and limit; as a man he is whole and robust and fully alive.

This cannot be said about Cadmus and Tiresias. For one thing, they are old men, their life force is diminished and stunted. This means that they cannot suffer as Pentheus can. It also means that they have come to terms with the world; there are no issues left for them to battle out, no difficulties over which to fret. Cadmus is a fine specimen of the *arriviste*,

proud of the achievements of his grandson, but even prouder of the in-
clusion of a genuine god in the family. The god must at all costs be kept
in the family, even if it becomes necessary to mince the truth a little.
Here is Cadmus' humble plea to Pentheus (333):

> And if, as you say, the god does not exist,
> keep this to yourself, and share in the fine fiction
> that he does; so we may say that Semele bore
> a god, for the greater glory of our clan.

The distinction between truth and falsity, between order and disorder,
is of no importance to him. At his time of life, a good reputation is a
finer prize than a noble life, no matter whether the reputation is deserved or not. Tiresias likewise is not concerned with essentials. This
Tiresias is not the Sophoclean man of truth, the terrible mouthpiece of
mystery and damnation, but, of all things, a clever sophist, a pseudo-
philosopher who strips away the mystery and the strangeness of the superhuman world and is content to worship a denatured, an ungodded god.
A squeamish deist, he does not hold with the miracles and the barbarisms
of popular faith. In his lecture to Pentheus he pares down the stature of
Dionysus to render him manageable and unoffending (272ff). Point one:
he is the god of wine (280)

> which liberates suffering mortals from
> their pain.

That is to say, he *is* wine (284), precisely as Demeter *is* grain. By alle-
gorizing the old stories and identifying the gods with palpable substances,
we can dispense with whatever is not concrete and intelligible in the
traditions about Dionysus. Point two: he is a perfectly natural god. The
distasteful tale about Zeus sewing him up in his thigh produces a quite
satisfactory meaning once it is understood that the grating feature is due
to a pun. Like Max Müller in a subsequent era of facile enlightenment,
Tiresias believes that the mystery of myth is caused by a linguistic aberration; with the discovery of the cause, the mystery disappears.

Finally, in the third part of his lecture, Tiresias does pay some attention to the irrational virtues of the god, to his mantic powers and his
ability to inspire panic in strong men. But this part of the assessment is
underplayed; it is briefer than the other two, and one feels that Tiresias
adds it only in order to have a weapon with which to frighten Pentheus.
The reference to soldiers strangely routed and to Dionysiac torches at
home in the sanctuary of Delphi is not a confession but a threat, calculated to appeal to Pentheus in the only language he understands: the

language of military and political authority. Tiresias' heart is not in the threat; what interests him is the theological and philological sterilization of the god. Neither he nor Cadmus really understands or even wants to understand what the god has to offer. But they know that his triumph is inevitable, and so they try to accept him within their lights. They are fellow travelers, with a good nose for changes of fashion and faith. To take them seriously would be absurd; a Tartuffe has no claim on our sympathy.

They do not understand; hence nothing happens to them.[1] Pentheus, on the other hand, is fully engaged, and he is a big enough man to perceive the truth beyond his own self-interest. He is capable of appreciating the real meaning of Dionysus; though he does not approve, he understands. But understanding, in a man of his power of commitment, is tantamount to weakening, and in the end, to destruction. This is what Euripides dramatizes with the sudden break-up of Pentheus' royal substance. Abruptly the officer of the State turns into a Peeping Tom. One shout of the god (810) and the manly general becomes a slavish, prurient, reptilian thing, intent on watching from a safe distance what he hopes will be a spectacle to titillate his voyeur's itch. The civilized man of reason is gone, and in his place we find an animal, living only for the satisfaction of his instinctual drives.

Is the rapid change psychologically plausible? Once more, the question is not pertinent. There is no character in the first place, only a comprehensive life-image to symbolize one side of a conflict which transcends the terms of a uniquely experienced situation. Whether it is possible for such a man as Pentheus is shown to be in the first half of the play, to turn into the creature he becomes after his conversion by Dionysus, is a question on which psychoanalysts may have an opinion but which does not arise in considering Euripides' purpose. The truth is that the change is not a transition from one phase of life to another, much less a lapse into sickness or perversion, but quite simply death. When a tragic hero in the great tradition is made to reverse his former confident choice, especially if this happens at the instigation of the archenemy, the role of the hero has come to an end. We remember Agamemnon stepping on the crimson carpet, after Clytemnestra has broken down his reluctance. The blood-colored tapestry is a visual anticipation of the murder. Instead of the corporeal death which will be set offstage, the audience watch the

---

[1] The metamorphosis which Dionysus inflicts upon Cadmus in the epilogue is a datum from mythology. Because of the bad state of preservation of the final portion of the play we do not know how Euripides motivated the metamorphosis, and what the punishment—for such it is said to be (1340ff)—is for.

death of the soul. With Agamemnon slowly moving through the sea of
red the contours are blurred and the king of all the Greeks is annihilated
before our eyes. Aeschylus uses a splash; Euripides, less concretely but no
less effectively, uses a change of personality.

That the hero has died in his scene with Dionysus becomes even clearer
when the god, with a Thucydidean terseness, announces the physical
death (857):

> Now I shall go and dress him in the robes
> he'll wear to Hades once his mother's hands
> have slaughtered him . . .

His death, then, is an agreed fact both while the chorus sings their ode
to Natural Necessity and also during the terrible scene which follows
in which Pentheus arranges his woman's clothes about him. The King
joins the Maenads, but he goes further than they, for he adopts the
bisexuality of the god. All this is meaningful as a picture of the complete and devastating victory of reality over unreality, of the natural
over the institutional life. But it is not without its psychological aspect, and here, curiously, we may see an ironic parallel to one of Plato's
most troublesome concerns. In his discussions of dramatic poetry, Plato
takes it for granted that the spectacle affects the soul of the spectator,
even to the extent of transforming it in its own likeness. This is what
drama demands; the audience must allow what they see to shape their
souls, without struggling against the impact. Plato recognizes the legiti-
macy of the demand, and decides that therefore drama is too dangerous
to have around in a healthy body politic, except the kind of drama whose
effect is beneficial. Pentheus also is about to see a spectacle, a Dionysiac
drama of the type which as a responsible man of the city he had condemned. Euripides knows that Plato's act of censorship is in a hopeless
cause. A life which does not reach out to embrace the sight of a greater
reality which tragedy affords is incomplete. Watching a play may mean
a partial sacrifice of the soul, a surrender to the unlimited and the irrational, but we cannot do without it. Pentheus holds out against it for
some time, but in the end he throws down his arms, with such finality
that his soul comes to be transformed and enriched even before he goes
off to spy on the mysteries.

Pentheus is drunk, without the physical satisfaction of strong drink
(918):

> Ho, what is this? I think I see two suns,
> two cities of Thebes each with its seven gates!

This is one way of formulating his conquest at the hand of Dionysus.
Drunk he sees more keenly, or at any rate more completely:

> And now, leading me on, I see you as
> a bull . . .

And Dionysus replies:

> Yes, now you see what is for you to see.

For the first time Pentheus' eyes are sufficiently opened to see the god
in his animal shape. His vision is broadened; but his role as Pentheus
is finished. The disintegration of the king is made particularly painful
by the emphasis on the feminine clothing. With Dionysus assisting as
his valet (928) the one-time upholder of the *vita activa* becomes fussy and
vain about the details of his toilette. Does the cloak hang properly? Is
he to carry the thyrsus in his right or in his left hand? The energies
which had once been directed toward the mustering of armies and the
implementation of public decisions are now bestowed on the arrangement of his Bacchic vestments. Along with this attention to the correct
fashion—behold, another Tiresias—to the external signs of his newfound
anonymity, there goes an internal change which is equally preposterous.
The blocked doer turns into an uninhibited dreamer (945):

> I wonder if my shoulders would support
> Cithaeron and its glens, complete with Maenads?

His speech, formerly royal and violent and ringing, has become pretty
and lyrical; he pictures the women (957)

> like birds in the thickets,
> contained in the fond coils of love's embrace.

Compare this with his earlier comment (222) that the women

> slink off by devious ways into
> the wild and cater to the lusts of males.

His imagination has been fired, his surly prejudices are gone. The vision
which neither Cadmus nor Tiresias was able to entertain has come to
Pentheus and is inspiring him. The Bacchianized Pentheus is a visionary
and poet. But it is a poetry which lacks the saving grace of choice. He
contemplates the prospect of his mother carrying him home from the
mountains, and the prospect pleases him. The political man has become
woman *and* child. Having rid himself of the social restrictions and classi-
fications, he savors infancy, a sentient creature for whom the mother's

cradled arms offer escape and bliss. He is woman and child and beast, an amorphous organism susceptible to all influences and realizing itself in a life of instinct and unthinking sense. The victory of Dionysus is complete; the king is dead, and the man has been found out, in the god's image.

Chronology of Important Dates

484 B.C.	Euripides born at Salamis.
480	Greek naval victory over the Persians at Salamis.
468	Sophocles defeats Aeschylus in dramatic competition.
458	Aeschylus' *Oresteia.*
456	Aeschylus dies in Sicily.
455	Euripides' first play produced: *Peliades* (now lost).
442 or 441	Sophocles' *Antigone*
441	Euripides' first victory in dramatic competition (titles unknown).
438	*Alcestis*
431	Outbreak of the Peloponnesian War; *Medea*
428	*Hippolytus*
425	Aristophanes' *Acharnians,* his first extant comedy. Euripides appears briefly and is mocked for presenting "heroes in rags."
416	Athenians destroy the neutral Island of Melos.
415	*Trojan Women*; departure of the Sicilian Expedition.
414	Aristophanes' *Birds.*
413	Failure of the Sicilian Expedition; Athenian fleet destroyed.
412	*Helen.*
411	Aristophanes' *Thesmophoriazusae,* in which the women of Athens plot revenge against Euripides for slandering them in his plays. Euripidean "escape scenes" parodied.
409	Sophocles' *Philoctetes.*
408	*Orestes*; Euripides leaves for the court of King Archelaus in Macedonia.
407/6	Euripides dies in Macedonia; at Athens he is mourned by Sophocles' chorus.
406	Sophocles dies.
406/5	*Bacchae*; *Iphigenia at Aulis.*
405	Aristophanes' *Frogs,* in which there is an *agon* between Aeschylus and Euripides. Various aspects of Euripides' art come under comic attack. Aeschylus deemed the victor.
404	Fall of Athens.

Notes on the Editor and Contributors

ERICH SEGAL, editor of this volume, teaches Classics at Yale University. A playwright and the author of several major films, he has also written a study of Plautus, entitled *Roman Laughter*, and has published essays on Comparative Literature.

WILLIAM ARROWSMITH of the University of Texas is well known for his translations of Euripides, Aristophanes, and Petronius. A former Rhodes scholar, Guggenheim Fellow, and winner of the *Prix de Rome*, Professor Arrowsmith is at work on studies of Euripides and of American Higher Education.

ANNE PIPPIN BURNETT teaches Classics at the University of Chicago and has published essays on several plays of Euripides. She is on the editorial board of *Classical Philology*.

G. M. A. GRUBE is head of the Department of Classics in the School of Graduate Studies at the University of Toronto. He is the author of *Plato's Thought*, *The Drama of Euripides*, and, most recently, *The Greek and Roman Critics*.

ERIC A. HAVELOCK is Sterling Professor of Classics and Chairman of the Department at Yale University. He is the author of *The Lyric Genius of Catullus*, *The Crucifixion of Intellectual Man*, *The Liberal Temper in Greek Politics*, and *Preface to Plato*.

BERNARD M. W. KNOX, formerly Professor of Classics at Yale University, is now Director of the Center for Hellenic Studies in Washington, D. C. He has written two books on Sophocles, *Oedipus at Thebes* and *The Heroic Temper*.

THOMAS G. ROSENMEYER teaches Classics and Comparative Literature at the University of California at Berkeley. Author of *The Masks of Tragedy*, a co-author of *The Meters of Greek and Latin Poetry*, he also translated Bruno Snell's *The Discovery of the Mind*.

JEAN-PAUL SARTRE's translation of *The Trojan Women* was not the first encounter with Greek drama for the French writer-philosopher. His play *Les Mouches* was an existentialist retelling of the Orestes myth.

EILHARD SCHLESINGER is a German scholar who has published on Pindar and Sophocles as well as Euripides, and has taught Classics both in Europe and at the University of Buenos Aires.

CHRISTIAN WOLFF, who teaches at Harvard University, is a talented composer as well as a Classicist. He is completing a book on the later plays of Euripides.

Selected Bibliography

Arrowsmith, William, "Eliot and Euripides." *Arion,* IV, No. 1 (1965), 21-35.

Blaiklock, E. M., *The Male Characters of Euripides.* Wellington, 1952.

Burnett, Anne Pippin, "Euripides' *Helen:* A Comedy of Ideas." *Classical Philology,* LV (1960), 151-63.

―――, "Human Resistance and Divine Persuasion in Euripides' *Ion.*" *Classical Philology,* LVII (1962), 170-72.

Diller, Hans, "Die Backchen und ihre Stellung im Spätwerk des Euripides." *Akademie Mainz. Geistes-und Sozialwissenschaftlichen Klasse* (1955) no. 5, pp. 451-71.

―――, "Umwelt und Masse als dramatisches Faktoren bei Euripides," *Fondation Hardt, Entretiens sur l'antiquité classique,* tome VI. Geneva, 1960. [Hereafter referred to as *Fondation Hardt.*]

Dodds, E. R., "Euripides the Irrationalist." *Classical Review,* XLIII (July 1929), 97-104. Cf. Dodds' *The Greeks and the Irrational.* Berkeley and Los Angeles: University of California Press, 1951. Invaluable is Dodds' introduction to his edition of the *Bacchae.* Oxford, at the Clarendon Press, 1944.

Friedrich, W. H., *Euripides und Diphilos (Zetemata 5),* Munich, 1953.

Greenberg, N. A., "Euripides' *Orestes:* An Interpretation." *Harvard Studies in Classical Philology,* LXVI (1962), 157-92.

Greenwood, L. H. G., *Aspects of Euripidean Tragedy.* Cambridge, England, 1953.

Grube, G. M. A., *The Drama of Euripides.* London: Methuen & Co., Ltd., 1941 (reprinted 1961).

Harsh, Philip W., *A Handbook of Classical Drama.* Stanford: Stanford University Press, 1944 (reprinted in paperback).

Kamerbeek, J. C., "Mythe et Réalité dans l'oeuvre d'Euripide." *Fondation Hardt, op. cit.,* pp. 1-25.

―――, "Unity and Meaning of Euripides' *Herakles.*" *Mnemosyne,* Series IV, vol. xix, fasc. 1 (1966) pp. 1-16.

Kitto, H. D. F., *Greek Tragedy,* 3rd ed. New York: Barnes & Noble, Inc., 1961. Second edition in paperback, Doubleday Anchor Books, 1954.

Lattimore, Richmond, "Phaedra and Hippolytus." *Arion,* I, No. 3 (1962), 5-18.

Lattimore, Richmond, *The Poetry of Greek Tragedy*. Baltimore: The Johns Hopkins Press, 1958.

————, *Story Patterns in Greek Tragedy*. Ann Arbor: The University of Michigan Press, 1964.

Lesky, Albin, *Greek Tragedy*, trans. H. A. Frankfort. London: Ernest Benn, Ltd., 1965.

————, *A History of Greek Literature*, trans. James Willis and Cornelis De Heer. New York: Thomas Y. Crowell Company, 1966, pp. 360-409.

————, "Psychologie bei Euripides." *Fondation Hardt, op. cit.*, pp. 123-68.

Lucas, D. W., *The Greek Tragic Poets* (2nd ed.), New York: W. W. Norton & Company, 1964.

Martin, Victor, "Euripide et Ménandre face à leur public." *Fondation Hardt, op. cit.*, pp. 243-72.

Murray, Gilbert, *Euripides and His Age* (1918), reprinted as an Oxford paperback, 1965.

Norwood, Gilbert, *Essays on Euripidean Drama*. Berkeley and Los Angeles: University of California Press, 1954.

————, *Euripides and Shaw*. London: Methuen & Co., Ltd., 1921.

Reckford, Kenneth J., "Heracles and Mr. Eliot." *Comparative Literature,* XVI (Winter 1964), 1-18.

Reinhardt, Karl, "Sinneskrise bei Euripides" in *Tradition und Geist*. Gottingen, 1960, pp. 227-56.

Rivier, André, "L'élément démoniaque chez Euripide jusqu'en 428." *Fondation Hardt, op. cit.*, pp. 43-72.

————, *Essai sur le tragique d'Euripide*. Lausanne, 1944.

de Romilly, Jacqueline, *L'évolution du Pathétique d'Eschyle à Euripide*. Paris, 1961.

Rosenmeyer, Thomas G., *The Masks of Tragedy*. Austin: University of Texas Press, 1963.

Segal, Charles Paul, "The Tragedy of the *Hippolytus*." *Harvard Studies in Classical Philology*, LXX (1965), 117-69.

Snell, Bruno, *Scenes from Greek Drama*. Berkeley and Los Angeles, University of California Press, 1964.

Strohm, Hans, "Euripides, Interpretationen zur dramatischen Form." *Zetemata*, XV (1957).

Winnington-Ingram, R. P., *Euripides and Dionysius: An Interpretation of the* Bacchae. Cambridge, England, 1948.

————, "Hippolytus: A Study in Causation." *Fondation Hardt, op. cit.*, pp. 171-91.

Wolff, Christian, "Design and Myth in Euripides' *Ion*." *Harvard Studies in Classical Philology, LXIX* (1965), 169-194.

Zuntz, Günther, "On Euripides' *Helena:* Theology and Irony." *Fondation Hardt, op. cit.*, pp. 199-227.

———, *The Political Plays of Euripides*. Manchester, 1955.

Zürcher, W., *Die Darstellung des Menschen im Drama des Euripides*. Basel, 1947.

EDITOR'S NOTE: As this volume was going to press, the following works were about to appear:

Conacher, D. J., *Myth, Theme and Structure in Euripidean Drama*. Toronto, University of Toronto Press, 1967.

Webster, T. B. L., *The Tragedies of Euripides*. New York, Barnes and Noble, 1968.

TWENTIETH CENTURY VIEWS

European Authors